LOVE IS IN THE EARTH-

THE EARTH-

LAYING-ON-OF-STONES

THE JOURNEY CONTINUES

Cover Art: "**THE KIVA**" created by the mineral kingdom in the lovely land of Brazil.

"The Kiva" is comprised of amethyst crystals, quartz crystals with amethyst phantoms, and thin needle-like quartz crystals which have a delicate calcite druse overlaid upon them. These geodes are between 24" and 25" high and between 9" and 10" across the middle [larger at the base]. "The Kiva" presents the sacred energies of the universe to all.

Illustrations created by Julianne Guilbault.

I would like to thank Julianne Guilbault for assisting in the lay-out and for creating the illustrations shown within **LOVE IS IN THE EARTH - LAYING-ON-OF-STONES**. Julianne and I have been friends through many lifetimes and have worked together toward the furtherance of the "brotherhood" of "All That Is" and toward the actualization of the inner light. She has been active in the crystal awareness movement and the practice of Native American spirituality for years and is truly the personification of creativity, both living and being the essence of originality and ingenuity. She has been involved in graphics design and illustrating for over twenty years, utilizing the mediums of watercolour, pastels, charcoal, pen and ink, and acrylic. She has produced lovely avantgarde sculptures of fantasy art deco crystal/crystal ball holders; previous sculptures, including flower faeries and crystal holders, are in private collections throughout the world. She has also begun her first fiction/fantasy novel which recounts an exciting journey into the varied dimensions of the mind. I thank her also for her love, her encouragement, and her support in both the illustration of **LOVE IS IN THE EARTH - LAYING-ON-OF-STONES** and in the compilation and illustration of my workshop materials. Julianne may be contacted c/o Earth-Love Publishing House.

Back cover Photography by Lyle Hansen.

I would like to thank Lyle Hansen for the photography of both the author and the illustrator, shown on the back cover of LOVE IS IN THE EARTH - LAYING-ON-OF-STONES. Lyle and I have been friends for many lifetimes. He has traveled extensively in both mind and body and has photographed many countries of our beautiful Earth. He is active in the Native American traditions and bridges the gap between the "old ways" and the future. Lyle delivers! He brings love, joy, and peace to everyone.

Front cover Photography created by Ken Anderson, Tucson, Arizona, USA.

Colour separations by Peter Hoyt, Pacific Scanning, Medford, OR, USA.

Back cover photographic processing by Les and Debbie Litzenberger, Kennewick, WA, USA.

The author may be contacted c/o Earth-Love Publishing House.

LOVE IS IN THE EARTH-

LAYING-ON-OF-STONES

THE JOURNEY CONTINUES

BY: ♪ ♪ **MELODY** ♪ ♪

illustrator: **Julianne Guilbault**

EARTH-
LOVE

PUBLISHING
HOUSE

3440 YOUNGFIELD STREET, SUITE 353
WHEATRIDGE, COLORADO 80033

Published by
EARTH-LOVE PUBLISHING HOUSE
302 Torbett, Suite 100
Richland, Washington 99352

First Printing 1992
Second Printing 1993
Third Printing 1994

This book is a reference work based upon research by the author and by those who are mentioned in the acknowledgements. The opinions expressed herein are not necessarily those of, or endorsed by, the Publisher. The information as stated in this book is in no way to be considered as a substitute for consultation with a duly licensed holistic physician.

Library of Congress Catalogue Card Number: 91-771320

ISBN: 0-9628190-1-8

DEDICATION

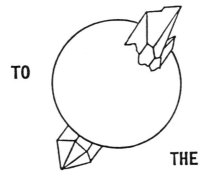

TO

THE

EARTH

♥♥♥
♥♥♥

IN TRIBUTE TO OUR EARTH,

THE "LOVE IS IN THE EARTH..." Books

EVERYONE LAUGHS AND SMILES IN THE SAME LANGUAGE -
SO EASILY TRANSLATED, SO LOVELY TO SEE

ACKNOWLEDGEMENTS

I would like to thank the following people for their assistance in helping to make this book a reality.

Charley Berryhill - for his love and encouragement and for taking time to teach me more about the Native American ways.

Bob Beck - for his being and for my first introduction to the Chevron amethyst.

Carlos do Prado Barbosa - for his being and for my first introduction to Phenacite.

Mike Brown - for his love and encouragement in all areas of my life, for his sensitivity to the sanctity of the Native American ways, and for his awareness and practice within crystal-consciousness.

Bruce Cairncross - for his love and encouragement.

Dawn Cairs - for her love and encouragement and her research into the alchemical philosophy of actualization and into the energies of colours.

Edward Salisbury Dana - for teaching me, via his textbooks of mineralogy, about the multitude of crystalline structures which exist today.

Jan and Raymonde de Vries - for their love and encouragement and for their assistance in working with the mineralogical formations and geometrical arrays.

Howard Dolph - for his being and for my first introduction to the Nephrite/Quartz structures and the violet sheen and electric-blue sheen Obsidian.

Lynn Fielding - for his love and encouragement in pursuing my path; this book, nor "Love Is In The Earth - A Kaleidoscope Of Crystals", would have been possible without his guidance and advice.

Arthur Goldstein - for my first introduction to Charoite from Russia.

Gypsy Blue Eyes - for his being and for his emanation of the ideal that minerals are truly alive.

Lucy and Joe Gross [Mama & Papa] - for their being, their love, encouragement, reassurance, motivation, patience, and support in all that I attempt and all that I am, for stimulating my interest in all of the kingdoms of the Earth, and for further helping me to both recognize and understand my heritage.

W. R. Horning - for his love and encouragement, for stimulating my interest in the mineral kingdom, and for my first and recent introduction to the Faden crystal.

Bob Jackson - for his love and encouragement in my life, for his patience, for his assistance in editing the text of the material, for his quotable words shown herein, for making available [via Pleasant Company Ltd., 3440 Youngfield, Suite 353, Wheat Ridge, CO 80033, USA.] the wonderful minerals of the world, for his creations as a silversmith/goldsmith which represent the configurations shown herein, and for being a part of the many and varied adventures in the journey toward the self.

Marguerite Martin - in her memory and for stimulation of my interest in the greater realm of minerals, and for their love and encouragement toward continuing interest in the mineral kingdom.

Anthony Malakou - for his love and encouragement, for his efforts with Zimbabwe phenacite, and for my first introduction to the Ajoite phantom crystal from Africa.

♫

Scot Nelson - for his love and encouragement and for his assistance.

Osho - for his being, in a time when many of us were ready to consciously experience.

Chris Pittario - for her love and encouragement and for her assistance in the applications of the zodiacal and planetary signs and symbols.

Antar Pushkara - for his love and encouragement in my life, for being my kinsman, and for sharing his radiance and manifestation of inner calm, peace, and understanding.

Rafael - for his love and for calling at the "right" time.

Gregory Sluszka - for his love and encouragement, for giving of himself to further the advancement of all, and for his continuing support and assistance in the application of the mineral kingdom to elevate both collective and personal development.

Milt Szulinski - in his memory, and for his love and encouragement toward personal development.

Jean Schroeder - for her love and encouragement and for assisting in making this book a reality.

LaSonda Sioux Sipe - for her love and encouragement, for working with me in the investigation of aspects of the Native American ways and in the application of the mineral kingdom to healing.

Rob Smith [African Gems & Minerals, Johannesburg, RSA] - for his love and encouragement, for my first introduction to the Ajoite crystal, for organizing and creating, and for making available the wonderful minerals from the African continent.

Petal & Ainsley Smith - for their love and encouragement and for their research and information concerning the opening of the chakras relative to the potentials for divergence with respect to the rotational axis of each chakra.

Layton Talbott - for his love and encouragement and for my first introduction to the gold/silver inclusions in quartz.

Angel Torrecillas - for my first introduction to Peacock Rock and to Ruby Silver, for his many gifts of minerals, and for his lovely smile.

Liza Van De Linde - for her love and encouragement, for her openness and care, and for her assistance in providing this material in the Republic of South Africa.

Bertha Yates [Gramps] - in her memory and for her being, for her love and encouragement in my life, for her support and approval of all that I attempt, and for her inner light which leads the way toward development.

In addition, I want thank all of the lovely South Africans who shared, during the September workshops in South Africa and during the Namibian gem tour, in the finalization of this book via their participation in the first workshops which applied a variety of these techniques. Thanks also to my lovely friends throughout the world who have shared in the practical application of these techniques.

Thanks also to those friends who provided the quotations and poetry which are included herein.

I especially want to thank all of those people who have acted as the focal point of the configurations and those who have touched my life and have, thereby, assisted in the furtherance of my being. Thanks to my many friends on this wonderful Earth. Love to All.

♫

TABLE OF CONTENTS

THE UNIVERSE ... MIRROR IMAGE

Mother Earth, Our Body
Father, the Sky, Our Vision
Grandfather the Sun, Our Warmth
Grandmother the Moon, Our Reflection
Brothers & Sisters, the Stars, Our Learning
One's Spirit, Our Insight

Oh Great Spirit, Our Understanding

Marie Mockers
In honor to the North American Indians
Kyoto, Japan, 1989

To The Reader

The information contained within this guidebook has been derived from "hands-on" experience, historical research, and experimentation; any channeled information which is included was first validated via experimentation. The information provided in the first book, **LOVE IS IN THE EARTH - A KALEIDOSCOPE OF CRYSTALS** is, for the most part, not repeated herein; terms and examples of methodology which were previously defined are not defined again. The utilization of this book presupposes the knowledge of the methods and processes which were formerly reported. Appendix A of this guidebook, entitled "Mineralogical Update", contains information for several "new" crystalline formations; supplementary information applicable to the vibratory rates of Master Numbers is given in Appendix B. In addition, Appendix C provides cross-referencing of astrological signs and mineralogical associations.

The illustrations, for each of the arrays which are described, are primarily represented with quartz crystals. The reader is encouraged to utilize additional crystals/minerals in the construction of each of the configurations. The recommendations for supplementary crystals which are, occasionally, included are based upon personal experimentation. Please note that the total number of crystals which are shown in the illustrations are not required to facilitate the configurations - the minimum number required would be the number through which the flow of energy can be maintained. Note also that several of the arrays may be used for similar "work"; however, one practitioner may find the utilization of one array to be easier than the utilization of another array which can perform the same function.

One may advance considerably in the realm of crystal healing by remembering that one element of the crystal healing system is the understanding that blocked emotions and blocked energies can eventually cause illness in the body, mind, and spirit; the energies of the arrays which are described herein, in conjunction with the energies of the mineral kingdom, can assist in relieving blocked emotions and energies. Many years of practice was required to produce the prodigious extent of detail, and the many examples of exercises, which are provided; they are meant to assist the neophyte as well as the expert.

The journey into the multi-faceted energies of the mineral kingdom has begun; the journey now continues toward the actualization of the perfect state. May you continue to harvest the benefits of the stones, begin to harvest the benefits of the configurations and methodologies presented, be receptive to the wisdom from within, and enjoy your life in this physical form while maintaining respect for the Earth which sustains you. As you journey to sacred fulfillment, I wish you peace within yourself, love to guide you, and the understanding leading to bliss. May you heal yourself in all ways♥

LIVE, LAUGH, AND LOVE

INTRODUCTION

This book is meant to facilitate the continuance of ones intimate journey into the subtle realms of crystal energy, via the application of "laying-on-of-stones" in symbolic arrays from ancient times. The combinations bring one toward additional avantgarde adventures in the world of the mineral kingdom. The multi-dimensional arrangements, coupled with the crystalline formations, provide for an energy that works simultaneously with the multi-facets of a person and helps to harmonize conflicting elements in the body, mind, and spirit.

Throughout the text, the members of the mineral kingdom are designated as crystals. A crystal is defined as any portion of a mineralogical body which exhibits characteristic internal structure and is enclosed by symmetrically arranged plane surfaces, intersecting at definite and characteristic angles. It is the "regular" form which a substance tends to assume, during the process of solidification, through the inherent power of cohesive attraction. Crystals are the blossoms of the mineralogical portion of the Earth; the recognition of the beauty and the acceptance of the loving energies of these forms can greatly enhance ones personal development. The configurations of arrangement which are reported may be used to assist one in healing the emotions, the mind, and the body, furthering ones recognition, acceptance, and inviolate consummation of the perfect self.

Crystals have been scientifically proven to possess vibratory energy, to generate and to emit electrical charge, and to possess the vital energy force which sustains all that exists. The energies of the mineral kingdom are "universal energies" and are available to those who are willing to both receive and meld this energy with their own. The arrays in this guidebook assist one in the exercise of personal creativity, merging with the Higher Will, contacting and synthesizing the energies from which the entire universe is comprised, and in healing the self and/or facilitating the healing of others while continuing on the path to enlightenment.

The power of each configuration is supplemented by the types of minerals which are selected as a part of the array. The combination of these energies is so very powerful that the applications may only be used through the highest consciousness of the individual. The individual universal energies contained within the combination of the configuration and the mineralogical structure is activated and directed by interaction and/or contact with same. Right intention during the exercises stimulates the melding of ones personal energy with that of the mineral kingdom, furthering the propagation of the light, the love, and "the good of all".

The significance that each of us has the infinite power of the universe within the self is not overshadowed by the application of crystals and crystal configurations. Although we tend to find it more effortless, and are inclined to accept support from that which is from outside of ourselves, the use of the arrays bring us back to the realization and application of out intrinsic power. Arrays may be used for healing and "being" on all levels. Many early explanations of existence stated that since the supreme being cannot be anything but perfect and all powerful, dis-ease and all negative conditions cannot exist because they are not of the supreme being who is perfect. One may recall the adage that the truth may easily be blown away, while stones hold the energy with a steadiness and strength to facilitate transmission of same.

Each array has its own individual energy and its own "personality". The addition of the varied mineralogical structures tend to activate the diversity of each configuration. Each can be used in unique ways to assist one in understanding the multi-faceted nature of existence on the Earth plane.

The increasing consciousness of the planet is directing humanity to the re-discovery of the ancient and neglected healing arts in which the utilization of crystals and symbolism is prominent. Dis-ease and disorder in ones life usually entails lessons which will allow one to release the burdens of unconsciousness. Although one must ultimately heal oneself, the healing process may be facilitated by the catalytic presence of many things. To experience dis-ease is to experience a total or partial disconnection from wholeness, a loss of awareness of the innate and universal source of perfection. The members of the mineralogical kingdom have been used for centuries to act as catalysts and to assist one in becoming re-united with that source; the employment of newly founded and ancient symbolism, in conjunction with ones creative energies, enhances ones quest toward the ultimate.

The utilization of each array via the "laying-on-of-stones" involves placing the members of the mineral kingdom upon the body of the self or the body of another. Those from ancient civilizations have used this art to facilitate healing of another on all levels; first affecting an aligned connection between the perfection of the etheric body and the physical form and, subsequently, promoting the energy transfer from the minerals to the physical form.

The "laying-on-of-stones" can be used to initiate healing, astral travel, travel to the center of ones being, etc. The processes can facilitate the awareness of the unconscious patterns of behavior which may assist in actualization and/or which have contributed to dysfunctions.

There are no set procedures and no rules; the intuition is the teacher; one will make no mistakes because there are no mistakes - let your creative energies flow. It is recommended, however, that during the application of an array, in the conditions when the subject is in need of assistance in grounding and/or centering, that initial centering be facilitated by holding the feet of the subject and/or that appropriate minerals be used at the areas of the hand and feet chakras; this centering/grounding assists one in the acceptance of the transfer of the mineralogical healing energies during ones participation in the exercises listed.

SETTING THE STAGE

The arrangements may be used via placing the array within ones environment and allowing it to remain and/or via placing the array upon/around the self or another. Gridding is another method of using the arrangements.

If the arrangement is placed within ones environment, it can be placed in a location where it can be used daily [e.g., during meditation] and/or can be placed surrounding something material [e.g., affirmations, material which one desires to transfer to another via teleportation of thoughts/written information, photographs of the self or another for healing or connected-ness, etc.

SELECTING THE STONES

The shapes and structures of the members of the mineralogical kingdom vary with natural occurrence and with enhancement by humanity. Both unpolished/natural and polished crystalline forms of any given crystal configuration embrace and provide the same energies. Some shapes which are fabricated provide for properties identical to those shapes found within the Earth; fabrication of other shapes will not produce identical properties. Other fabricated shapes provide unique properties of both direction and use to the contained energy.

Throughout this publication, the recommendations for the application of selected stones are based upon successful experimentation. The practitioner is urged to explore and to intuitively discover the most suitable arrangement and minerals for each situation.

The assignment of a type of crystal to a specific chakra is not given within the text of this book; it is recommended that the crystal which contains the colour associated with the chakra is used when one is beginning to practice chakra stimulation and balancing, auric healing, and the "laying-on-of-stones" in the art of crystal lay-outs.

In addition to the qualities listed which are relative to each array, the organs located in the area of each chakra and the properties inherent to each chakra can be treated with minerals exhibiting the colour associated with said chakra. As one becomes more attuned to the crystals _and_ to the self, intuition will guide to the most beneficial crystals and the most beneficial locations for placement. When one utilizes these arts with a loving and open heart, there can be no errors and there can be no detrimental or adverse effects.

ENVIRONMENTAL ARRANGEMENTS/LAYOUTS FOR YOUR SPACE

1. Write exactly that which you wish to actualize. Be specific and provide sufficient detail. You can never be too grandiloquent in your detail. Success has been obtained via writing the desire in the future tense [e.g., "I will have no pain by 6AM

tomorrow morning"], or in the present tense [e.g., "I have no pain"]. Please note that the examples in the previous sentence do not contain sufficient detail and are not adequately specific.

Notes: It should be noted that in the everyday routine, most people send the Higher Self a continuous flow of jumbled conflicting wishes, plans, fears, hopes, etc. Each hour or day, they change and/or modify the thoughts relevant to these ideas. The person who decides precisely what is wanted, and holds to this decision emphatically, striving always in that direction, can present to the Higher Self the proper thought forms from which to build the future as desired and planned.

It should also be noted that if your wishes are harmful to another, success cannot be expected.

It is also quite helpful to include in the written word that "I deserve ...[whatever the wish]".

2. Cleanse the area and the material which will be used [e.g., crystals, stones, written matter, photographs, etc.]. Assure that all of the stones have been pre-programmed; program them for the operations for which they will be used. Request protection and assistance from the divine perfection.

3. Attune - between self and the stones and between the self and the subject[s]. Relax, center the self, and initiate deep circular breathing,

5. Speak aloud [this reinforces that which is precisely what is desired] eight times [or a sufficient number of times so that which you wish to actualize is deeply impressed upon both your conscious mind and your subconscious mind]. That which you speak aloud is either memorized verbatim or read from the written word that was generated in step one. One will intuitively recognize when one becomes "one" with the desire.

6. Arrange the stones in accordance with the pattern of your choice.

7. The environment in which the array is located is a lovely place for daily meditation and for relaxing. It is necessary, for the maximum beneficial results, that the practitioner attune with the stones, the array, and the wish[es] at least daily. Cleansing of the area daily may or may not be required.

BODY ARRANGEMENTS/LAYOUTS

1. Prior to the arrival of the subject upon whom you will be arranging the stones, the practitioner attunes to the stones; the practitioner would always be well attuned

to the stones which are used in the arrays. In the case of the practitioner and another person or multiple persons being a part of a patterned configuration, all involved would attune to the stones.

2. Cleanse the area and the material which will be used [e.g., crystals, pillows, etc.]

3. Upon arrival of the subject, discuss the reason for the visit, determine that which is desired to be actualized, and together write the precise words describing the condition desired.

4. Request protection and assistance. Open to your Higher Self and request that the universal perfect vital force flow through you to the subject.

5. Attune your self with the subject. [e.g., via the utilization of attunement stones such as herkimer diamonds, Faden crystals, and/or a crystal which has been programmed for the purpose].

The process which follows the attunement includes opening the chakras of the subject, followed by the conscious relaxation of the subject and the practitioner and the initiation of deep-breathing [circular breathing has been quite effective]. The subject continues deep-breathing until the arrangement of the pattern is completed. The purpose of the arrangement is stated via the reading of the written word [at least eight times] which was generated in step three. The stones are arranged in accordance with the pattern which has been selected, and are placed upon the body of the subject intuitively or via a pre-determined method. The ritual that you have personally chosen or developed to augment the arrangement of the stones is then performed [e.g., guided meditation is a relaxing way to begin].

6. At the end of a healing session, and after removing any stones which have been placed upon the subject, instruct the subject to place his/her hands palms down on his/her solar plexus area. Place your hands over the hands of the subject [palms down] and direct the subject to relax and to allow the healing power of the universal source to run through you, from your hands into his/her hands, in order to facilitate energization, well-ness, and/or relief of pain [physical, emotional, or spiritual].

GRIDDING ARRANGEMENTS

The localities within the Earth and in which minerals reside are connected by an inter-dimensional grid. This grid allows, for example, for the transmittal of energies from one mineral to another. Those minerals which are removed from within the Earth tend to retain an ethereal connection to those remaining within the grid. In order to activate and to enhance the connection between the minerals which are on the Earth plane and those which are a part of the interdimensional grid, a graphic design is accessed via the alignment of the energies of the specific tangible selected minerals and those minerals which remain within the Earth.

When gridding a specific location, the tangible minerals are placed on ley lines within the location of concern. This placement facilitates enhanced energy transfer and subsequent results due to the increase in the focusing ability of the minerals between the points of the grid.

"LAYING-ON-OF-HANDS" DURING "LAYING-ON-OF-STONES"

The following techniques have been used successfully with many of the arrangements shown in the following sections. During a "laying-on-of-stones" session, the "laying-on-of-hands" provides for further stimulation of both the transfer of the energy of the stones and the transfer of the universal perfect energy.

The "laying-on-of-stones" and the "laying-on-of-hands" has been used for centuries to heal physically, mentally, and spiritually. Many types of stones and many methods of "touch" have been used to the benefit of the receiver.

It should be noted that the vital force which maintains the body must have a certain strength in order to maintain a state free of dis-ease. If this force is permitted to become depleted [due to, for example, programming of the self to "believe" that he is susceptible to dis-ease, aches, pains, etc., or dissimilar programming of the self by others - "You'll catch a cold if you go outside with your hair wet", "If you get cold, you'll catch cold", "The whole family is sick with the flu, so you will be too", etc].

Well-ness and dis-ease are the actions of ones conscious and sub-conscious selves; when the connection is maintained between a non-complexed conscious self and the Higher Self, via the non-complexed sub-conscious self, the result is well-ness. The use of the hands in conjunction with stones has produced intensified contact of the unique energies of the stones and the universal healing energy; they assist the practitioner in connecting with the electrical energy flow within the subject and in directing the vital flow to remove and melt energy blockages.

In the situations of healing specific conditions, it is suggested that the practitioner use both crystals and "touch" to promote the healing of the subject. Transmission of energy has worked successfully in the amelioration of emotional and physical traumas and illness and energy blockages in body. It has been used to promote ease of birth, stability of the birth environment, and the integration/release of pre-conception choices including past-life karmic patterns. Touch helps to bring that vital quality of health to every level of the body/mind/spirit.

One of the methods used for healing via "laying-on-of-hands" utilizes the accumulation of a surcharge of Prana [universal life force] and laying of ones hands upon another. It has been reported that there can be a transference of the malady to the healer - this does not need to occur since one sends the universal life charge through the subject, cleansing and purifying as it travels through the body, and being released at a pre-determined location. It is recommended that the healer pre-determine the location of release such that the unwanted energy is discharged to a black hole filled with white light, through which the essence of the product of cleansing is transformed/purified and not released into the environment; it was historically known that the essence of the product of cleansing was an invisible substance which would cling to localities or persons if not directed toward purification. When you lay your hands on another, make a centered audible request that the universal vital force enter the other and correct the condition of concern.

In addition, research has also supported the application of the "laying-on-of-hands" with the "laying-on-of-stones" techniques to the removal of unwanted entity implants and to the detachment of unwanted entities. In these cases, the implant/entity is <u>not</u> "pulled" from ones physical body, but "pushed" from the body and discharged to the black hole filled with white light. Since we are all "working" toward universal love, it seems much kinder to send the unwanted and/or negative energies to a location of purification.

The "laying-on-of-hands" can be applied to a multitude of arrays; the technique serves to assist in physical, emotion, mental, and spiritual healing. One method of combining the "laying-on-of-stones" with the "laying-on-of-hands" is as follows:

- ♥ After "Setting The Stage" and placing the crystals in the arrangement of the chosen pattern, crystals may also be placed on the body [e.g., at the areas of the chakras]. One may either use stones the colour of the chakras and/or stones which are totally intuitively selected. Please note that one cannot cause harm by combining stones - the stones are from our Earth and have lived in a similar environment for eons; in addition, ones intuitive and/or Higher Self will guide one toward the stones that are optimally beneficial.

- ♥ Opening of the chakras is then performed. Chakras can be opened by a variety of methods. One method is via the use of a wand-type crystal, rotated in a counter-clockwise direction [in the northern hemisphere]. Research in Africa in 1989 has supported the opening of chakras [in the southern hemisphere] via rotation of the wand-type crystal in a clockwise direction. Research in The Republic of South Africa during the 1991 workshops has provided data indicating that the energy rotations of ones chakras is not consistently in either the clockwise or the counter-clockwise direction; hence, it is important to "feel" the direction of rotation of each chakra, independent of each other chakra, prior to determining and performing each directional opening. Closure of the chakras is accomplished via the opposite manipulation.

♪ 7 ♫

- The practitioner may remain either within or outside of the bodywork pattern as the remaining exercises are performed.

- The practitioner centers the self by concentrating on a point two inches below the navel, by lightly pulsing the area of the thymus, or by any means which is comfortable. The subject is requested to center and to relax [circular breathing is in progress during this time] and to allow the energy of the stones to permeate the body.

- The practitioner can then direct the subject to feel each specific stone, allowing several minutes per stone for both the conscious and sub-conscious awareness to occur; beginning with the lower part of the body allows the subject to understand grounding, while continuing through the chakras to the crown, allows the healing energies to be acknowledged.

Please note that when energy blockages, healing, implant/entity removal, release of karmic carry-overs, etc., are being facilitated, the stones may be placed upon either the front or the back of the subject. This reverse application, where the subject lays "front-down", may provide for easier access to the location of the unwanted condition; it further provides for an integration and an acknowledgment of the energies existent in the back which have, for many years, been ignored by our civilization. Integration of the left/right brain, the front/back, the top/bottom, the inside/outside, etc., can bring each of us to wholeness.

- The practitioner opens to his/her Higher Self and asks that the universal perfect vital force flow through him/her to the subject. It should be noted that when one requests assistance for a subject through ones Higher Self, the request is also communicated to the Higher Self of the subject; this is predicated on the premise that all Higher Selves are linked as a "multiplicity in singularity" and "singularity in multiplicity" - they are "unity in separation" and work both together and separately.

- The practitioner locates north [or behind the head] of the subject and places his/her hands over the eyes of the subject for several minutes. [The easiest way to position the hands during this activity is with the fingertips of each hand covering one eye while the remaining portion of the hand rests on the forehead or temples of the subject.] This assists the subject to further relax and to allow trust to permeate the environment.

One may notice that the hands are pulsing with the heartbeat and/or are becoming warmer.

♥ Now, location by location, beginning at the crown [or at the feet] of the subject, cover the stones with your hands. Each position will require several minutes of quiet time.

If a single stone is in a location, the practitioner can lay one hand upon the other - the first hand covering the stone and touching the body, while the second hand covers the first hand. If multiple stones are in a location, the practitioner can use both hands, covering one or several stones with one hand while covering another or several other stones with the other hand - covering the stones and touching the body concurrently. If a stone is located at an extremity, the subject can, for example, hold the stone in one hand while placing this stone against the foot of the subject; the other hand is placed on top of the foot of the subject.

♥ Upon completion of the "laying-on-of-stones/hands", the practitioner can proceed to guide the subject toward the recognition of the cause of dis-ease or disorder and can, hence, assist in facilitating the release of the causes. The combination of these techniques seems to help the energies of the crystals to penetrate the physical, emotional, and spiritual bodies to a greater degree.

♥ The chakras of the subject are then closed, by the practitioner, by the manipulation opposite of that which was used for opening.

The subject is now informed that the healing does not end when he/she leaves the realm of the array; his/her Higher Self has been made aware of the condition which is desired, and energies will continue to flow from the Higher Self during both waking and sleeping hours. The subject is also directed to read the written information several times each day until the condition is facilitated and/or corrected.

The "laying-on-of-hands" may also be performed via the utilization of Tibetan pulsing techniques, where the practitioner allows the hands to pulse upon the stones and the body in a rhythmic harmony with the pulse of the subject. When the subject is in accord with the pulsing, there is a dissolving into the self, and an increase of the energy which is transmitted; energy blockages which are identified with trauma, emotional repression, denial of feelings, etc., become evident and one is provided the stimulus with which to release personal identification and to allow the distress to dissolve.

GEOMETRICAL PATTERNS FOR BODYWORK

The ensuing information is provided as guidance for those who wish to practice the art of "laying-on-of-stones". The methods which are presented include examples of techniques which have achieved the desired results; the reader is encouraged to intuitively develop and to subsequently implement additional methods which relate in the application to personal energy and/or accelerate ones personal progress upon the physical, mental, emotional, and spiritual paths.

The patterns which follow describe a variety of arrangements which have been used to facilitate specific qualities and/or conditions [e.g., healing, meditation, ascension, chakra alignment, self-actualization, etc.]. The number of crystals may vary from the number shown in the illustrations; the general configuration of each may be maintained with significantly fewer crystals/minerals.

Where recommendations are provided for the utilization of specific minerals, the application of at least one of the minerals [in an "and/or" description] is suggested.

The vibrational frequencies are given for the zodiacal and planetary configurations due to the dynamic energies emitted by their progression through time and space.

It should be noted that the following configurations also have been successfully applied to the realm of metaphysical jewelry; the wearing of the configuration [or placement of same within ones environment or upon a photograph] acts to transfer, to the user or to the environment, the multi-faceted qualities of the array. Bob Jackson, of Richland, Washington, USA, has combined the mineral kingdom with the energy patterns of the configurations to produce lovely and highly energized metaphysical jewelry. He may be reached through Earth-Love Publishing House.

CHAKRA ARRAY

OPEN THEIR HEARTS

Those whose Hearts
Are closed
Only need
A little bit
Of Love and Understanding
For their Hearts
To Awaken

Marie Mockers
Paris, France, 1990

CHAKRA ARRAY

The "Chakra Array" is established by placing crystals upon and in circumvention to the chakras; Figure 1 illustrates the location of eight major and four minor chakras.

CHAKRA DEFINITIONS

Although chakras were defined in **LOVE IS IN THE EARTH - A KALEIDOSCOPE OF CRYSTALS**, to promote ease in utilizing this book, the explanation and a further description of the chakras is provided.

Chakras [translated from Sanskrit as "wheels" of rotating energy and pronounced as "shock-ras"], as defined by the Eastern Masters, are intersections of vital energy flows which are present in the ethereal body and in related locations of the physical body.

There are hundreds of these intersections, each related to an acupressure/acupuncture point. Of these hundreds of points, there are seven [or eight] major chakras associated with the physical body; these major chakras are the areas where the major energy flows intersect.

The health of an area of the physical body and the condition of its associated chakra are considered interdependent [e.g., when a chakra is clear and vital, the associated portions of the body should also be in the optimum state]. As chakras are cleared, vitalized, and expanded in clarity and development, one may experience the actualization of qualities which have not previously been manifest. It should be noted that each chakra functions to awaken a certain power of response in the particles which flow within and through it; hence, the response mechanism would be holistically considered so that all chakras are integrated [and treated, when required].

Base Chakra - The base chakra [first chakra] is located in the area of the base of the spine in the area of the lumbar. It is the center of vitality, physical energy, and self-preservation. It activates and strengthens the will [e.g., the will to live, to survive, to manifest, etc.], assists one in living on the physical plane, and stimulates the life-sustaining energies. It is the location of the resting Kundalini, a force which exists on all planes, and that which awakens all other chakras. It is the center which vitalizes the kidneys, the suprarenal glands, and the spinal column in the physical body. The colours associated with the base chakra include red [representing the essential, idealistic, and confident passion for life] and black [representing stability and grounding to the source of security].

Sacral Chakra - The sacral chakra [second chakra] is located in the area 1" to 2" below the navel. It is the center of desire, emotion, creativity, sexuality, and intuition; it provides for sensitivity to the influences of the outer world. It stimulates the creative life force, the forces required for existence on the physical plane, and the bases of life, itself. It is the center which vitalizes the digestive system, reproductive organs, sexual activity, and the gonads where sex hormones are produced. The second chakra has been known as the pathway to health; it is attuned to emotions and thoughts concerning well-ness and is, usually, the center which allows the condition of dis-ease to manifest in order to cleanse the body, mind, and/or emotions.

The second chakra has also been said to be located under the area of the rib cage, at the location of the spleen. It has been called the <u>splenic chakra</u> and is considered, by some, to be a major chakra. In addition to the attributes of the sacral chakra, it is the center which allows for vitalization of the entire physical form. It also acts as an open door to both the receipt and the assimilation of the life-giving energies of the universe. Although considered by some experts to be the enabling energy to allow one to travel consciously [with partial understanding of that which is seen and experienced] in the astral body, the solar plexus chakra is usually awarded that attribute.

The colour associated with the sacral chakra is orange [representing wisdom, equity, creativity, and benevolence to all]; the colour associated with the splenic chakra is blue/green [representing the synthesis of Divine guidance in the areas of healing.

<u>Solar Plexus Chakra</u> - The solar plexus chakra [third chakra] is located at the solar plexus area, below the breastbone and behind the stomach. It is sometimes considered to be located at the navel. Looking at the solar plexus chakra from the back of the body, the location is just below the shoulder blades. It is the center of personal power, ambition, intellect, astral force [conscious astral travel with concomitant partial comprehension of same], desire and emotions based on intellect, and touch.

The third chakra contains a protective energy, protecting against any negativity which is contained within any of the other chakras. It is the center which vitalizes the stomach, liver, gall bladder, sympathetic nervous system [activating involuntary muscles which enhance the mobilization of the physical body], pancreas, and adrenal glands. The colour associated with the third chakra is yellow [representing meditative analytical thought and intellectual activity].

<u>Heart Chakra</u> - The heart chakra [fourth chakra] is located in the center of the chest, at the level of the heart. It is the center of compassion, love, group consciousness, and spirituality associated with a "oneness" with "All That Is". The fourth chakra provides for a desegregation between the loving energy of the heart and the analytical energy of the intellect; it provides for a "sprinkling" of love and compassion to all of the chakras.

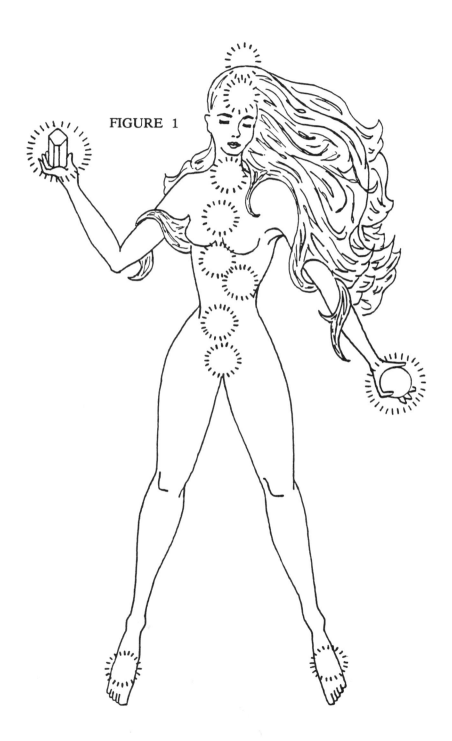

FIGURE 1

It also enables one to attune to the vibratory rates of other astral entities such that one may instinctively perceive the emotions of same. It is the center which vitalizes the heart, thymus, circulatory system, blood, cellular structure, and the involuntary muscles which assist in the restoration of both physical and loving energy. The colours associated with the fourth chakra include pink [representing softness in strength, compassion, empathy, and unconditional love to all that exists] and green [representing soothing, smoothing healing, ecstasy and exhilaration, and a joyful and fulfilling anticipation].

Throat Chakra - The throat chakra [fifth chakra] is located at the neck, the center being recognized as the area of the throat located above the collar bone. It is the center of communication, sound, and expression of creativity via thought, speech, and writing. The fifth chakra has been called the communication center, acting to provide the energy for, and the understanding of, both verbal and mental communications. It also enables one to utilize the sense of hearing on the astral plane. It is the center which vitalizes the thyroid gland, throat and jaw areas, alimentary canal, lungs, vocal cords, and the breath. The colour associated with the fifth chakra is blue [representing the knowledge of, and oneness with, Divine guidance].

Third-Eye Chakra - The third-eye chakra [sixth chakra], also known as the brow chakra, is located between and about one finger-breadth above the eyebrows. On the back of the body, the corresponding location is at the base of the skull in the area of the medulla oblongata. It is the center of psychic power, higher intuition, the energies of the spirit, magnetic forces, and light. It enables focusing of the higher intuitive information and stimulates the wisdom for "right" intent. The sixth chakra, when activated and clear, is the center for outside guidance and the intuitive "aha". It facilitates the power of magnification on the astral plane.

It also assists in the purification of negative tendencies and in the elimination of selfish attitudes. It further enables one to distinguish [with clarity] that which is encountered on the astral plane. It is the center which vitalizes the cerebellum, nose, central nervous system, the pituitary gland, and the left eye. The combined interaction of the pineal and pituitary glands activates this center. The colour associated with the sixth chakra is indigo [representing the attainment, the search, and those who search for the spiritual purpose of life].

Crown Chakra - The crown chakra [seventh chakra] is located at the crown of the head. It is the center of spirituality, enlightenment, dynamic thought, and energy. It allows for the inward flow of wisdom from the ethers and brings the gift of cosmic consciousness. When stimulated and clear, it enables one to see the truth concerning illusory ideals, materialistic pursuits, self-limiting concepts, pride, and vanity; it further allows one to experience continuous self-awareness and conscious detachment from personal emotions.

It is the center which vitalizes the cerebrum, the right eye, and the pineal gland. The colours associated with the seventh chakra are violet [representing royalty in enlightenment and the search and attainment of the true meanings of spirituality, life, and existence] and a shimmering golden-white [representing the state of perfection in body, mind, emotions, and spirituality].

Minor Chakras - The areas where few energy flows intersect are called minor chakras. These minor chakras include, for example, centers at the palm of the each hand, at the sole of each foot, behind each eye, in front of each ear where the jawbone is connected, above each breast, and at the back of each knee.

CHAKRA ARRAY UTILIZATION

All emotional experiences are stored within the body; the areas of the chakras are vortices through which energy transformation may be facilitated [e.g., transformation of energy blockages and/or diminished energy flow, which may be obvious from conditions manifest during dis-ease]; the blockages may be gently removed via the utilization of the "Chakra Array" pattern. Energization, implant/entity removal, guided meditation, etc., can also be facilitated via this array.

Chakras are awakened by the Kundalini energy [see also the "Kundalini" pattern]; they may be opened by a variety of methods. One method is via the use of a wand-type crystal, rotated in a counter-clockwise direction [in the northern hemisphere]. Research in Africa in 1989 has supported the opening of chakras [in the southern hemisphere] via rotation of the wand-type crystal in a clockwise direction. Research in The Republic of South Africa during the 1991 workshops has provided data indicating that the energy rotations of ones chakras is not consistently in either the clockwise or the counter-clockwise direction; hence, it is important to "feel" the direction of rotation of each chakra, independent of each other chakra, prior to determining and performing each directional opening. Closure of the chakras is accomplished via the opposite manipulation.

Vitalization of the chakra may be provided by crystals of the colour corresponding to the chakra. The assignment of a type of crystal to a specific chakra is not given within the text of this book; it is recommended that the crystal which contains the colour associated with the chakra is used when one is beginning to practice chakra stimulation and balancing, auric healing, and the "laying-on-of-stones" in the art of crystal lay-outs.

Many massage and bodywork therapists place the minerals, which are associated with each of the chakras, below the table on which the subject rests -the location of each mineral being placed in an area parallel to the location of the associated chakra; this activity tends to assist in both the alleviation of energy blockages and the release of tension and constriction within the body.

In addition to qualities which are attributed to each stone, the organs located in the area of the chakra and the properties inherent to each chakra can be treated with minerals exhibiting the colour associated with said chakra.

As one becomes more attuned to the crystals <u>and</u> to the self, intuition will guide the practitioner to the most beneficial crystals and the most beneficial locations for placement. When one utilizes these arts with a loving and open heart, there can be no errors and there can be no detrimental or adverse effects. Please note that *all members of the mineral kingdom are totally compatible and all crystals function efficiently with all other crystals.* The "semi-exceptions" to this practice are those minerals which are highly-radioactive/highly-toxic, and which the energies of humanity have not yet been enabled to utilize without detrimental effects.

The following exercise has been utilized to vitalize the chakras, to provide for consciousness on the cellular level, to remove implants, to promote healing, etc. The application of "laying-on-of-hands" to well-ness exercises involving the chakra array is also recommended.

♥   Crystals, which correspond in colour[s] to the chakra associations listed above, are selected and cleansed; additional intuitively selected minerals may also be utilized.

♥   The practitioner and the subject attune to one another; concurrent holding of an attunement crystal [e.g., herkimer diamond, Faden crystal, or a crystal which has been programmed for attunement] - the receiving hand of one [palm "down"] resting upon the receiving hand of the other [palm "up"] and the crystal in the center of the hands.

This attunement exercise opens the practitioner and the subject to each other and facilitates an atmosphere of trust and non-restraint.

♥   When an additional array is not employed, the subject centers the self, initiates deep circular breathing, and relaxes the body and mind. The deep breathing process is continued for approximately five-minutes. The circular breathing is continued during the entire process.

♥   The practitioner centers the self, opens the chakras of the subject, and [after the "deep" phase of the circular breathing has been completed by the subject] places the crystals upon/around the appropriate locations.

Grounding of the subject, when necessary, may be accomplished via the placement of black tourmaline, smokey quartz, etc., at the bottom of the feet and directed away from the body. [Grounding, during this exercise, is not usually required; it would, however, be helpful for those who are emotionally volatile.]

Receptivity may be reinforced via the placement of quartz crystals upon the arms, and in the hands; the termination, when singly terminated, would be directed toward the upper body.

Ones perception of the changes in the chakras may be facilitated via the placement of quartz crystals in the areas of the crown chakra [directed toward the crown chakra] and at the feet [directed toward the bottom of the feet].

♥ Placement of the crystals upon the subject is usually initiated at the base chakra [unless grounding stones are utilized]; the additional crystals are placed with intuitive timing. The differences in experience, with respect to the step-wise progression in placement, is not often noticeable.

♥ The practitioner, beginning with the crown chakra, places his/her hands upon each chakra/crystal. The hands are held in this position for three to five minutes. Centering, e.g., via concentration upon the area two-inches below the navel, is recommended each time the hands are transferred to another chakra.

During the process, the subject may desire to comment on the feelings and the sensations which are experienced; in some cases, comment is deferred until the end of the session.

♥ At the end of the process, the practitioner removes the crystals, solicits experiential response from the subject, and discusses the results. The chakras of the subject are then closed.

♥ After the first session, it is a lovely custom for the practitioner to give the attunement stone to the subject; in future sessions, the subject may return with the stone to reinforce attunement [or a hug may more than suffice].

The "Chakra Array" is one of the finest for healing via crystals. Prior to the initiation of the array, the auric field is scanned in order to determine energy blockages and/or the existence of auric "holes" which allow the drain of energy from the physical body. Appropriate crystals are selected to cleanse and stabilize the aura and the crystal is directed toward the auric field; a "sweeping" motion is performed from the top to the bottom or from the bottom to the top of the auric body; both a pre-determined direction and an intended receiving source for any negativity are recommended. In addition to the quartz crystal, there are numerous other minerals which are quite useful for balancing, cleansing, stabilizing, and scanning and correcting any problematic areas in the aura. After these processes, the practitioner opens the chakras, selects the crystals which will assist in the healing, and intuitively places them upon the body of the subject. Information will be forthcoming from the subject which will guide the practitioner and the subject to the determination of that emotional issue or prior programming which has provided the bases for the dis-ease; release of the bases is often accomplished during subsequent "laying-on-of-stones" sessions - often, with a variety of distinct and dissimilar crystals.

The "Chakra Array" has also been utilized to stimulate the immune system, activating the primary physical line of defence. It assists one in consciously recognizing the impact that the emotional and psychological states have upon ones state of well-being; it promotes stress reduction and the diminishment of emotional factors which are devitalizing ones system. The Echinacea extract and/or tincture, used in conjunction with this array has produced excellent results.

Guided meditation and past-life ascension have been successfully performed via the utilization of this array.

FIRST PRINCIPLE ARRAYS

RULES ARE FOR FOOLS
AND THE WISEST OF MEN -
WHICH ONE ARE YOU?

Paul Snook
Johannesburg, RSA

DRUID CIRCLE

The "Druid Circle" configuration is established by placing the crystals in the design of a Celtic cross, the center located upon the body at the solar plexus; the entire arrangement is then surrounded by a circular field [See Figure 2]. The arms are perpendicular to the body. The number of crystals used is left to the intuition of the practitioner.

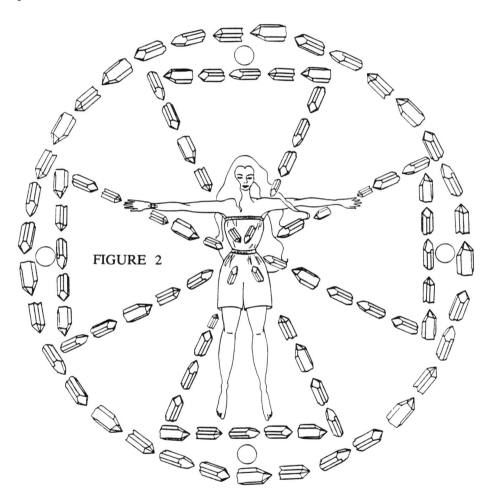

FIGURE 2

This array assists in future-telling via auguries from the world of natural phenomena [e.g., the stars, clouds, wind, smoke, plants, minerals {the Faden crystal, the ajoite phantom, the red phantom, the electric-blue sheen obsidian, and the nephrite with quartz crystal structures have successfully facilitated a direct link between one and the depth of wisdom and energy of the elements of the mineral kingdom}, the flight and/or the call of birds, the rain, etc.].

It also induces memory of incidents which are antecedent to the issue being addressed; the memory not being, necessarily, from present-life physical experience, but also arising from past-lives and other worlds. This operation is initiated via entry to the array and opening the area of the solar plexus to the outer realms of nature; the question is verbalized and the natural images begin to float through the mind. Ones intuitive awareness, which is also augmented via the array, will provide for total understanding of the answer to the question.

Within this array, a "touchstone" may also be used to verify the authenticity of the messages which are given. The "touchstone" provides for a connection with the "absolutes of nature" which govern ones actions - i.e., honesty, purity, love, and unselfishness. If the message contains these qualities and does not contradict ones intrinsic morality, the answer may be safely implemented. The question which is normally posed to the energies of the "touchstone" is "Will the action resulting from this advice enhance ones efficiency, strength, and loving progress?" A "touchstone" is intuitively selected by the user and placed within a smaller version of the array for a period of time in which total energizing can be completed [usually several days, or twenty-four hours if the energizing is performed during a distinct phase of the moon, during an eclipse, and/or during the celebrations of the equinox/solstice periods]. Subsequent re-charging is also recommended. In several cases, the "touchstone", after empowered with the smaller version of the array, has been successfully used without ones entry to the normal-sized array.

The removal of unwanted other-worldly implants has also been facilitated via this array, allowing one to recognize the disparate pattern of thought or conditioning, to determine the precise location of same, and to perform an ethereal removal which may either return the infusion to the source or provide for the disintegration of same; in this application, the method of disposal is determined prior to entry to the array and the appropriate minerals, to facilitate the process, are placed within the array at the initiation of the exercise.

The "Druid Circle" further assists one in "judging with spirituality", allowing one to recognize prior to concluding, that each person and object in ones reality is connected to ones individuality and that "all" comprises "All That Is". Entry to the array, prior to any judgment, is recommended; a broad-based loving attitude is facilitated and understanding becomes adjunctive to perception.

THE YOD

"The Yod" configuration is established by placing the crystals in the pattern of a "Y" with the intersection located between the breasts of the subject [See Figure 3]. The number of crystals used is left to the intuition of the practitioner.

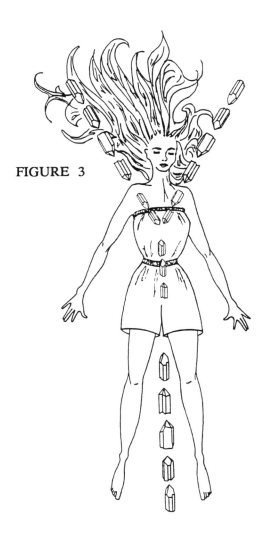

FIGURE 3

For the truly intelligent and evolving person, the foremost principles in reality are comprised of ones consciousness of that reality <u>and</u> the degree of the strength of realization which is available. When there is manifestation in ones actuality [all dimensions], there is first the element of action which initiates the process. This configuration assists in the origination and the initiation of the actions which are necessary to both fulfill and complete the transaction.

It brings the positive, active, and dynamic forces to ones actualization and fashions one to reflect the role of the "white magician". Supplying impulse, via the location of the intersection of the array, it facilitates the projection of energy to create, to sustain, to change, to modify, ...

It provides the primary energy toward the activation of the divine nature and the infinite perfection which is within the self. "The Yod" brings a "right" transmission of that which is "willed" such that a balance of ones world of physical needs is facilitated with the supplementation of the element of realization.

The configuration instills authority over ones circumstances, and promotes concentration in any endeavor which is recalled within the array.

A smaller version of "The Yod" placed upon ones photograph, continues the stimulation of these qualities. It further enables one to recognize the duality of "facts" and to, subsequently, find and live the "middle truth".

Duality situations, of which one is a part, can be analyzed objectively and, subsequently, remediated. The utilization of the array by two persons [where one array is the inverse of the other, where the bodies form a straight line, and where the head of one person is in direct connection with the head of the other] has assisted in resolution of differences and in the determination of appropriate and agreeable compromises. The array tends to liberate the energy of anger and to direct that energy toward constructive enterprises. It prompts a "flowing outward" toward the environment such that ones energy does not become locked into internal efforts of repression and control.

"The Yod" provides for the introduction of creativity, the exploration of all aspects, and the consummation of the resultant form. It promotes independence and ready response to inspiration, cultivation, and healing; the use of this configuration with the chakra healing arrangement is highly recommended.

STAR YOD

The "Star Yod" configuration is established by placing the crystals in the pattern of a "Y" with the central portion continuing from the location between the breasts to above the top of the head of the subject [See Figure 4]. The number of crystals used is left to the intuition of the practitioner.

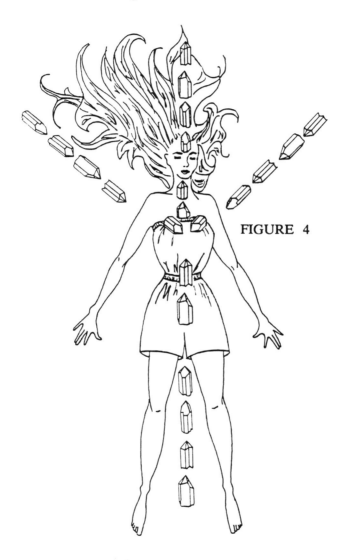

FIGURE 4

This configuration is one which stimulates, as Aristotle succinctly described, the first principles of learning, the first principles of being, and the absolute unity of being and thought in which all differences of finite thought and existence are overcome. In brevity, it provides for the management and understanding of abstract ideas.

The "Star Yod" assists one in recognizing logic as a form of thought which can be, altogether, separated from *matter*, and by the application of which, *matter* can not be affected or changed. It furthers one understanding that the separation between the mind and its object can only be a division on the basis of a unity and, therefore, the self-abnegation of the mind in its investigation of facts, cannot be an absolute renunciation, but is only the first step on the path to discovering that the facts are intelligible and, hence, essentially related to the intelligence. It assists one in the realization of self-revelation with respect to the object such that the world may completely reveal itself, in its harmony, with itself and with the mind.

The "Star Yod" stimulates the unification of the intellect, the physical, the emotional, and the spiritual. It assists one in achieving the knowledge relative to disorders within the physical and emotional systems, and provides for a clear understanding of the logical process through which the disorders may be released. It has also been used to produce the integration between intellectual information and intuitive awareness, helping one to apply the cooperative result of the synthesis of these two realms.

It also acts to reveal the foundation of inner knowledge upon which a new world may be built, bringing the application of logic to the implementation of love. It has been used to stimulate the mental processes and to enhance ones mathematical, deductive, inductive, and productive capabilities.

Placement of a smaller version of the array upon ones photograph can concurrently amplify ones reasoning abilities and ones intuitive faculties such that the two sets of qualities may be combined to promote a cooperative effect.

It further releases self-imposed "imperative" requirements and eliminates constraining forces which have been self-implemented. The application of logic, without the opposition of structured and limiting separatist attitudes, can further ones progression in all areas of life and in all aspects of the mental, physical, emotional, and spiritual realms.

An exercise which has been quite useful involves retrieval of a memory that will awaken a profoundly emotional response, and the application of the intellect to the remembrance. After objectively examining the memory, one "re-files" the information and then clears the mind of all thoughts relevant to the topic. Upon the next entry to the array, the memory is again retrieved to evaluate whether it continues to elicit a significant emotional response; if so, the same process is initiated - if not, the memory is again "re-filed" and another memory is retrieved and relegated to the same process.

CREATIVE FORCES - RECEIVING

The "Creative Forces - Receiving" configuration is established by placing the crystals in the pattern of a single-lined cross, with the intersection located at the solar plexus of the subject, and the arms of the subject relaxed at the sides of the body [See Figure 5].

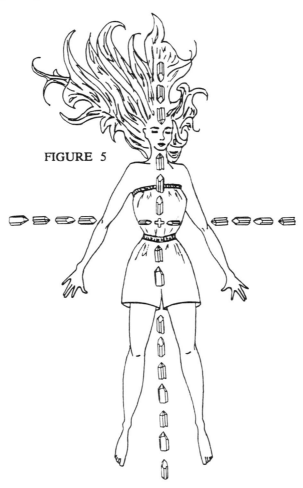

FIGURE 5

This array is placed such that ones head is in the northerly direction. Crystals in multiples of seven and in multiples of four have been used successfully in this arrangement. When available, a fairy cross [staurolite], is placed upon the solar plexus intersection.

This configuration is one of "being" a part of the world of elements and "being" within the complex of all the influences of ones surroundings. It promotes the receipt of positive energies from the physical, astral, and extra-terrestrial planes, and assists in the alignment and balancing of the mental, physical, and emotional bodies.

It is an array for receiving information from all realms, for "tapping into" the universal source of power, and for bringing strength and determination to ones life. It represents the creative forces and facilitates the application of the energies of each cardinal direction via the electrical force fields which are established in the pattern.

"Creative Forces - Receiving" is an excellent array for healing situations. It facilitates the internal adjustment to ones external environment, providing for a direct receipt and an appropriate routing of vibratory energies to the proper nerve centers, with subsequent transmission, via the sympathetic nervous system, to the appropriate organs of the body. The stimulating vibrations are enhanced and provide for proper metabolic responses.

Based on the premise that dis-ease is an alteration of the oscillatory state of the equilibrium of an organism which is affected in the physical and psychic fields, one may align the internal and external rays of vibration to correspond to each other, and to produce a state of balance and well-being. The array tends to ameliorate the disruptive energies to which one has been externally, or internally, exposed, in order to initiate healing on the physical and emotional levels.

It is an array of response to, and identification with, the energies of the mineral kingdom and the energies of others. A double arrangement [the subject being within the "Creative Forces - Receiving" pattern, and the practitioner being within the "Creative Forces - Earth Healing" pattern] also facilitates a timely transmission and an immediate receipt of energy.

The array has also been utilized as a pattern for receiving the creativity of the universe, furthering ones pursuit of inventive and original ideas, and prompting an endless flow of relevant and insightful information to the user.

In addition, it has been used to energize elixirs, tinctures, and plants, and to provide a protective barrier around that which it grids [e.g., via a photograph of that which is to be protected].

CREATIVE FORCES - EARTH HEALING

The "Creative Forces - Earth Healing" configuration is established by placing the crystals in the pattern shown in Figure 6. The intersections are located at the solar plexus and at the throat chakra of the subject. The number of crystals utilized in the array is left to the intuition of the practitioner.

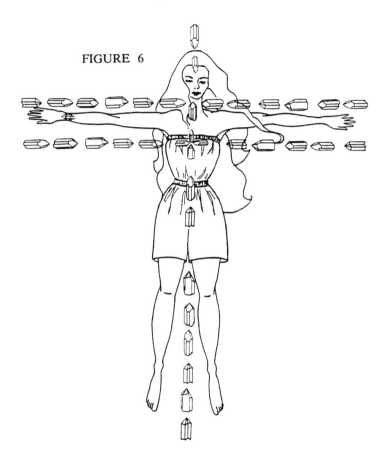

FIGURE 6

The Earth both maintains and sustains ones reality and existence physically and metaphysically, connecting one to all other life forms and enlivening ones spirit of continuity. In this age of science and technology, the populous has tended to become oblivious to these actualities, and the ecological imbalances of the Earth and the physical form have developed into a reflection of this state. This configuration has been used to assist one in understanding that which is inappropriate and that which can be performed to ameliorate the depressed perfection of the physical world. It promotes insight into the methods which can be utilized to transform ones daily life in order to further consciousness and health and the extension of the self toward others who are initiating the same quest. One is provided with the techniques to inspire and educate others to create a holistic relationship with the Earth and to re-connect to the Earth in a personal and individual manner. The array assists one in acting such that "too little is not done too late"; helping one to act purposefully and effectively. It facilitates constructive change in ones consciousness and in ones world, promoting mental clarity such that one may fathom ones inherent responsibilities as a citizen of the universe.

As the Earth experiences changes, we experience changes; this array assists in the synthesis of these changes such that the state of balance between humanity and the Earth is re-initiated. Gridding of the Earth with this array [both via photography and in actual locations of instability] is also recommended.

The utilization of the array to connect with others in order to produce the worldwide healing operations, via the transmittal of energies to both the Earth and to others who enter the array, has been accomplished by the following exercise: One first defines whether the connection will be between the self and others who are cultivating Earth healing, or between the self and the Earth. Next one centers the self, enters the array, and commences deep circular breathing. The flow of the connective energy is visualized as flowing through the arms and as being released to the directions in which the hands are located. [It is recommended that the array be rotated ninety-degrees after each exercise so that the energy can be sent in all directions; with this array, the field of energy transfer has been determined to be forty-five degrees above and below the plane of the arms.]

One may initiate pre-determined times with others through-out the world such that a great amount of energy is transferred toward Earth healing; the thirty-minutes prior to, and after, the actual times of the solstices, equinoxes, full moon, and new moon, are currently being used to connect with others for Earth healing. One is encouraged to establish additional times to initiate the exercise singularly and with friends in proximity; these exercises are usually directed toward specific areas and specific needs of the Earth, as well as, to the remediation of conditions of the populous which have tended toward the hinderance of healing [in this case, energies are directed which are programmed to diminish destructive attitudes and to instill a perspective of love to be given to ones environment].

The philosophy of the ancient Aztecs and Nahuas reflects the ideal that every phase of nature was sustained and personified by a representative guardian spirit. This array assists one in connecting to the spiritual plane of both the singular and collective natural forces and components of same. It has been used to bring balance to the natural forces and to promote the healing of our Earth. Many of the traditional protective energies of historical times have been contacted via the utilization of the array {e.g., the guardian of volcanos and earthquakes [Zotzilaha], the nourisher [Tonacayohua], the guardian of renewal [Cihuapipiltin], the healer [Ixtlilton], the guardian of the earth dwellers [Mosilikatse], and the universal life giver/patron divinity of birth and growing vegetation [Quetzalcoatl and/or Itzamna]}.

TAU

The "Tau" configuration is established by placing the crystals in the pattern of an inverted "L" with the long portion of the "L" located on a line at the center of the body and ending above the head of the subject, and the short portion of the "L" initiating above the center of the head and continuing toward the left side of the body of the subject [See Figure 7]. The number of crystals used is left to the intuition of the practitioner [multiples of two have been successful].

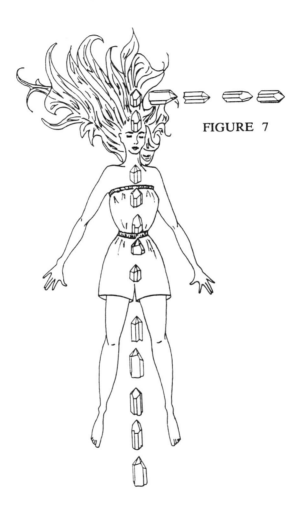

FIGURE 7

This configuration represents the bringing forth and/or emergence of the self. It is representative of the Southern Cross, in the night sky of the southern hemisphere, conveying a time of plentitude and rejoicing. It represents the Tau, the great primary forces which were, at one time, referred to as the builders of the universe and the originators of all realms.

The array can be used to stimulate the total advent of the potential self, stimulating the condition of abundance within ones life. It acts to further the inherent wisdom of the self, bringing exhilaration in all activities, and bringing strength to purpose.

It serves to bring innovation and beauty to ones life [concurrently] and assists in all exploratory activities.

It is a royal array of decision, assisting one in realizing a conclusion which would be beneficial to all who are involved. Said to have once been the seat of Osiris, it promotes the furtherance of all judgments based upon the loving heart. It promotes insight and provides for the non-exclusion of all possibilities prior to decision-making. It is said to stimulate an equilibrium between the user and that which is being evaluated.

It allows one to release conformity, and to maintain a community spirit where the collective mass is not divided into classes according to worldly status.

It is an array of the stratosphere, providing for uniformity in action and energy. It brings one ethereal connections between ones brothers and sisters of all worlds. It represents the "one", the unification of all into one totality. It further acts to relieve the "closed" aspects of ones character and to allow for the opening of the self to others.

The "Tau" is said to bring "luck" to the user; placed upon a photograph of the self or a facsimile of that from which one may, by chance or conscious effort, gain profit, it is said to send the energies of success to the environment and to promote the attainment of that which, otherwise, may be termed as coincidental.

The utilization of the array with another [head toward head, bodies in a straight line], has been reported to facilitate a fellowship which is beyond personal love. It tends to stimulate the release of adversarial feelings and emotions, and to produce a devotion to the well-being and care of others. It is quite useful when one is in the position to serve another, helping one to understand the intrinsic value of the service and to understand the concept that "I am also a 'you'♥"

It has been used successfully in homeopathic and naturopathic treatments. It can also be used in the treatment of disorders relating to the heart, hands, liver, muscular structure, lung tissue, lymphatic glands, the skin resilience, and the ears.

TAU GROUNDING

The "Tau Grounding" configuration is established by placing the crystals in the pattern of a "T" with another row of crystals above the "T" [See Figure 8]. The number of crystals used is left to the intuition of the practitioner.

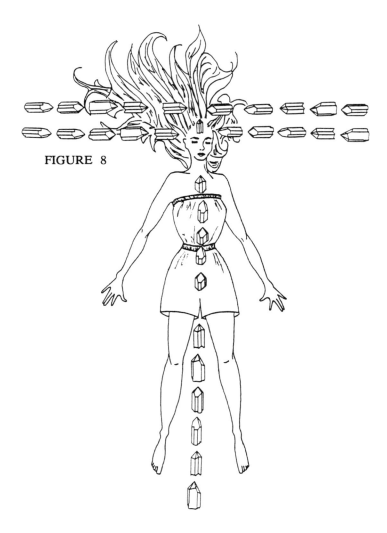

FIGURE 8

The energies which are emitted from this array are elemental energies, the subtle force which sustains the physical body. When we ground the self, we also ground the etheric body. Grounding prior to the initiation of psychic exercise prevents the depletion of ones elemental energies and allows one to draw energy from the universal source. Grounding, which is also regarded as "centering", can be facilitated via the utilization of crystals, via concentration on the area of the body which is located two-inches below the navel, via the "Tau Grounding" array, etc. Grounding via the array is recommended prior to the implementation of psychic activities.

This array is utilized to teach one to become grounded with the Earth and all substance which surrounds ones life. It helps one to live on this plane in a contributing and effectual manner, such that one may promote comfortable conditions and compatible living.

"Tau Grounding" has been placed upon "star people" to assist them in the transition from their world to ours, helping them to understand the modulation of passage and the adjustments which will be conducive to successful participation within the society.

A smaller version of the configuration may be placed upon ones photograph to facilitate grounding during the utilization of crystals/minerals. It allows for the handling of a variety of energies without the disturbance of the auric field.

The array has also been useful for visualization, re-birthing, and for generating a dynamic charge of energy which may be applied toward protective activities, visualized creative endeavors, operations involving the evocation of the goddess within the self. It assists one in confronting challenges and in re-directing the self when necessary; it acts to stimulate conscious movement which will be catalytic to ones progressive growth, and to promulgate new and innovative views.

It can be applied to suppress the disintegration of molecular cohesion, acting as a healing array to raise the vibrational frequency of the specified location such that the perfect state is consciously recognized and transmitted from the ethereal body to the physical. It is also useful for the stabilization of depression and emotional trauma, again, balancing the vibratory energies and then infusing the aura with a cleansing force.

It has been used in the treatment of disorders associated with less than adequate motor skills and in the amelioration of conditions associated with dysfunctions of the brain, the pineal gland, the thymus, and the legs/feet.

TAU ARISING - MEDITATION

The "Tau Rising - Meditation" configuration is established by placing the crystals in the pattern shown in Figure 9. When available, the utilization of isomorphic minerals [e.g., phantom and included crystals, chevron amethyst, pyrite replacement minerals, rutilated/tourmalinated/goethite included crystals, etc.] are recommended for the array. The number of crystals used is left to the intuition of the practitioner.

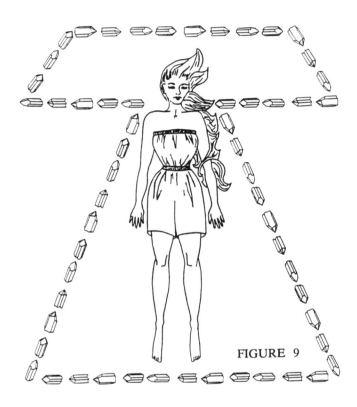

FIGURE 9

Meditation is one of the most powerful techniques which are available to improve ones health and well-ness on the physical, intellectual, and emotional planes. This array provides an ideal climate for the practice of the meditative techniques, such that the understanding of meditation is resonant with the self-guided experience. One may resolve major obstacles that have detained the entry into the deep meditative state which can increase ones mindfulness and, subsequently, facilitate clarity, inner peace, serenity, joyfulness, creativity, and positive energy.

This array assists one in consciously cultivating the attitudes and thought patterns leading to the quality of mindfulness which enhances dynamic intuition on all levels. It serves to relieve negative attitudes, helps one to listen to the inner voice, and helps one to discover the enjoyment of ones mind and its hidden potentials. It further acts to release hidden potentials, to increase ones experiences of harmony, and to induce self-confidence which enables one to "be" both dynamically and fully.

Bringing together all of the disparities of ones nature [i.e., emotional, personal, physical, and intellectual], it fosters the integration of the right and left brain, the present and past experiences, and the conscious and unconscious dimensions of ones being. Vitality is experienced and balance with inner clarity is advanced. Note that the integration of the right and left brain may be accomplished via entry to the array, conscious deep circular breathing, and the visual merging of the dual portions of ones mental processes; the continuance may be facilitated via the placement of ones photograph within a smaller version of the array together with a missive of direction describing that which is desired.

This meditative array enhances ones introspective capabilities, increasing self-reliance, self-design, and self-direction. It intensifies the meditative state and allows one to "go within" in order to transcend the self and to exist in the present moment such that one does not identify the self with ones thought patterns. We all live in an age which is, at least partially, governed by time; we are constantly busy and oriented toward that which is external to the self - it is *time* to take *time* for yourself to experience the blissful state of meditation. One exercise which is conducive to the enhancement of the meditative state is as follows: One centers the self and enters the array; deep circular breathing is initiated and one focuses on the area of the third-eye. As thoughts and images appear, they are watched, but not prevented from continuing through the mind; one allows the thoughts to flow in, and through, the mind until emptiness remains and the weight, of all that one has carried within the mind is released. The "time" will pass and one will become a part of the totality of "All That Is".

Placement of a smaller version of the array upon ones photograph also assists in the entry to, immersion within, and completion of, a deep state of meditation. It helps one to rise above the intricacies of ones life and to return refreshed and renewed.

The actualization of mindfulness during all daily activities may be enhanced by placing ones photograph within the array with a missive describing that which is desired. The "absent", yet ethereal, stimulus, assists one in "being the doing", in total absorption with the present activity and in all activities relative to the pursuit of tantra, the total experience.

The entry of two persons to the singular array has acted to further both intuitive and verbal communication skills; in addition, the attainment of oneness through the shared meditative state and/or via tantric communion, has been elevated. In actuality, a union is fostered in which the consciousness of the selves have disappeared, and in which the participants are "one".

QUADRATE

The "Quadrate" configuration is established by placing the crystals in the pattern shown in Figure 10. The number of crystals used is left to the intuition of the practitioner.

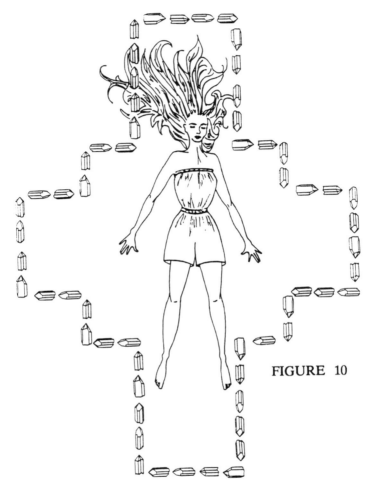

FIGURE 10

This array has assisted in promoting the understanding of the art of symbolism, the knowledge and treatment of symbols, primarily in reference to that which is spiritual, invisible, and based upon the ideal. It allows one to attach emblems and/or signs to an object or activity such that the illusion and the object/activity are likened to coincidence. The array also serves to enhance the understanding of the reality which "speaks" to each of us in a multitude of subtle ways, reminding one of "things", suggesting manners of behavior, and fore-shadowing future events. One may recognize the eternal dance of symbols and allegories which have been in ones environment since ones inception on this planet; it assists one to recall each pattern in all of life and to recognize that all is alive with signs and symbols; it helps one to become aware of the symbols and promptings which have a direct pertinence to ones daily life. "Quadrate" has produced insight to that which can be given and/or utilized to stimulate a bonding memory of activities between the self and others. A symbol defined and/or developed within this array can produce an instantaneous recall, of that to which it is attached, each time the symbol is encountered; the many applications of this concept are far-reaching and of an unlimited magnitude. The configuration has promoted access to the hieroglyphics and pictorial portrayals of the ancient societies and has further instilled the understanding of the animal forms and the combinations of animal/human figures which were used in their ancient texts and tablets. It has fostered an understanding of a symbolism of all that is created, and facilitates the understanding of the application of allegorical symbolism to each activity, to each person, and/or to each object. The capability to distinguish between the conventional and the sacred essence which is represented in ceremonies and in mundane activities, has also been provided. Symbolic representations of numbers [e.g., vibratory rates], mathematics, chemicals, architectural and art forms, religion, etc., and the multitude of metaphysical disciplines [e.g., the Runes, I Ching, Tarot, Neo-Tarot, astrology, etc.] have been presented to the user in an intuitive manner such that total and complete understanding was forthcoming. It assists one in opening to the sepulchres of the ancient world, in beholding the monuments of the past, and in understanding the enigmas of each symbolic representation.

The placement of a smaller version of the array upon a photograph of a person or object can act to stimulate the inner knowledge of an appropriate symbol for representing same; this application requires a written missive to be included which states the purpose of the array.

For the metaphysical applications, one may perform future-telling within the array. The state of dreaming has also been promoted during sleep within the array; in this case, the symbology of the dreams which occur are totally obvious; in addition, the translation of dream symbology can be furthered via the placement of a smaller version of the array upon ones photograph, with a missive stating the purpose of the array.

The concept, that symbols and words represent ideas, is implemented such that an analogy between the symbol and the idea is presented in an understandable manner. One is presented with ideas which symbolize, in mental imagery, the "thing" in the outside world; the ideas serve to assume a dynamic force through which one relates the self. Overall, the personal understanding of symbolism is heightened and the ability to apply the art of symbolism in ones world is enhanced. "Quadrate" brings the knowledge of ancient symbolism from the four corners of the ancient world, providing for correspondence to, and synthesis within, ones life.

The array has also, quite by accident, been utilized to ameliorate bone disorders, stiffness of joints, and calcium deficiencies.

POTENTATE

The "Potentate" configuration is established by placing the crystals in the pattern shown in Figure 11. The number of crystals used is left to the intuition of the practitioner.

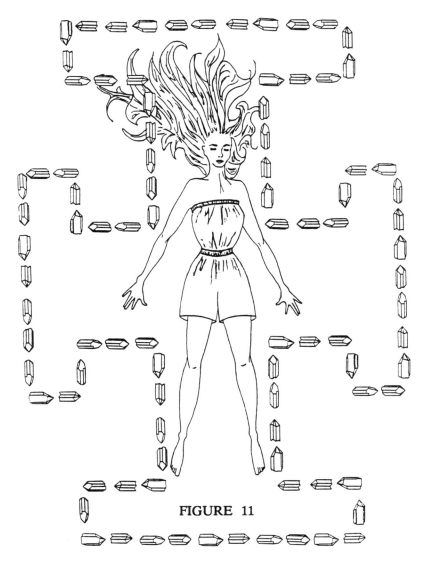

FIGURE 11

This configuration is applicable to the development of ones spirituality via assisting one in the recognition of a supreme, all pervading and indwelling power, in which unification of "all" is manifest. It helps one to understand the ideal of direct communication between the self and the infinite, not via external media [e.g., revelation, oracles, etc.], but by a variety of ecstatic transfusion or identification in which one becomes, in very truth, the partaker of divine essence. With this understanding, the infinite ceases to be an object and becomes an experience.

It provides for an immediate movement from a mechanical philosophy of reason to an assertion of sensitive comprehension which can not be articulated, but can be known [i.e., it is actually an intellectual intuition of the infinite perfection, the Absolute]. "Potentate" encourages the pursuit of the deepest ground of ones being in order that one may dispel that which separates the personal self from ones true and perfect life. It expedites the inward turning of the sight, demanding a faculty surpassing reason, and providing for a union with the divine; the union, often momentary in duration, is realized in the submission of the will and in the ethereal harmony of ones life being reduced to a passive experience.

The union with the infinite is not produced via knowledge or intellectual stimulation, but through the realization of absolute truth. As the air fills with sunlight and is transformed into the same brightness as the sunlight, such that it does not appear to be illuminated, but to be light in itself, ones feeling and inner understanding of the divine is self-dissolved and wholly transferred into the experience.

The array assists one in the recognition that all "things" are as divine as is in their nature to be, and furthers ones understanding of the unity and divinity in all which exists, all which will ever exist, and all which has ever existed. It tends to heighten the delight in natural beauty, providing for an enraptured bliss.

It further serves as a catalyst to quicken ones exploration as a "seeker" and to provide for identification and transformation of the elements of the mind which are burdens on the path toward wisdom.

The initiation by ancient masters, into the mysteries which transcend ordinary human knowledge, has also been experienced, and an immediate state of intuitive knowledge has been facilitated. Occasionally, during the encounter with the masters, instruction was dispensed with respect to the rites and bases for the "scientifically unexplainable". Further contact with the masters has been initiated with subsequent visits to the array.

A smaller version of the array placed upon ones photograph has acted to facilitate the improvement in the continuance of the wisdom which is experienced.

While within this configuration, one experiences a melding with the inner light, a fusion with the ultimate reality of "things", and an enjoyment which cannot be articulated. There are no procedures or rules, one may just experience the transition from the mundane to the sacred.

PYRAMID CROSS

The "Pyramid Cross" configuration is established by placing the crystals in the pattern shown in Figure 12. The utilization of at least four fluorite octahedrons and at least one piece of red granite [placed at the intersection] is recommended. Pyramidal shaped crystals may also be used to enhance the energy transmittal. The number of crystals used is left to the intuition of the practitioner.

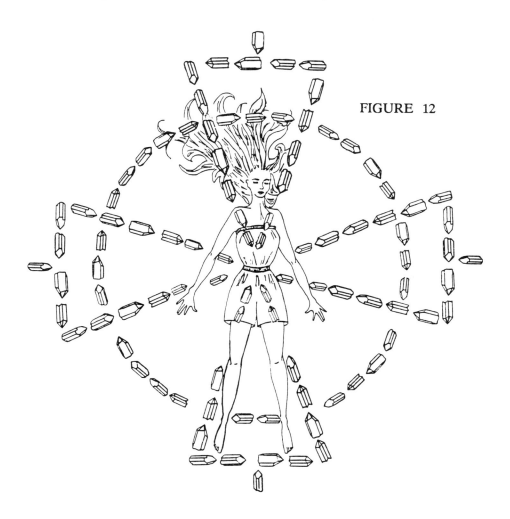

FIGURE 12

This configuration is representative of bringing the powers of the four corners to the pinnacle of power. The intersection represents the sepulchral chamber wherein the sovereign of life is placed; it is the magnified location of energy in the array.

The "Pyramid Cross" may be used to preserve and protect, assisting one in healing and in the recall of ancient remedies; it has been used to clear a pathway for communication between the self and those of the Egyptian civilizations ranging from 4750 B.C. to 3000 B.C. These communications have produced both naturopathic and technological information.

Placed upon the body, it serves to stimulate the alignment of the primary vibratory forces of the body, acting to align the energy fields and to activate the axes of each chakra. It is an array of vitality, bringing stamina and endurance in all situations.

Not only does it enhance ones energy, but it also incites ones awareness of the pulsing fluctuations of same. It further promotes the growth of the auric field and the radiation of ones inner light. One can, both via the senses and by the intuitive perception, recognize the growth of the aura, and can more readily locate those areas which are retaining tension and/or those areas which restrict the flow of energy due to the presence of energy blockages.

If one breathes "into" the areas of tension while within this array, the obstructions seem to dissipate, allowing the free flow of energy throughout the body. This exercise may require several entries to the array. Breathing "into" an area of tension may be described as:

♥ First, one visualizes the area of blockage or tension;

♥ Second, during exhalation, one visualizes the breath flowing to [and eventually through] the obstruction. The flow "through" the obstruction may require several sessions; however, improvement will be apparent after the first exercise.

The "Pyramid Cross" is also utilized for gridding "anything and everything" which will be enhanced by an addition of energy; when applied to objects, the focal point of intersection would be located at the midpoint of the object. Similarly for a photograph, unless the photograph is of a person - in this case, the focal point would be placed at the same intersecting point as in the normal-sized array.

This is one of the finest arrays for producing supplemental energy.

MALTESE

The "Maltese" configuration is established by placing the crystals in the pattern shown in Figure 13. The number of crystals used is left to the intuition of the practitioner.

FIGURE 13

This configuration assists one in transforming any problem or self-limiting situation into a stimulus for "becoming". It stimulates curiosity such that ones actions are generative, and are not remedial. It is an array for fortification, bringing sustenance and supplementing ones strength. It can enhance ones problem-solving capabilities and is helpful to the facilitation of succinct communication; it further serves to provide one with "an edge" during situations of debate.

The following exercise has been conducive to facilitating ones change from that which is undesired to that which is preferred:

- ♥ The problem, habit, or situation is precisely identified and the preference is stated in a written missive and also stated verbally. The missive is placed beneath a smaller version of the array.

- ♥ One centers the self, enters the array [dexterity is required if the exercise is performed without assistance], and initiates deep circular breathing.

- ♥ The condition which one desires to eliminate is reviewed within the mind and one visualizes that which initiates, or is a precedent to, the condition. For example, of the condition which is chosen for elimination is smoking, one would visualize ones actions and/or environment, and experience the emotional feelings which would occur, at the moment just prior to lighting the cigarette.

- ♥ Next, one visualizes the actions which would be actualized if the cigarette were not readied for smoking; the images would be in the positive vein, bringing a delightful sense of attraction to the idea of, for example, the non-smoker.

- ♥ Now, return to the first image and place the second image as an overlay. Recognize the diminishment in the clarity of the first image and the strengthening of the second.

When the second image totally eradicates all traces of the first image, attempt to visualize the first image; when the first image can no longer be "easily" retrieved, the exercise is ended and resumed again the next day.

The exercise to eliminate this habit, situation, or problem is terminated when the problem no longer exists.

Placement of a smaller version of the array upon the written negation of the problem, habit, or situation, can also enhance the positive accomplishment of the exercise.

The smaller photographic arrangement has also been used to facilitate protection for animals.

It can be used in the treatment of disorders of the joints and the spleen, and to ameliorate fevers, pain, and swelling.

CELTIC

The "Celtic" configuration is established by placing the crystals in the pattern shown in Figure 14. The number of crystals used is left to the intuition of the practitioner.

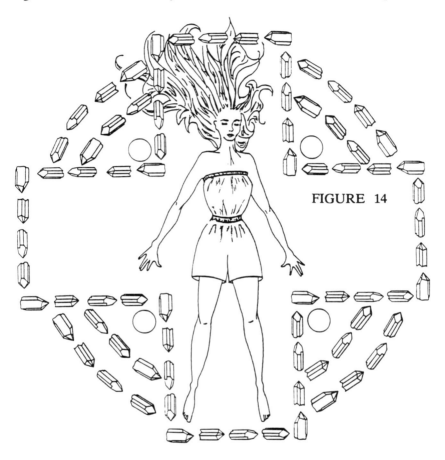

FIGURE 14

This configuration assists one in comprehending the product of the fusion of all religions; it acts as a central energy point which consolidates the concepts of ones existence and the after-life. It can provide a connection between the self and those of ancient times, promoting a rich stream of treasured information flow toward the self in return for an open channel of beauty and love flowing from the self. Blessings and privileges are often bestowed and visions are prompted. Fragments of ancient texts, lost and unknown, have been channeled during the use of this array. It also assists in the mastery of illusion and in the encouragement of vaticinal activities, whereby one may assist another with the prophesy.

It has promoted clairaudience and the opening to the ethereal harp of spirituality. It further advances ones creativity in the areas of art, poetry, fiction, genealogy, literature, history, storytelling, design, dance, and song, providing strength of purpose in all endeavors.

It can be utilized to assist in the suspension of any activity, advancing ones courage and tenacity in the alleviation of conditions which are undesired.

The "Celtic" enables one to correspond respectively to others and to speak that which is required in a loving manner. One recognizes the methodology through which all statements may be given in a positive and loving manner if one pauses prior to verbalization. The array has been used as a refuge from the outer world, serving to separate the self from the physical world during intervals of crisis; a calming and protective energy is provided during this application. It assists one in recognizing the way of life and living which would be both benevolent and beneficial to the self and to others.

This configuration is the terrestrial representation of the energies which can stimulate the intuitive knowledge and facilitate further historical knowledge to help one understand the arts and sciences of our world; it further helps one to understand that ones power is bounded only by ones breadth and depth of imagination.

It has been used to facilitate the understanding of Runic information and symbols. When one selects a Rune for future-telling activities, entry to the array has stimulated intuitive translation and the advent of further information.

It is a patron of merchants and has been used to assist in the restoration of ones property, which has been removed by another, without permission. The thought of the property being returned is held within the mind during array employment; the results have varied, from the return of same within twenty-four hours, to the compensation for loss and/or an apology provided [physically or intuitively] by the one who removed the property.

Energizing and "blessing" of plants, elixirs, and tinctures is enhanced via the "Celtic".

It is an array of gentleness, health, and posterity and works well when placed [as a smaller version] upon a photograph of that which is in need of these attributes; in all cases of photographic use, a missive is necessary which defines the purpose of the array.

The "Celtic" has been used in the treatment of disorders relating to the arms, the muscles, the voice and vocal cords, the pancreas, and the blood [relative to toxins]. It has inhibited over-eating and over-consumption, and has facilitated the amelioration of infertility, chills, spasms, dysfunctional metabolism, and less than adequate coordination.

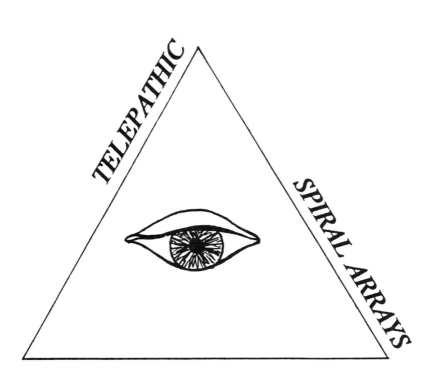

THE INFINITE STREAM
TO ETERNITY
LAYS IN THE UNDERSTANDING
OF THE WHIRLING
ASCENT TO PERFECTION

TELEPATHIC SPIRAL ARRAYS

The Spiral Telepathic Arrays are comprised of the "Left Spiral" and the "Right Spiral" arrangements which are illustrated in Figure 15 and Figure 16, respectively.

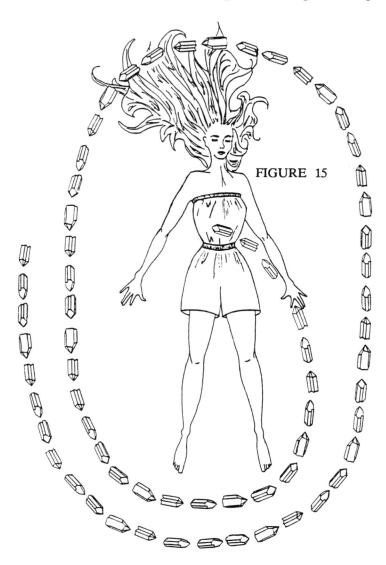

FIGURE 15

The "Left Spiral" configuration is established by placing the crystals, starting at the right side of the subject and progressing from the right side of the subject, in a helical pattern, ending at the navel. The "Right Spiral" configuration is established by placing the crystals, starting at the navel and progressing from the right side of the subject, in a helical pattern, ending on the left side of the subject. The application of the Faden crystal formation or the fulgurite configuration tends to enhance the realization of the following activities. The total number of crystals used is left to the intuition of the practitioner.

The "Right Spiral" and the "Left Spiral" arrays have been utilized successfully to facilitate and to strengthen the teleportation and reception of thoughts. The background information which provides the foundation for the methodology is based upon the premise that the ethereal/astral body which is associated with the subconscious, adheres to anything which is contacted by any of ones senses, via thousands of invisible threads. These filaments provide for a connection between the self and the object [e.g., the astral cord which connects the astral body to the physical body]. The filaments have been seen when heavily charged with vital force and have become almost solid enough to touch. The kahunas [of the Huna philosophy] and those of theosophical inclination, regard all "things" [i.e., physical bodies and thought-forms] as possessing continual and substantial [although, not normally visible] astral bodies. One may recall the general acceptance of, albeit not usually supported philosophy that, "thoughts are things".

Telepathy can be demonstrated via the utilization of these invisible fibers. Experimental studies have demonstrated that distance causes no appreciable difference in the strength or clearness of the messages. The threads of ethereal material appear to be perfect conductors of vital electrical force through which singular thought-forms, or clusters of thought-forms which comprise complete messages or impressions, can be transmitted to and from dispatcher and receiver; the assistance of the subconscious is enlisted in order to facilitate the sending and receiving of messages in this manner. The spiritual unity of all which exists facilitates the connection via the etheric threads.

In accordance with the Huna theory and the practice by the shamen of the West Indies, psychometry, and its related phenomena, also depend upon the similar mechanisms; the exception being that the ethereal cord or thread does not connect two similar persons.

The following exercise has been effective for the transmission of thoughts via the "Right Spiral":

- ♥   One transcribes the precise message which is to be relayed and places the missive beneath a smaller version of the array.

The time most conducive to the reception of that which one transmits is during the "bewitching hour" or when one knows that the other person will be in a receiving state.

- ♥   One enters the array, after centering the self, and initiates deep circular breathing.

This form of deep breathing is a common preliminary to teleportation, telepathy, and psychometry - these activities depend upon the movement of thought-forms along a filament of the ethereal essence. Deep circular breathing assists in promoting a connective flow between the consciousness and the subconscious, such that the subconscious is notified that its services are required.

If the Faden crystal or the fulgurite is utilized, it is now placed upon the area of the body beneath the solar plexus.

♥ After several moments of relaxation [via the breathing exercise], one repeats the message while centering two-inches below the navel and while maintaining a mental image of the intended recipient. One then consciously directs the subconscious to transmit the information.

♥ During transmittal of the message, it is helpful to visualize a white beam of crystalline light, tied to ones senses, and radiated from the area just beneath the solar plexus area, upon which the message is "riding" and, such that when the light ray encounters an obstacle, it detours and locates a clear pathway for continuance to its destination. The visualization of golden Prana, and the utilization of golden crystals [occasionally with rutile or goethite] in conjunction with the Faden crystal, have also produced excellent results.

When the Faden crystal is used, the visible thread within the crystal acts to facilitate the transmittal of the information; the ethereal filaments of ones body tend to be directed through the Faden crystal to increase the strength of the message and the thread which is carrying the message. When the fulgurite is used, the tubular structure acts as an unobstructed tunnel through which the transmission occurs.

Upon reaching the defined destination, the ethereal threads enter the ethereal body of the subject; if the intended recipient is aware of the occurrence of this connection, he/she can repel [via consciously directing his subconscious to not accept] the entry. Once the contact has been made, however, the electrically-charged invisible thread connects the two individuals; the strength or weakness of the connection is dependent upon the reinforcement, of the connection by one or both participants.

♥ Ones intuitive self will provide notification when the transmission has been completed; it will also provide feedback with respect to any unsurmounted obstacles which precluded the fulfillment of transmission [i.e., deflection and/or refusal by the recipient].

When not within the "Left Spiral", the recipient may not immediately become consciously aware of the received message. In this case, the subconscious selects the "right" time to transfer the information to the center of consciousness; occasionally the resultant sensation is similar to that of recalling a memory,

- ♥ At the conclusion of the broadcast, one exits the array and removes the smaller version of the array from the written message.

The "Left Spiral" may be used to facilitate psychometric operations. A psychometrist usually rests quietly and touches a letter, ring, etc., through which psychic information may be transmitted [e.g., information relative to the past history of the object which is being held or the contents of a letter and the nature and environs of its writer]. The point is - one practicing this form of "magic" reaches-out along the etheric threads which are attached to an object, following them to their ends, and finding there the things and people presently and/or formerly associated with the article. For example, if the object is a piece of lava, images would be descriptive of the volcanic eruption from which is was formed; if the object is a meteorite, the thread will lead only to the source of the meteorite. The following exercise has produced successful results in the realm of psychometry:

- ♥ One centers the self and enters the array; deep circular breathing is initiated and one allows the reasoning processes to cease.

- ♥ After placing the object of the psychometric operation within or beneath the left hand, affirmation is verbalized that the perception which will be received is in the light and love of universal perfection. At this time, one releases ones energies to allow for the reception of spiritual and/or physical sensations.

One may open to the images of the third-eye and follow the etheric threads of the object to the originator. The images will then appear at the termination of the threads and be relayed back to the area of the third-eye. One may also notice that when reasoning ceases, a flow of vital energy [electricity] surges through the body for a moment; after this occurs, lucidity takes control and pictures will arise. The lucid state sometimes arises immediately and sometimes takes several hours; this depends upon the environment [e.g., skepticism or even attention by others may delay the transmission of information].

The above exercise has also been utilized to access the world soul or Akasa, upon whose memory is impressed all that happens; the process is conducive to visual contact with, and understanding of, the Akashic records. A similar exercise may be applied to the art of crystal gazing; in this situation, the thought of a certain person may be held in mind while one gazes into the crystal in the expectation of seeing a vision form in its depths. The thought held in the mind provides the seed for the psychometric action via the ethereal thread. During the act of crystal gazing there is a relaxation, similar to sleep, but with the conscious self in a "stand-by" condition in the waking-state such that one may observe that which is sensed by the subconscious through the images centering around/within the crystal.

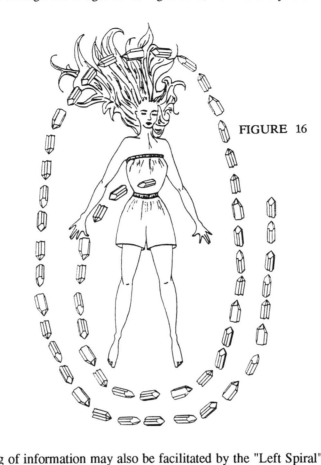

FIGURE 16

The receiving of information may also be facilitated by the "Left Spiral". If one is cognizant of a message being sent at a specified time, one may enter the "Left Spiral" to expedite the process. The utilization of a Faden crystal or a fulgurite [placed below the solar plexus] in this activity assists in providing an unobstructed field for entry of the message. The recipient may experience a faint electrical tingling or warmth, often accompanied by a tactile response of a chill to the skin when the message reaches the ethereal body and ones attention is necessary for conscious recognition of the completion of the transmission. In the cases tested, the recipient has accurately received the message, has recognized images which were relayed, and has experienced a type of translation which is performed by the subconscious and provides for the translation of the message into terms which are readily understood by the consciousness.

In addition, the "Left Spiral" has been employed during "mind-reading" experiments via the following method from the ancient cultures; from these cultures we have been given the insight that thought-forms and sensations of touching provide for a bridge between the self and other selves. These ethereal threads remain as a permanent connecting-mechanism of contact or communication; they are not usually activated until a vital sustaining force is directed from the initiator to a receiver. The following procedure has been utilized to prepare the ethereal threads for contact and to promote the receipt of impressions from the source.

- One places a smaller version of the array upon a photograph of the person with whom one desires information.

- After centering the self, one enters the "Left Spiral" and commences the deep circular breathing. The departing breath is visualized as creating a large sphere of vital force which is, subsequently [after a size comparable to a bushel basket is attained], sent to the etheric connecting thread. This vital force facilitates the enlargement and strengthening of the thread for the moments of contact, and provides for the connection to the other person via an electrically charged invisible thread.

- With ones conscious and deliberate intention focused upon the area just beneath the solar plexus, ones subconscious projects the essence of ones sensory organs, through the thread, to the intended recipient.

One then may observe the thoughts which are passing through the mind of the subject, the sensory impressions or thought forms of memories, and/or the environment in which the subject is located and the activities in which the subject is participating; this observation is facilitated via the duplication of the thoughts of the subject as thought-forms and the return of these thought-forms through the open channel of the ethereal thread. The Faden crystal is of immense assistance during this portion of the exercise.

Upon return of the information, the center of consciousness is presented with the information [this process is analogous to the mechanism which produces the projection of a memory by the subconscious when one consciously desires to remember events or circumstances from ones past]. These thoughts and impressions are received by the consciousness from the location below the solar plexus, which has been considered the primary home of the subconscious when actively engaged in sending or receiving messages or sensory impressions. It should be noted that the etheric body of the subconscious possesses duplicates of every cell and tissue of the physical body, thus duplicating all sensory organs such that the etheric eyes can be projected to see, the etheric ears to hear, etc. This array allows one to "see" without the physical eyes, to "hear" without the physical ears, and to perceive intuitively more than one would sense with any physical capabilities. It provides for the ethereal communication with others, with distance being not a barrier.

ARRAYS OF THE

GOLDEN

AGE

When you take inventory
Of the people you consider
To be your true friends -
The really important individuals
Who have given unselfishly
To help you achieve
Your goals and desires,
*Be sure to include **yourself** on the list.*

Julianne Guilbault
1991

SEVEN-RAY CIRCLE

The "Seven-Ray Circle" configuration [See Figure 17] is established by placing seven [or multiples of seven] crystals in a concentric circle around the subject, while placing at least three crystals pointing toward the subject at the location of the long ray, and at least two crystals pointing away from the subject at the location of each of the shorter rays.

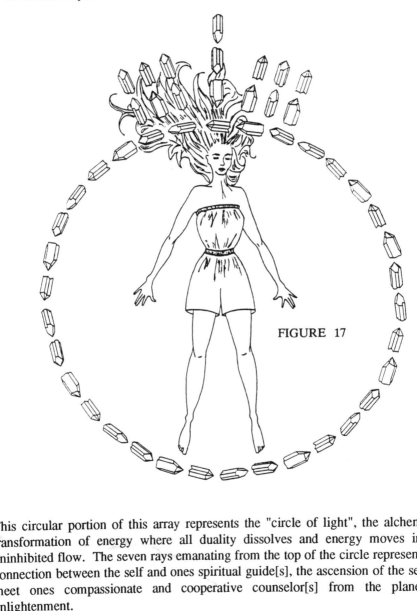

FIGURE 17

This circular portion of this array represents the "circle of light", the alchemical transformation of energy where all duality dissolves and energy moves in an uninhibited flow. The seven rays emanating from the top of the circle represent the connection between the self and ones spiritual guide[s], the ascension of the self to meet ones compassionate and cooperative counselor[s] from the plane of enlightenment.

The following exercise has been utilized to facilitate the meeting of, and/or to further communication with, ones spiritual guide[s]:

♥   A photograph of the self is placed within a smaller version of the array, with the long ray pointing in the same direction as the long ray of the standard-sized array. This acts to initiate further protection in the light and love of the universe.

♥   After centering the self, one enters the "Seven-Ray Circle". Deep circular breathing is initiated and focus is directed to the crown chakra. At this time, one can feel the inflow of pure energy from the universal source via the six outer rays and the outflow of pure energy to the spiritual plane via the center ray.

♥   One now visualizes a grand version of ones "favorite" crystal [an extremely powerful protective mechanism] located on the spiritual plane at the end of the center ray of energy. One follows the ray to inside the crystal, envisioning comfortable conditions [e.g., a beautiful lush garden, the top of a mountain, the serenity of the autumn, the vitality of the ocean], and establishes a comfortable location in which to await the arrival of ones guide.

♥   When the guide materializes, an effusion of energy usually fills the subject. At this time, introduction of the self is recommended [this assists in the relaxation of "formality programming"]. Communication will ensue and one will emotionally understand that the guide is a "best friend". The sojourn may continue indefinitely; one usually terminates the visitation with a verbalized intention to meet again at a future time [either specified or unspecified].

♥   After the meeting is concluded, one returns via the energy ray to the "Seven-Ray Circle".

One may return to within the array whenever, and as frequently, as is desired. Visualization of a different "favorite" crystal located at the end of the center ray of energy has facilitated the encounter of other guides. It is recommended that one visualizes the same "favorite" crystal each time contact with the same guide is desired.

EARTH-HEAVEN

The "Earth-Heaven" configuration is established by placing crystals around the body of the subject as shown in Figure 18 and surrounding same with a concentric circle. Some of the crystals which are a part of the six-pointed star configuration shown within the center of the circle may also be placed upon the subject. It is also important to place at least one crystal on the throat chakra. Success has been attained via the utilization of multiples of six in this arrangement and via the use of a triangular-shaped crystalline formation [natural or formed by lapidary] on the area of the third-eye.

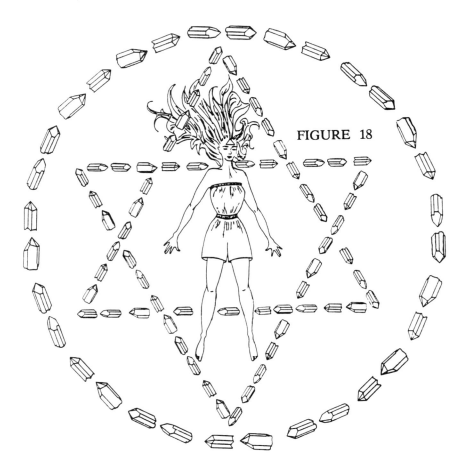

FIGURE 18

This array can be utilized to assist one in connecting with the ancient civilizations of Lemuria, Atlantis, Mu, etc., and in traveling to the original cultures representing the native tribes of the world. It has been used successfully to reach these territories via the accessing of parallel dimensions where the cultures continue to exist.

The following exercise has facilitated contact with those of these past civilizations and has furnished information concerning rites, rituals, and ceremonies associated with same:

♥ One of the ancient civilizations or original cultures is chosen and the name is transcribed to paper and placed within a smaller version of the array.

♥ After centering the self, one enters the array and initiates deep circular breathing.

♥ Focus is directed to the third-eye. A pathway is visualized and one may follow this passage to the predetermined location.

♥ One may participate in communication with others, may read information from recorded history books or other records, may receive information via observing conversations, and may even be permitted to participate in ritualistic activities.

♥ For some, a recognition of a "homeland" and the connection with kinsmen have been reported; other participants have, occasionally, received stimulus to produce memories of localities, structures, and people from past-lives.

♥ Upon each return, recording that information which was gleaned, is recommended. It is also recommended that "harmonious time" [e.g., meditation] be initiated daily to reinforce the continuance of any relationship which has been formed and that dream journals be updated daily to record the relevant information which is received during the dream state.

Quite often ceremonial instruction is presented after utilization of the array and during the dream state.

In addition, one may access other parallel dimensions and the astral plane via the above exercise.

UNIVERSAL CONNECTION & INTER-GALACTIC CONNECTION

The "Universal Connection" configuration is established by placing multiples of four crystals upon and around the body as shown in Figure 19. One of the methods which has been shown to produce results uses only red hues of crystals [to represent the "+"] and white/clear crystals to represent the remaining patterns.

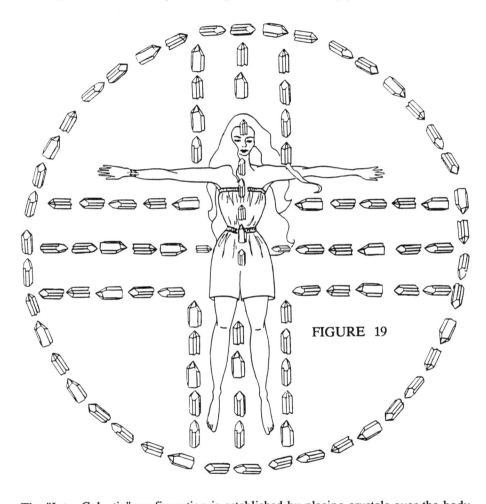

FIGURE 19

The "Inter-Galactic" configuration is established by placing crystals over the body of the subject as shown in Figure 20. Success has been attained via the utilization of multiples of five in this arrangement.

The "Universal Connection" arrangement is utilized for astral/mind travel to within the universe of which the Earth is a part; the "Inter-Galactic" arrangement is utilized for astral/mind travel to other galaxies.

These are arrays to stimulate cooperative efforts between those of extra-terrestrial origins and those who are experiencing life on Earth. Each can assist one in transcending the illusions of life and in re-connecting with the forces which assisted ones transition to this plane. They can be used to facilitate direct interdimensional travel and to promote future communication with other realms.

They can awaken the euphoric emotions of the self and, acting to promote the production of endorphins, can allow one to vanquish stress and/or states of depression.

The configurations may also be used to facilitate ones understanding of present circumstances and past patterns, to allow for knowledge with respect to whether one is a "star person", to further define the lifetime in which one was a "star person", to discover the reasons for coming to Earth, and to ascertain the point of origin. The arrays also facilitate inter-planetary and/or inter-galactic communication.

The following exercise is applicable to the utilization of either array:

♥ One prepares a list of questions relevant to the issues in the preceding paragraph.

♥ One question is specifically chosen [others may also be answered, but only one is chosen to be represented during each entry to the array].

♥ A photograph of the self and a copy of the written question is placed within a smaller version of the array, such that it is totally enclosed within the circular portion if the "Universal Connection" configuration is selected.

♥ After centering the self, one enters the selected array and initiates deep circular breathing.

♥ Focus is directed to the third-eye. A pathway is visualized and one may follow this passage to ones "home in the stars". The travel, in itself, is very enjoyable.

♥ One may participate in communication with others, may read information from recorded history books or other records, and may receive information via observing conversations.

Upon each return, recording that information which was gleaned, the conversations in which one has shared, the participants with whom one interacted, etc., is recommended. It is also recommended that "harmonious time" [e.g., meditation] be initiated daily to reinforce the continuance of any relationship which has been formed <u>and</u> that dream journals be updated daily to record the relevant information which is received during the dream state.

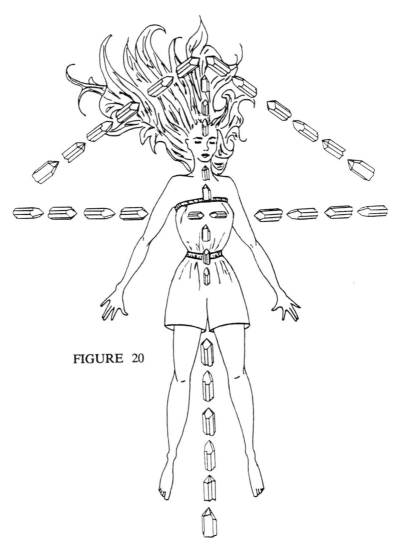

FIGURE 20

The utilization of moldavite, boji stones, and bi-coloured tourmaline has further facilitated the actions of the arrays; placement of the moldavite at the area of the third-eye, the boji stones in each hand, and the bi-coloured tourmaline at the area of the solar plexus, has promoted the initiation and continuity of the communicative aspects of the array.

SACRED FOUR

The "Sacred Four" configuration is established by placing the crystals in a semi-circular pattern of half-moons around the body [See Figure 21]; the array is oriented in the direction of north. Success has been obtained via the utilization of multiples of four crystals in this arrangement.

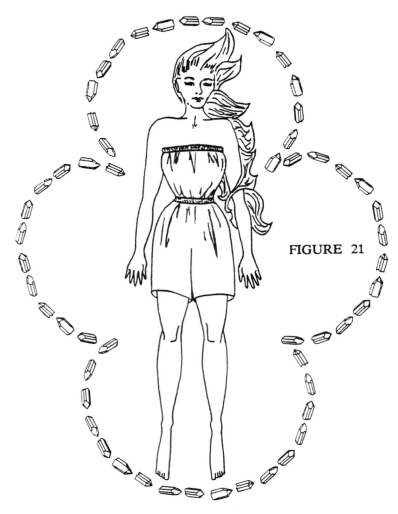

FIGURE 21

Small spherical [or semi-spherical] crystalline configurations are placed under the hands of the subject; it is recommended that these "spherical crystals" are used only for connecting with the "Sacred Four"; the crystals may also be carried in a pouch, and used during the ceremonial of the array, during "harmonious time", and/or during sleep [when they are placed under the pillow and/or worn/affixed upon the body. Selection of the "spherical crystals" which will be used for this connection would be intuitive; note that similar size is not required and that dissimilar minerals may be chosen.

Prior to use of the array, smudging and cleansing of the environment is recommended. Following use of the array, thankfulness and love is sent to the "keepers of the four sacred directions".

This array can be employed to assist one in connecting with the sacred four directions; historical information describing the Oglala Sioux has defined the sacred West as representing growth and renewal, the sacred North as symbolizing life and breath, the sacred East as signifying the benefit of wisdom, and the sacred South as exemplifying vitality and transition.

One exercise which can facilitate the connection is as follows:

- ♥ A photograph of the self is placed within a smaller version of the array. One determines which direction will be accessed, and places a crystal at the apex of that location; the colours of crystals which have been assigned to these directions include: black [West], red [North], yellow [East], and white [South].

- ♥ One centers the self, enters the array, and establishes the self such that the head is in the same "half-moon" of the array as is the black, red, yellow, or white crystal [i.e., the crown chakra and the chosen crystal are in the same area, with the crown chakra "open" to the direction which has been chosen].

- ♥ Deep breathing is initiated, and one opens the self to the material which will be made available from the "keeper of the sacred direction".

Another exercise has been utilized to assist one in the "vision quest":

- ♥ A photograph of the self is placed within a smaller version of the array, with a red, a white, a yellow, and a black crystal placed at the corresponding sacred directions.

- ♥ The normal-sized array is prepared with a red, a white, a yellow, and a black crystal placed at the corresponding sacred directions. If one desires to meet ones totem animal, the crown chakra would be "facing" South and two additional white crystals are placed on either side of the southern crystal. If one desires to pursue a vision, the crown chakra would be "facing" East and two additional white crystals would be placed on either side of the eastern crystal.

♥   After centering the self, the array is entered and deep circular breathing is initiated. Assistance from the "keeper of the sacred direction" is requested when one is the direction associated with that "keeper".

♥   One rotates the body in a counter-clockwise direction, after approximately thirty minutes [or more] in a location. The ending location is the same as that which was the initiating position; an additional thirty minutes is utilized at this time to assist in the assimilation of the information gained via the quest.

The minimum time for this exercise is two and one-half hours. When possible, additional time is given to the activity.

The array can also be used to assist one in recovering lost articles. In this case, the additional coloured crystals are placed in the appropriate directional locations and, after centering the self, one enters the array, rotates in a counter-clockwise direction after at least ten minutes in each location, and ends with an additional ten minute receptive state in the originating position. Assistance is requested from the "keeper of the sacred direction" when one is entering that direction. A message is usually provided from one of the "keepers of the sacred directions" during the time the crown chakra is in that area.

The array is also an excellent reinforcement to activities involving crystal healing. The additional crystals are placed in the appropriate locations and the subject is rotated, in [approximately] fifteen minute intervals, through the array. Assistance from the "keeper of the sacred direction" is requested during the time the subject is located with the crown chakra in that direction. When rotation is completed, the ending position is again the originating position, and additional time is utilized in this location to synthesize the information and the energies which were provided. Additional crystals representing the Zenith [blue] and the Nadir [green] are added to the array - the blue crystal in the North and the green crystal in the South. The employment of the "Chakra" array in conjunction with the "Sacred Four" can also further the healing session.

DIVINATION

The "Divination" configuration is established by placing the crystals in the pattern of an arrow, beginning below the feet and ending above the head of the subject [See Figure 22]. The number of crystals used is left to the intuition of the practitioner.

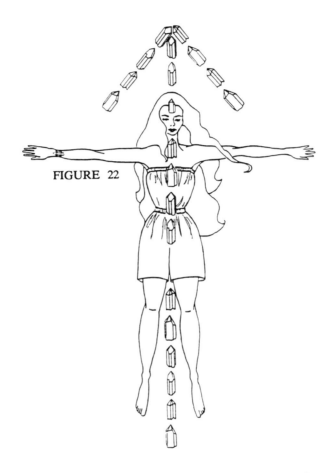

FIGURE 22

This array can be utilized to facilitate a mental/emotional connection with another person or object which is located in the direction in which the arrow is directed [i.e., a directional connection]. It is conducive to enhancing the art of divination, providing for insight via communication from those on other planes or from the divine source of the universe; the information given is, usually, of hidden places or things, or future occurrences. Occasionally the hawk [divine bird of the Bornean culture], brings messages of the future. "Divination" stimulates a change in the consciousness of the subject such that sensory and mental impressions are intensified. Arousing a state of auto-hypnotism, a trance may be induced through which automatic-speaking, as a result of inspiration, is facilitated. Mental conceptions and visions are also common. An exercise which has been utilized is as follows:

> ♥ A smaller version of the array is placed upon a photograph, facsimile, or description of that with which one desires contact.

If divination is with respect to a person or a location <u>and</u> one has knowledge of the direction [north, south, east, west, etc.] in which the person or location can be found, the array is constructed so that the apex is directed toward same. If one is not cognizant of the direction, the array is placed such that the apex is focused toward the location which was intuitively provided.

> ♥ A precise question is formulated and repeated aloud. One enters the normal-sized array after centering the self. [For "Divination", one can also lay above the structure.] Deep circular breathing is initiated and one allows the self to travel through the apex of the array toward that which has been requested.

If the intuitive alignment of the configuration is used, and that which is desired is not found in this direction, blankness of the mind usually ensues and, occasionally, a flash of light which indicates the proper direction, is "seen" by the subject; when the direction is not "seen" by this method or a method which is personal to the subject, the array is rotated until the location is found.

> ♥ After obtaining the correct position, the path to that which was requested is followed and information is gleaned.

Please note that each time the array is used, one verbally repeats a precise question or request; the array which is upon the photograph will continue to stimulate the receipt of information until removal of same <u>or</u> until the question/request is replaced by another.

The art of crystal gazing has also been renewed and enhanced by the subject holding two crystal spheres while being above or below the array; after approximately thirty-minutes, the receipt of messages via the sphere has been expedited.

Placement of a smaller version of the array upon a photograph, facsimile, or detailed description of a person, place, or object, can assist one in locating and determining information with respect to position, situation, surroundings, etc. It is also conducive to the enhancement of forecasting via the tarot, the Neo-tarot, the Runes, and the I Ching. It has been used to promote the arts of palmistry, "throwing the bones", and shell-hearing. Often times, dreams are provided which provide additional information to a query conveyed during the construction of the smaller array.

THE GREAT MYSTERY - JOURNEYING

"The Great Mystery - Journeying" configuration is established by placing the crystals in a three-fold pattern: a triangular shape surrounding the subject, a circle surrounding the triangle, and a square surrounding the circle [See Figure 23].

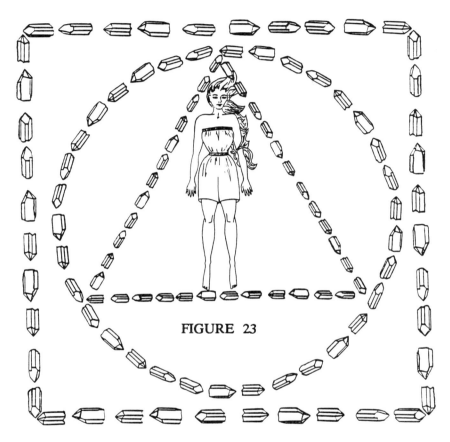

FIGURE 23

The Incas and Mayans used lapis lazuli, iron, and sulphur during ceremonial activities involving these forms.

Excellent results have been attained via the placement of an electric-blue sheen obsidian sphere or an ajoite crystal at the apex of the triangular formation and/or beneath the left hand of the participant.

A chevron amethyst placed over the third-eye has enhanced the array. The number of crystals used is left to the intuition of the practitioner.

This array supports the achievement of a shamanic technique, which has been used since ancient times on all continents by the various tribal shamen, to facilitate a conscious journey of ecstasy to the realms of the unknown via the transcendence of the profane.

It is recommended that solitary initiation of this process is not executed until many guided journeys have been completed successfully. The practitioner guides the subject through the journey, being ever mindful of conditions and circumstances experienced, and assisting the subject in an effortless return.

"Journeying" can be used for travel to within the body, to within the mind, and to within the heart of "All That Is".

Prior to the commencement of the following exercise [journey to the heart of "All That Is"], the room is smudged with sage, cedar, juniper, or incense, and purified with sweetgrass, elephant grass, or another cleansing herb:

- A smaller version of the array is placed upon/around a photograph of the subject; the subject centers the self, enters the array, and initiates deep circular breathing.

- A feather is placed within the array and in contact with the subject.

- Drumming and/or rattling [rhythm to be intuitive] may be introduced at this time by the practitioner or by a pre-recorded drumming/rattling cassette tape. [The rattle is often fabricated from a gourd in which small crystals are placed.]

The drumming/rattling assists the mind to release thoughts of this physical realm and to "break-through" the dimensional limitations; the drum represents the microcosm of the sky, the Earth, and the multi-dimensional realms.

- A slower softer drumming/rattling is continued throughout the journey-time.

Note that when one becomes proficient in journeying, and travels alone, drumming and/or rattling can be achieved via a self-recorded or a professionally recorded cassette tape.

- The subject is requested to envision, and to climb, a mountain, a rainbow, or a birch tree [the sacred "World Tree"], or to imagine crossing a bridge.

During the travel, guardian spirits are encountered and information is transferred to the subject.

One may meet ones guardian animal[s], from whom secrets of the future are given; information may also be imparted concerning the correct path and the "right" course of action for the subject with respect to the physical realm. The guardian animal may lead one to a personal future scene and/or may communicate the messages verbally. [During subsequent journeys, one will repeatedly meet the same guardian animal; however, additional guardian animals may also surface when additional considerations are held within the conscious mind.] Ancient tribal teachings indicate that the Eagle, the father of the first shamanic journey, granted power to both the ancestral/guardian spirits as well as to the animal, plant, and mineral kingdoms to act as guides for those traveling through the dimensions. It is quite interesting to experience ones guides from all kingdoms and to listen with both the heart and the mind to the knowledge that is given.

One may meet ones guardian spirit[s] or ones ancestral spirit[s], who will travel as companion[s] and will take one beyond the physical dimension to a consciousness in which mysteries are revealed, varying subjects are taught, prophecies are conferred, or in which one is educated in the methods by which dis-ease is recognized and through which subsequent healing is facilitated.

The guardian[s] may also guide one to times past, such that one can view past-lives, the creation of the world, etc.

One may meet healing spirit[s], of whom one may request healing for the self and/or for another. The healing spirit for a specific condition may agree to repossess the dis-ease or may perform the healing during journey-time.

One may also be traveling "for joy" and will be given information with respect to life in other realms. Many use this journey-time for meditation, solitude, and visiting with guardians.

> ♥   The subject communicates each scene and experience to the practitioner concurrent with the occurrence of the event. At the end of the session, the tempo of the drumming/rattling is increased and the subject is returned to the physical realm.

Often ones guardian spirit[s] will accompany one to the door of the physical realm so that there is no confusion with respect to the path of return. In many cases, the descent from the mountain, the rainbow, or the tree, or the reversed crossing of the bridge, is envisioned to facilitate the homecoming.

For journeys to within the body, the same procedure is utilized [the feather and the drumming/rattling are not required, but may enhance the activity]. One crosses to the inner realm to examine conditions within the body and to act to eliminate same. Ones guardian[s] will be met and one will be shown the precise condition which needs rectification. At this time, often the healing guardian[s] appear and one may watch during the removal of dis-ease; occasionally, the process is taught to the subject at the same time.

For journeys to within the mind, the same procedure is utilized [the feather is not required, but may enhance the activity]. This journey-time facilitates the examination of deep-rooted emotional difficulties and complex intellectual self-limiting ideas. The guardian[s] also appear and assist in the evaluation and solution of the problems.

In addition to the above journey-time ventures, a small version of the array placed upon/around ones photograph can provide protection against all forms of negative energy.

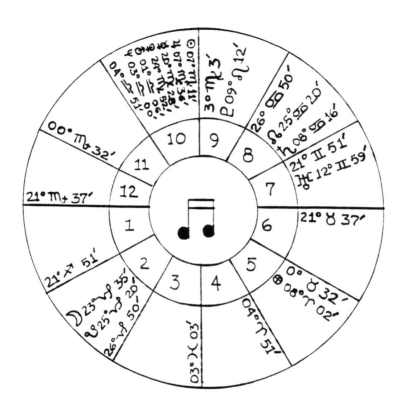

ZODIACAL ARRAYS

The Ten Thousand Things
Intrude, Surround -
Obtrude Upon The
Essential Soul -
Within Your Love
All Time Is Bound -
My Wandering Path
Attains The Round.

R.R. Jackson
1991

AUTONOMY

The "Autonomy" configuration is established by placing the crystals in the pattern shown in Figure 24. It represents Aries, a zodiacal constellation located between Pisces and Taurus. When using the array, the crown chakra of the subject would be toward the East with the intersection of the array located at the heart chakra. The number of crystals used is left to the intuition of the practitioner.

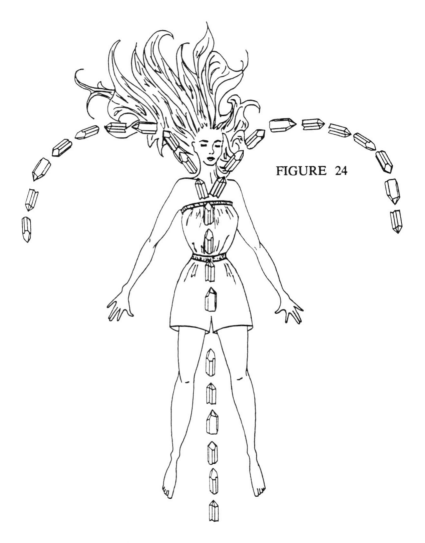

FIGURE 24

The array stimulates ones latent forces into action; it assists one in recognizing and in taking appropriate action during the "turning points" in ones life. It furthers spontaneity and pioneering adventures. It promotes motivation, inspiration, creativity, assertiveness, and courage.

It has also been employed to arouse the pursuit of ones personal spiritual path and the awareness of ones personal potential, helping one to remain aware of individual objectives. "Autonomy" can be also be used to assist one in identifying and removing obstacles in ones avenue of progression. It can encourage the inspiration of others toward independence and self-direction. It furthers ones access to desired seclusion which can be utilized for spiritual renewal.

The array has been placed upon a photograph of the self/another to facilitate continuance of the state attained during the physical gridding of the self or another. It can also be placed upon a photograph of areas which are being, or have been, affected by fire, stimulating control of the fire and spiritual renewal of that which is consumed. Used to grid ones photograph, it can bring success in fire-walking.

The movement of the Kundalini can be initiated and/or stimulated to continue upward toward the crown chakra. It can also be used to open, to activate, and to energize the base chakra.

Dual arrays, placed upon/around each person, can be used to promote shared courage in the unknown and assistance in the development of new endeavors. It can be used to enhance the appreciation of individual and cooperative freedom, helping each participant to express consideration of the other concurrent with personal expression of assertiveness.

"Autonomy" can effectively facilitate psychic surgery, assisting in the extraction or repair of areas of the body.

During the vernal equinox [varying from March 20-March 22], it has been used to cleanse, to activate, and to energize crystals.

This configuration can be used to assist in the relief of vertigo, neuralgia, mumps, nosebleeds, fevers, skin eruptions [including acne, measles, smallpox], anemia, insomnia, migraine headache, inflammation, encephalitis, convulsions, burns, apoplexy, cerebral congestion, hemorrhages, and convulsions. It can also be used in the treatment of disorders associated with the adrenal glands, the cerebrospinal nervous system, the cerebrum, the ears, the optic nerves, retina, and iris, the mouth, gums and upper teeth. "Autonomy" can assist in the assimilation of potassium. Placement of the array upon/around a photograph of one during and after physical surgery can assist in awakening recovery mechanisms.

The optimally utilized "Autonomy" array would also contain stones associated with the astrological sign of Aries. It is recommended that, when available, crystals from France, Poland, Spain, Peru, Italy and/or from meteorite deposition be utilized in the construction of the array.

Vibrates to the number 7.

RESOLUTION

The "Resolution" configuration is established by placing the crystals in the pattern shown in Figure 25. It represents Taurus, a zodiacal constellation located between Aries and Gemini. The number of crystals used in the array is left to the intuition of the practitioner.

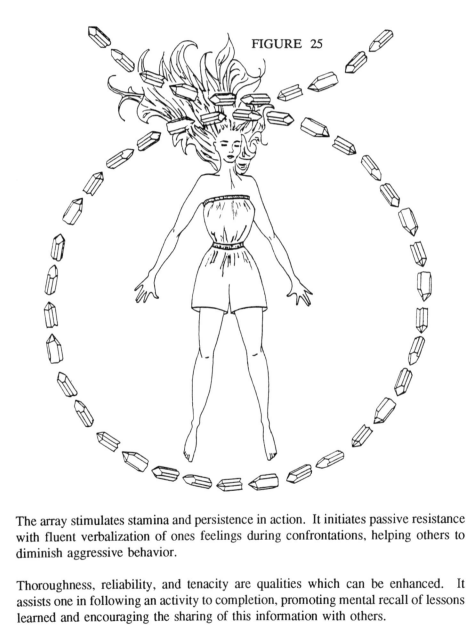

FIGURE 25

The array stimulates stamina and persistence in action. It initiates passive resistance with fluent verbalization of ones feelings during confrontations, helping others to diminish aggressive behavior.

Thoroughness, reliability, and tenacity are qualities which can be enhanced. It assists one in following an activity to completion, promoting mental recall of lessons learned and encouraging the sharing of this information with others.

It has also been employed to arouse the innate talents to facilitate financial gain, helping one to revel in busy circumstances, to excel in over-populated areas, and to enhance success and security in ones career and in "life after work".

The array has been placed upon a photograph of the self/another to facilitate continuance of the state attained during the physical gridding of the self or another. It can also be placed upon a photograph of a subject or a facsimile of a plan to encourage care in strategy and subsequent ease of action. Used to grid a garden, or a photograph of same, germination, abundance, and dis-ease resistance can be furthered.

It can also be used to open, to cleanse, and to stimulate the solar plexus chakra. It is an excellent array to combine with the art of massage.

Dual arrays, placed upon/around each person, can be used to promote shared ideas, the affectionate nature, and the opening to emotional relationship; it furthers understanding of conflicts and stimulates conflict resolution. It can also assist the participants in understanding the disadvantages of possessiveness, helping each to work toward building a tangible and reliable reality, while remaining open to the transformative processes. It can further act as a stimulant for releasing and/or resolving that which is unattainable - the unattainable being defined as that which is desired by one and is not desired by the other.

It is a configuration for the Earth, stimulating equilibrium and strength; it is a grid which can be used for areas and photographs of areas of the Earth, to assist in the stabilization of those areas of unrest [e.g., areas of volcanic or earthquake potential] which are below the surface. It can also work with the pyramidal structure to assist in preservation and stability of foods, elixirs, tinctures, etc.

"Resolution" can be used to assist in the relief of tonsillitis, chromosomal imbalance, mumps, gout, goiter, glandular swelling in the area of the neck, lower gum dis-ease, gluttony, abscesses, angina, apoplexy, lack of the sensation of taste, and circulatory disorders. It can also be used in the treatment of disorders related to the throat, esophagus, larynx, trachea, cervical vertebrae, thyroid, lower jaw, the adrenal glands, the cerebrospinal nervous system, the cerebrum, the ears, the eustachian tubes, cerebellum, the optic nerves, retina, and iris, the mouth, gums, upper teeth, and Vitamin B deficiencies. The array can assist in the assimilation of protein and iodine. Overall, it enhances ones recuperative abilities.

The optimally utilized "Resolution" array would also contain spheres. Additional stones would be associated with the astrological sign of Taurus. It is recommended that, when available, crystals from Asia, England, Australia, Austria, Cyprus, and/or Russia be utilized in the construction of the array.

Vibrates to the numbers 1 and 4.

DUALITY

The "Duality" configuration is established by placing the crystals in the pattern of a rectangle surrounding the body of the subject, with the top and bottom of the rectangle extending past the vertical lines of the rectangle [See Figure 26]. It represents Gemini, a zodiacal constellation located between Taurus and Cancer, and containing the bright stars Castor and Pollux. The number of crystals used is left to the intuition of the practitioner. Due to its multifaceted nature, this is one of the most favoured lay-out patterns and is related to the chlorite mineral which is conducive to healing.

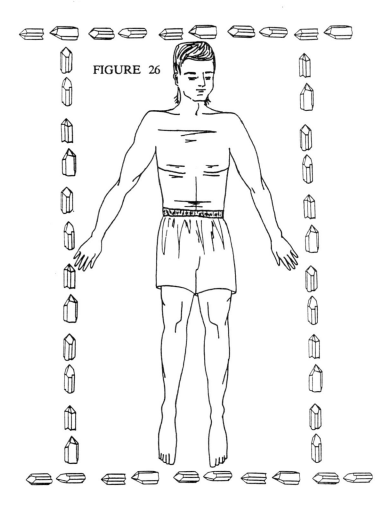

FIGURE 26

The configuration can be used to assist one in the manifestation of the qualities representing the multi-faceted nature which is inherent in humanity; it acts as a stimulus to incite the varying natures of one toward growth. It promotes both the mentality and the spirituality, providing insight with respect to purpose while promoting ones incentive to the integrity and distinction of ones life. The energies operating through the array tend to permeate the physical body awakening the vitality which leads to innovation and action. It also provides insight to the "yardstick" by which one may measure ones progress.

It serves to enhance the morality and to initiate guidance with respect to the definition of and reasons behind ones principles.

It further assists one in cascading with the times, encouraging one to be as "the rolling stone which gathers no moss". "Duality" can help one to be less inflexible, less demanding, and less structured; it can assist one in the actualization of the liberty of the "free spirit".

"Duality" has been employed to arouse the instinct and to expedite accomplishments which bring value and contribution to the furtherance of unconditional love.

It can also be used to assist one in accessing and interpreting ancient writings during the meditative state and can provide for stimulus to inspiration.

The array has been placed upon a photograph of the self/another to facilitate continuance of the state attained during the physical gridding of the self or another. It can also be placed upon a photograph of a subject to sharpen the quality of perception, to enhance writing and/or speaking abilities, to promote opportunities for traveling, and to provide for increased protection for passengers during travel.

Dual arrays, placed upon/around each person, can be used to promote multi-dimensional experiences between the participants; stimulating verbal communication and exploration with respect to future plans. It can help the participants to recognize and integrate emotional responses, promoting clarity and practicality in discussions. It can also help one to understand another with respect to versatile relationships, stimulating acceptance of the conditions and the active transference of unconditional love *or* acting to change ones reality so that commitment to another and from another is feasible. It is said to assist in the re-birthing process, helping traumatic events and conditions of the past to become obvious and assisting one in the release of same [this is an excellent array for cooperative re-birthing].

It is an excellent energizer for plant elixirs and tinctures, and can be used to assist in the germination and growth of plants and seeds. It has also been used to sanctify and to energize crystal elixirs.

It can be employed in the activities of "pest" control; placing the array around/upon the photograph of the "offender" encourages departure of same. The arrangement can also be used in conjunction with radionics to facilitate similar results.

It is a configuration for the atmosphere, stimulating cleansing and purity; it is a grid which can be used for aerial photographs of the Earth, to assist in the stabilization of the total auric field and in the facilitation of the replenishment of the ozone levels; the arrangement can also be used in conjunction with radionics to facilitate similar results.

It can assist in the activities associated with "cloud-busting"; during cloud-busting activities the array has been placed around the rod; it has also been placed upon a photograph of the desired result.

It can also be used to open, to cleanse, and to stimulate the crown chakra.

The "Duality" pattern can be used to assist in the relief of personality disorders, nervous disorders, tuberculosis, asthma, pneumonia, pleurisy, allergies, emphysema, and bronchitis. It can also be used in the treatment of disorders related to the lungs, the ribs, the intestines, the kidneys, the organs related to speech, the pupils of the eyes, respiratory malfunctions due to nervous afflictions, the upper dorsal nerves, pulmonary circulation, the arms, the legs, the feet, the hands, the heart, the capillaries, the ovaries, the ears, the upper and lower teeth, the trachea, and less than adequate oxygenation of the blood. The array can assist in the assimilation of potassium. It can also serve as a stimulant for the thymus.

The optimally utilized "Duality" array would also chlorite phantom crystals and other phantom crystals. Additional stones would be associated with the astrological sign of Gemini. It is recommended that, when available, very "old" stones from the Earth be utilized in the construction of the array.

Vibrates to the numbers 2 and 3.

NURTURANCE

The "Nurturance" configuration is established by placing the crystals in the pattern shown in Figure 27. It represents Cancer, a zodiacal constellation located between Gemini and Leo. When using the array, the crown chakra of the subject would be toward the North; note that the circles of crystals are placed around the hands. The number of crystals used is left to the intuition of the practitioner.

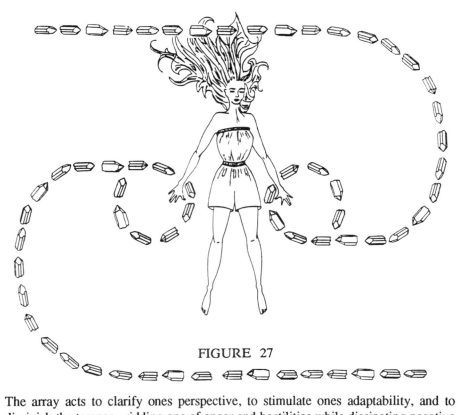

FIGURE 27

The array acts to clarify ones perspective, to stimulate ones adaptability, and to diminish the temper - ridding one of anger and hostilities while dissipating negative energies. It assists one in maintaining the courage of ones convictions, increases vitality and the flow of the universal life force, and helps to increase ones loving assertiveness. It helps one to evaluate situations with respect to security, protection, and tenacity. It further stimulates ones potential, helping one to remain aware of individual objectives.

The array has been placed upon a photograph of the self/another to facilitate continuance of the state attained during the physical gridding of the self or another. Placement of the array around a photograph or facsimile of a material item will assist the practitioner in attainment of same; it can also further the actions associated with the "collector", helping one to obtain material items for ones collections.

♪ 84 ♫

"Nurturance" can effectively facilitate merchandising and activities concerning the care of others. It can be also be used to assist one in experiencing positive sensitivity, in coherent expression of ones inner feelings and emotions, and in organizing the life with practicality and realism.

Dual arrays, placed upon/around each person, can be used to enhance an intuitive awareness of the others needs and desires. It can be used to enhance time shared and to freshen relationships. It can further dual participation in activities while helping each association to nurture the individuality of the selves. It stimulates "reaching-out" to one another in a communicative, loving correspondence. The dual array can also further the mother/child relationship assisting the mother in understanding the path of the child, albeit different from her own; it assists the mother in releasing the "smothering" overprotective manner while assisting the child to accept autonomy.

It also opens, stimulates, and cleanses the heart chakra, the solar plexus chakra, and the chakras located in the areas of the hands.

It is an excellent energizer for mineral elixirs, crystal and/or apophyllite pyramid waters. During the summer solstice [northern hemisphere] or the winter solstice [southern hemisphere] it is used to cleanse, to activate, and to energize crystals. The arrangement is reported to have greater strength in the southern hemisphere during this period. It is an excellent configuration for the stabilization of the oceans and waters of the Earth. It can be used for gridding springs, bringing the abundant energies and life forces of the ethers to the composition of the water. Gridding plants can also encourage the uptake of chlorophyll by same, stimulating the healthful state.

This configuration can be used to assist in the relief of chills, tumors, sclerosis, nausea, hypochondria, dropsy, alcohol addiction, dyspepsia, gastritis, heart burn, indigestion, gastric ulcers, iron-deficiency anemia, cancer, emaciation due to general ill-health, bronchitis, asthma, and abscesses. It can also be used in the treatment of disorders associated with the alimentary canal, urinal bladder, blood serum levels, chest, diaphragm, stomach, the esophagus, gall bladder, the upper portion of the liver, the lower portion of the lungs, the pancreas, the reproductive organs, the lower ribs, the teeth, the thorax, and the hands. It can assist in the assimilation of protein, iron, calcium, and Vitamins A and D; it serves to stimulate overall increase in the absorption of the nutrients required for the maintenance of the physical body.

The optimally utilized "Nurturance" array would also contain stones associated with the astrological sign of Cancer. It is recommended that, when available, crystals from Africa be utilized in the construction of the array.

Vibrates to the numbers 8 and 9.

SELF-EXPRESSION

The "Self-Expression" configuration is established by placing the crystals in the pattern shown in Figure 28. It represents Leo, a zodiacal constellation located between Cancer and Virgo. The number of crystals used is left to the intuition of the practitioner.

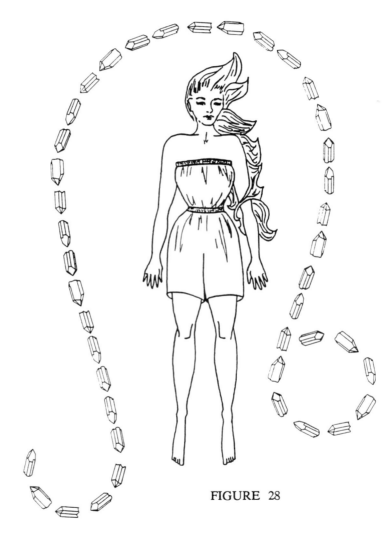

FIGURE 28

The array acts to stimulate the self-expression of ones individuality, inciting loyalty, affection, the release and verbalization of ones opinions, the diminishment of worry, and the release of ones self-limiting opinions. It promotes a positive mental, emotional, and spiritual attitude, stimulating the release of egotistic tendencies and vanity.

"Self-Expression" can also be used to assist one in the assertiveness and self-sufficiency necessary for single-parenting and/or single-living. It helps one to be aware of the self as a manifestation of the perfect Creator, opening and energizing the heart chakra and promoting loving leadership and administrative and interactive abilities.

It also assists one in the actualization of large-scale ideas and helps one to command the attention required to deliver projects and ideas to completion.

This configuration provides one with the meditative insight to "be in the moment", to act through the non-reactive state, and to foster the care of the self and others through self-actualization.

It can be used to open, to cleanse, and to energize the sacral chakra and to provide for balancing of the throat chakra.

Within this array, the movement of the Kundalini can be stimulated to continue past the throat chakra and on toward the crown chakra.

The array has been placed upon a photograph of the self/another to facilitate continuance of the state attained during the physical gridding of the self or another. Placement of the array around a photograph of the self/another promotes focus and determination in the pursuit of goals, persistence, and constructive thought processes which allow one to realize the state of non-hasty and totally methodical decision-making.

The photographic arrangement can also be used to stimulate the actualization of love affairs and romantic situations. It further promotes the utilization of the intellectual capabilities and provides assistance from other planes during discussions, public speaking, and debates.

Placing "Self-Expression" around the photograph of a jungle and/or islands can stimulate stability and healing of same.

Dual arrays, placed upon/around each person, can serve to help one to embark on permanency in relationships. It can instill faithfulness and can initiate the freshening of relationships.

The utilization of the dual array can also further the father/child relationship assisting the father to understand and/or release expectations of the child and allowing the child to grow at a personal rate in a personal way. It can also help one to understand that another is not on this Earth plane to "live-up" to *your* expectations or to *do* that which you desire. The array also assists one in recognizing *when* to implement control and when to release practical governing.

"Self-Expression" can effectively facilitate merchandising and activities concerning the care of others.

It also prompts the recognition of the etheric bodies, assisting one in the synthesis of the etheric with the physical.

It can be used to further ones advance toward spirituality, and intensifies the meditative and contemplative states.

This configuration can assist in the relief of fainting, heat exhaustion, anemia, sunstroke, meningitis, inflammations, hyperaemia, palpitations of the heart, fevers, frostbite, baldness, and infections of the mucous membranes which line the inner surface of the eyelids. It has also been used in the treatment of angina, baldness, and disorders of the membrane surrounding the heart.

It can be used in the treatment of disorders associated with the wrists, dorsal vertebrae and spinal cord, the middle dorsal nerves, the dorsal region of the upper region of the back, the sides, the forearms, the blood, and the manufacture and secretion of bile. Overall, it enhances ones recuperative and regenerative capabilities.

The optimally utilized "Nurturance" array would also contain stones associated with the astrological sign of Leo. It is recommended that, when available, crystals from Madagascar, France, Zimbabwe and/or the state of Washington, be utilized in the construction of the array.

Prior to manipulating the array and during the initial period of arrangement, burning of frankincense is recommended.

Vibrates to the numbers 5 and 6.

DISCRIMINATION

The "Discrimination" configuration is established by placing the crystals in the pattern shown in Figure 29. The intersection of the curved line of crystals, with the middle vertical line of crystals, is located between the base and solar plexus chakras. It represents Virgo, a zodiacal constellation located between Leo and Libra. The number of crystals used is left to the intuition of the practitioner.

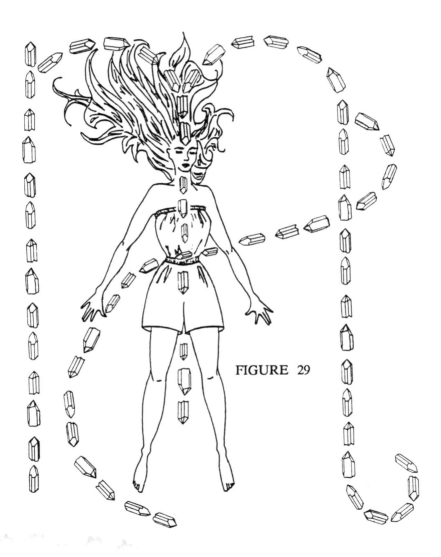

FIGURE 29

The array acts to stimulate linguistic abilities, elocution, fluency in writing, detail orientation, and precision. It can alleviate obsessions with respect to perfection, promoting the actualization of same without the excessive pondering.

It also serves to assist in the reduction of promiscuity without thought, promoting thought before action and providing insight to the subliminal causes of self-destructive actions.

It can help one to flow with conventional attitudes and opinions, promoting knowledge of when to do so in order to eliminate dissension; at the same time, however, it assists one in being open to contrasting opinions and in maintaining awareness of the differences.

It further opens one to both experiencing and exhibiting warmth of feeling; it also promotes insight with respect to the nature of being warm and loving, allowing for the understanding that one can be loving [and true to the self and others] without sharing time with those who are not on the same spiritual path. It actually supplies an extra energy which helps one to release all responsibility for entertaining and being with those who radiate negativity.

It can also be used to open, to cleanse, and to energize the crown chakra.

"Discrimination" can be used to assist one in "bringing the self away from the self" such that one can be an unbiased observer, acting the part which is required and/or chosen for the time. It helps the self to "*be*" the action and to more deeply understand the nature of this reality. *It is an array for analysis, examination, investigation, and evaluation.*

This configuration may be used to provide one with contact with the ancient ones of Babylonia, Egypt, and Mesopotamia, allowing for the transmittal of information concerning those ages and occurrences in the prior civilizations. The information tends to be with respect to the methodology used to care for others, to increase ones spirituality, and to further the practice of the multitude of metaphysical arts dealing with the advancement of the abilities of the mind.

The array promotes the expansion of clairvoyance, the reception of telepathic thoughts, and the acceptance of visions and images which are involved with psychometry.

"Discrimination" has been placed upon a photograph of the self/another to facilitate continuance of the state attained during the physical gridding of the self or another. Placement of the array around/upon ones photograph promotes focus and stimulation of knowledge related to mathematical pursuits. It also assists in diminishing psychological barriers with respect to frigidity and impotency. It is an excellent healing array to place around/upon the photograph of a pet.

Gridding of gardens and/or farms [or a photograph of same] with the array can promote healthy plants and an increase in the abundance of yield; it can also be utilized to expand the amount and diversity of grasses and grains. It is a configuration for the Earth, stimulating equilibrium and strength; it is a grid which can be used for areas and photographs of areas of the Earth, to assist in the stabilization of those areas of unrest [e.g., areas of volcanic or earthquake potential] which are below the surface.

Dual arrays, placed upon/around each person, can serve to help one to empathize with another, furthering a connected-ness, usually located in the region of the solar plexus chakra, which can promulgate understanding, openness, and warmth in the relationship. Since this array provides for receptivity of thoughts which are being sent from another, it is an interesting exercise for one participant to be gridded with "Discrimination" and another to be gridded with a planetary array which stimulates transmitting or which enhances both receiving and transmitting [e.g., the "Neptune" configuration].

Dual arrays of "Discrimination" have also been used to assist the practitioner in determining the cause of dis-ease, the pathway to increased well-being, and the nutritional provisions which would help the subject. It is interesting to note that this array also provides insight and understanding to both the nutritional requirements for, and the principles and ethics which support, vegetarianism.

The configuration can be used to assist in the relief of parasitic infestation, ruptures, appendicitis, malnutrition, dysentery, fractures and disorders of the hands, typhoid fever, inflammation of the intestines, dyspepsia, diabetes, colitis, eczema, and anaphalytic shock. It can also be used in the treatment of disorders associated with the spleen, the auto-immune system, the uterus, plasma, the pancreas, the lower dorsal sympathetic nervous system, the lower portion of the liver, the abdomen, the colon and intestines, the diaphragm, and the duodenum. It has been used to assist in the elimination of excess hair. It can also assist in the assimilation of potassium and Vitamins A, C, D and E, and can stimulate the metabolism of fats and carbohydrates.

The optimally utilized "Discrimination" array would also contain stones associated with the astrological sign of Virgo. It is recommended that, when available, crystals from Switzerland, Sweden, France, Zimbabwe, and/or Uruguay be utilized in the construction of the array.

Vibrates to the numbers 4 and 8.

COOPERATION

The "Cooperation" configuration is established by placing the crystals in the pattern shown in Figure 30. It represents Libra, a zodiacal constellation located between Virgo and Scorpio. When using the array, the crown chakra of the subject would be toward the North. The number of crystals used is left to the intuition of the practitioner.

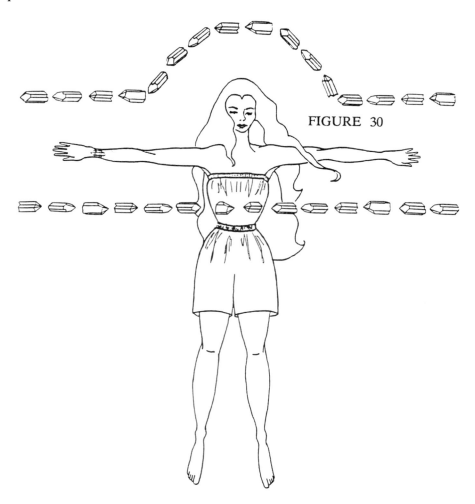

FIGURE 30

The array acts to stimulate the initiation and/or renewal of relationships and partnerships.

It instills the adaptability to changing circumstances such that one does not dismay, but becomes even more energetic when working to re-build that which is in the state of degeneration or that which has become deteriorated.

"Cooperation" can also be used to assist one in the actualization of artistic inclinations and scientific pursuits, via the enhancement of ones literary skills. It helps one to originate ideas and theories, furthering the talent for perceiving the "picture" in its entirety prior to determination of the resolution; it stimulates "option orientation", providing insight to the many and varied options which are available in any given circumstance.

It can also be used to open, to cleanse, and to energize the solar plexus chakra.

This configuration provides one with an enhanced appreciation of beauty and the willingness to pause to acknowledge same.

It further promotes the awareness of the cooperation between the conscious self and the Higher Self, stimulating the continuance of the direct conveyance of information.

It balances the chakras and the energies of the body, assisting in the elimination of energy blockages and elevating ones sense of well-being.

"Cooperation" has been used to awaken the automatic writing capabilities and to provide for the reception of information from those involved in the construction and use of the Egyptian pyramids.

It has also facilitated astral travel to the areas of the Indian Ocean where the vortices of Lemurian energy reside, assisting one in contact with those of the lost continent and in remembering the lessons of the enlightened members of that society.

The array has been placed upon a photograph of the self/another to facilitate continuance of the state attained during the physical gridding of the self or another. Placement of the array around/upon ones photograph also promotes ease in the attainment of the meditative state and in the performance of yoga and other meditative arts.

It can also sustain a balanced emotional nature, precluding the melancholy temperament and assisting one in understanding the inner reasons for depression and/or resentment.

Placement of "Cooperation" upon a contract or upon legal papers representing litigation serves to increase the positive outcome of same. It can also be used to stimulate interactions and/or romance [placed upon a photograph of that with which one desires interaction], cooperative efforts [especially for group endeavors], and mediation [when placed upon the photograph of the self and the other who is involved in the conflict].

It is a configuration for the atmosphere, stimulating cleansing and purity; it is a grid which can be used for aerial photographs of the Earth, to assist in the stabilization of the total auric field and in the facilitation of the replenishment of the ozone levels; the arrangement can also be used in conjunction with radionics to facilitate similar results.

Placing "Cooperation" around the photograph or facsimile of an area where inequality is prevalent can stimulate peaceful transformation of the imbalance and can assist in the elimination of pre-judgment tendencies and in the furtherance of correspondence between all involved. It also fosters cooperation in the environment of social gatherings.

It is an excellent energizer and stimulant for the germination of seeds, further assisting in the subsequent growth.

Dual arrays, placed upon/around each person, can serve to promote objectivity in conflict resolution and interaction between those involved; it assists each of the participants to maintain receptivity to the other, to be open to compromises, and to speak from the heart.

The dual array, when used by those involved in a relationship, can provide for insight to the shared soul-connection and can help the participants in managing circumstances and conditions which arise during the cooperative enterprises which are encountered.

During the autumnal equinox [varying from September 20-September 22], it is used to cleanse, to activate, and to energize crystals.

This configuration can be used to assist in the relief of Bright's dis-ease, diabetes, imbalance in the equilibrium, kidney stones, uremia, tularemia, and inflammation of the skin. It can also be used in the treatment of disorders associated with the veins, loins, lower abdomen, urinary system, metabolism, the internal generative organs, the ductless glands, fallopian tubes, the endocrine system, the upper portion of the kidneys, the lungs, the heart, the lower back/lumbar and spine and vertebrae, and the adrenal glands.

The optimally utilized "Cooperation" array would also contain stones associated with the astrological sign of Libra. It is recommended that, when available, crystals from Argentina, Germany, India, The Republic of South Africa, Namibia, and/or Tibet be utilized in the construction of the array.

Vibrates to the numbers 5 and 6.

TRANSFORMATION

The "Transformation" configuration is established by placing the crystals in the pattern shown in Figure 31. It represents Scorpio, a zodiacal constellation located between Libra and Sagittarius. The placement of an elestial crystal, if available, upon the area of the third-eye, is recommended. The number of crystals used is left to the intuition of the practitioner.

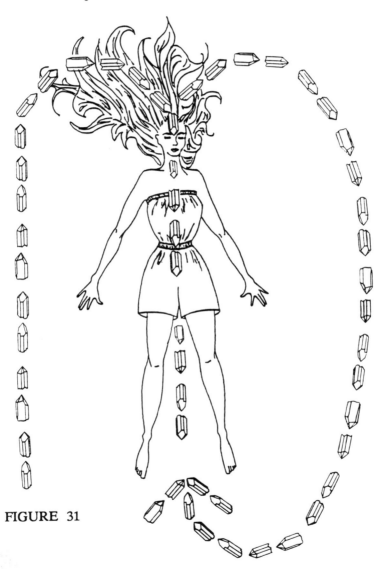

FIGURE 31

The array acts to eradicate sarcastic behavior, to augment ones courage [especially during the experience of danger], to provide impetus to progress, to assist one in the calm liberation of internal pressures, and to escalate ones stamina. *It assists one in all areas of psychic pursuits, white magic, and mysticism;* it actually expedites the elimination of skepticism by providing for experiences to dispel the doubts.

"Transformation" is quite effective for facilitating the understanding of reincarnation and for the promotion of activities related to past-lives; it provides for the state of ascension required such that one may view both past and future lives.

It can also be used during re-birthing sessions to enhance ones understanding of both the blockages which are removed and the reasons for which they existed.

The array has been placed upon a photograph of the self/another to facilitate continuance of the state attained during the physical gridding of the self or another.

Placement of the array around/upon a photograph of the self or another, it can also assist in the transition from one state to another - physically, emotionally, and/or spiritually; it helps one to attain a clear perception of the essence of the present and/or future state and to understand the reality of "progress via change" and/or "life after life".

The photographic arrangement also assists one in maintaining the will to deny imposition. Placed upon a photograph of another, it can encourage understanding, patience, and forbearance by the other. Placed upon the photograph of the self, it assists one in maintaining the mystery of the self, the privacy of ones inner thoughts, and the autonomy of ones experiences.

It is an excellent configuration for the stabilization of the oceans and waters of the Earth.

Dual arrays, placed upon/around each person, have been used to promote a double transmission of information from the ancients of Rome and Asia concerning spirituality and the manifestation of the perfect self; during this time, each participant is receiving information which is separate, unique, and which integrates as a subsection of the total "package".

The dual array can further enduring relationships, emotional intensity, empathy, and intimacy, and can assist in the understanding and release of jealousy. It can assist the participants in understanding that which is necessary to both jointly and successfully be a part of the cycles of transformation which are necessary for the growth of the individuals *and* the relationship.

If ones power animal is an eagle, the array can stimulate ethereal and/or dream visits by same. The visitations have been conducive to healing and/or to the awakening of the inner forces to actualize that which is desired.

The "Transformation" array is also an excellent energizer for mineral elixirs, and crystal and/or apophyllite pyramid waters. It can be used for gridding springs, bringing the abundant energies and life forces of the ethers to the composition of the water.

It can also be used to open, to cleanse, and to energize the base chakra.

This configuration can be used to assist in the amelioration of inflammatory swelling of the lymphatic glands. It can be used to relieve the symptoms of kidney stones, cholera, abscesses, gastric ulcers, toxemia, scurvy, frigidity, diphtheria, gall stones, allergies, and venereal disorders. It can also be used in the treatment of disorders associated with the thyroid, the spleen, the adenoids, the sense of smell, the secretory organs, prostate gland, pituitary gland, the small intestines, the generative organs, the excretory system, the ductless glands, the colon, red corpuscles and haemoglobin, the urinal bladder, the lower kidneys, the urethra, the appendix, the genitals, and the digestive system.

It can also assist in the assimilation of calcium and Vitamin C. It has been used as a stimulant for the thymus. It is conducive to assisting in the facilitation of the physical birth process, providing an increase in vitality to both the mother and the child.

Placement of the array upon/around a photograph of one during and after physical surgery can assist in awakening recovery mechanisms. It can also effectively facilitate psychic surgery, assisting in the extraction and/or in the repair of areas of the body.

The optimally utilized "Transformation" array would contain obelisks and additional stones associated with the astrological sign of Scorpio. It is recommended that, when available, crystals from Brazil, Spain, Arkansas, and/or Asia be utilized in the construction of the array.

Vibrates to the number 5 and the master number 66.

CONSCIOUS EXPANSION

The "Conscious Expansion" configuration is established by placing the crystals in the pattern of an arrow, beginning at the feet and ending above the head of the subject [See Figure 32]; the intersection is located at the area of the knees. It represents Sagittarius, a zodiacal constellation located between Scorpio and Capricorn. The number of crystals used is left to the intuition of the practitioner.

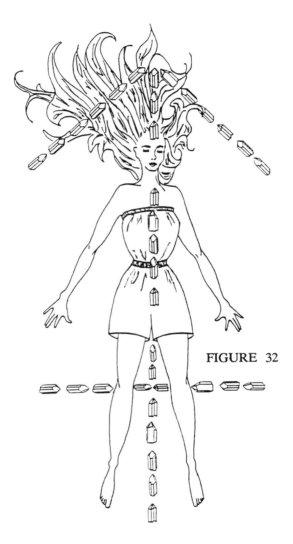

FIGURE 32

The array acts to stimulate integrity, benevolence, inspiration, enthusiasm, optimism, and physical/emotional stability. It promotes second-sight, opens and energizes the third-eye, and furthers the pursuit of "truth". It stimulates the quest for growth both mentally and spiritually.

"Conscious Expansion" can also be used to assist one in realizing "the self within the self" instead of seeking approval and/or realization from the external world. It further helps one to understand that one has "entered the school of life-experience", and that the events of ones life are those which will serve to affect the surmounting of limitations [self-imposed or other-imposed] *and* that by living in accordance with loving standards and by performing at ones highest abilities, ones ideals will become reality.

This configuration provides one with "permission" to accept the positive sides of self-indulgence, to be kind to the self, and to luxuriate the self with care.

The movement of the Kundalini can be initiated and/or stimulated to continue upward toward the crown chakra [when its progression has reached the third-eye]; the placement of electric-blue sheen obsidian in the location of the base chakra and violet sheen obsidian on the third eye is recommended.

Polarity can be enhanced and stimulated. It can also be used to open, to cleanse, and to stimulate the throat chakra and the sacral chakra.

Utilizing "Conscious Expansion" can facilitate automatic writing/verbalization, precognition, and visionary experiences; a sheen obsidian [electric-blue, silver, gold, rainbow, etc.] would be placed at the intersection of the configuration and/or at the crown chakra.

It has provided for contact with Native American spiritual guides and has advanced ones understanding of the Native American medicine practices; when one is "chosen" the guide usually remains in proximity to assist in the further development of ones spiritual self and to assist in protecting and guiding one during the daily events and circumstances which one encounters. For ventures to promote the Native American spiritual contacts, electric-blue sheen obsidian is placed upon the third-eye.

The array has been placed upon a photograph of the self/another to facilitate continuance of the state attained during the physical gridding of the self or another. Placement of the array around ones photograph also encourages "good-times" and good timing. It has been used to bring "luck" in games of chance, to induce spontaneity, and to protect one during air travel.

It can be placed on manuscripts and documents to stimulate publishing/publicity, and has been placed upon literature and legal documentation involving "animal rights" to further the success of the litigation for "animal rights" and to assist one in understanding both the personal and the individual parts that one can assume, to promote the conscious realization by others, with respect to the conditions which are occurring.

Placing "Conscious Expansion" upon documentation relevant to foreign trade can stimulate that trade; placed upon newspaper or magazine articles concerning foreign unrest, it can promote peacefulness; placement upon a photograph of people from other countries, it can promote telepathic connections and can assist in bringing that person [or those persons] to ones physical proximity.

Dual arrays, placed upon each person, can serve to help each of the participants to see into the inner self of the other; it stimulates the opening of a pathway to the depths of the self of the other, promoting insights and realizations with respect to past-life/future-life connections, and personal thoughts and manifestations. It actually assists one in obtaining the same closeness to another that one has with oneself.

Utilization of a dual photographic arrangement can serve to help each of the participants to see into the inner self of the other via looking deep within the physical eyes of the other. It should be noted that these dual configurations are placed such that the apex of one "arrow" is pointing toward the apex of the other "arrow".

The dual array can also be used to assist the participants in understanding the ideal of freedom in relationships.

This configuration can be used to assist in the relief of fevers, sciatica, degenerative dis-ease of the spinal cord, lumbago, baldness, rheumatism, and inflammatory disorders. It promotes the regulation of cholesterol and the metabolism of fats. It can also be used in the treatment of disorders associated with the feet, the hands, the sacral region and coccyx areas of the spine, the full range of spinal vertebrae, the thighs, the hips, the liver, the hepatic system, the blood, arteries, bone fractures and separations, and the eyesight.

The optimally utilized "Conscious Expansion" array would contain crystal obelisks and additional stones associated with the astrological sign of Sagittarius. It is recommended that, when available, electric-blue sheen obsidian [from Oregon] and crystals from Argentina, Czechoslovakia, France, Peru, Madagascar, Zimbabwe, Washington [USA], and Tibet, be utilized in the construction of this array.

Vibrates to the numbers 1 and 9.

ORGANIZATION

The "Organization" configuration is established by placing the crystals in the pattern shown in Figure 33. It represents Capricorn, a zodiacal constellation located between Sagittarius and Aquarius. When using the array, the crown chakra of the subject would be toward the South. The number of crystals used is left to the intuition of the practitioner.

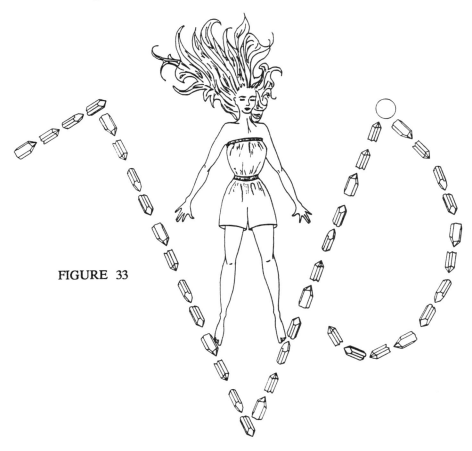

FIGURE 33

The array acts to stimulate ambition, seriousness when seriousness is required, light-hearted behavior when seriousness is not required, persistence, organizing capabilities, and conservation of ones personal resources [e.g., diminishment of over-spending, lessening of extravagance in the use of the natural resources of the Earth, etc.]. It can further assist in the acquisition of material wealth.

It also serves to provide for the recognition of action/thought patterns that are beneficial, promoting both the release of the detrimental modes of being and the retention of the quality systems. It promotes the management of emotional responses via prompting one to center the self prior to reply and/or "reaction". It also assists one in the determination of the appropriate protocol for any given situation or circumstance.

It further stimulates the recognition of the subversive actions of others, providing insights to allow for the detection of any potential destructive actions against one and promoting guidance in controlling the outcome in a positive manner.

It also helps one to understand that "one is always alone" - there is no requirement for loneliness, but there is the actuality that one must rely upon the conscious, the sub-conscious, and the Higher Self for actualizing that which one both needs and desires.

"Organization" can be used to assist one in understanding dis-ease and in allowing the dis-ease to depart. It is also useful when one is performing "bodywork" on another, helping the other to be open to releasing blockages and to be receptive to the supplementary energies which are being applied. It is an array conducive to promoting successful chiropractic manipulation.

This configuration has provided for contact with spiritual guides who are versed in the enlightened rites and rituals of the archaic orders of Freemasons. The information is usually granted during the meditative state when the participant is within the array. When "Organization" is utilized for the purpose of insightful guidance and/or to facilitate contact with the freemasonry spiritual guides, it is recommended that the procedure be repeated every six days.

The arrangement has also stimulated insights relative to the basis for, and the use of, the Runes.

The array has been placed upon a photograph of the self/another to facilitate continuance of the state attained during the physical gridding of the self or another. Placement of the array upon ones photograph also assists one in establishing a practical position in the mundane world; it also stimulates success in industrial pursuits.

It has been placed upon/around a photograph of an antique object to encourage the manifestation of the object; this application has been utilized to assist one in obtaining articles for antique collections. It has been used to grid ones office to stimulate both protection and business opportunities.

"Organization" can help in the discovery of mineral deposits and in the study of geology and geological forces. It can promote visions, given background information, with respect to locations of that which has not been discovered and/or that which has been "lost".

It is a configuration for the Earth, stimulating equilibrium and strength; it is a grid which can be used for areas and photographs of areas of the Earth, to assist in the stabilization of those areas of unrest [e.g., areas of volcanic or earthquake potential] which are below the surface. It has also been utilized in Earth rituals and in the cleansing and energizing of minerals.

It can also be used to open, to cleanse, and to energize the third-eye.

In addition, it has been used to grid wine, energizing, and occasionally, improving the taste of same.

Dual arrays, placed around each person, can serve to help each of the participants to understand a complete and loving platonic relationship. It can also be used to further contemplation of the other, providing for understanding of the depth and/or the superficial components of the personal structure.

This configuration can be used to assist in the relief of arthritis, skin eruptions [rashes, hives, etc.], rheumatism, poliomyelitis, paralysis, recurrent fever, frostbite, numbness, infectious disorders, hysteria, gall stones, hypochondria, gout, speech disorders, premature aging of the skin, inflammation of the mucous membranes, skin cancer, bruises, eczema, psoriasis, scabies, rashes, broken and/or dislocated bones, stiffening of the joints, and metabolic disorders.

It can be used in the treatment of disorders associated with the knees, kneecaps, throat, stomach, intestines, teeth, spleen, the arteries, the gall bladder, and the connective tissue. It can also assist in the assimilation of calcium, magnesium, and zinc. It is said to promote the growth of hair and beards.

The optimally utilized "Organization" array would also contain crystal pyramids and additional stones associated with the astrological sign of Capricorn. It is recommended that, when available, crystals from Afghanistan, India, Egypt, Zimbabwe, and/or Tibet be utilized in the construction of the array.

Vibrates to the numbers 5 and 7.

WAVE AND FORM

The "Wave And Form" configuration is established by placing the crystals in the pattern of two zig-zag lines, one placed on each side of the body of the subject, and each line having seven apexes [See Figure 34]. Success has been obtained via the utilization of multiples of seven crystals in this arrangement. It represents Aquarius, a zodiacal constellation located between Sagittarius and Pisces.

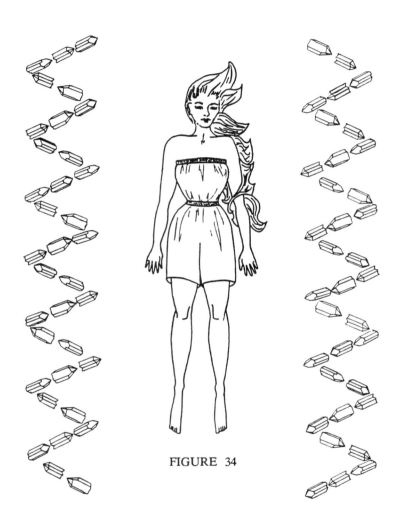

FIGURE 34

It should be noted that "Wave And Form" provides for a total healing and protective environment for that which is within the field of the array. It acts to transmit a white healing light around the subject which also provides for the safety and security of the subject [and/or that which is within the array or represented within the array via photograph or facsimile].

The array acts to stimulate altruistic pursuits, providing insight with respect to the ideal towards which the world would progress in order to produce a loving environment and humaneness to all. It allows one to recognize and to practice that which would bring the highest good to the reality of this lifetime.

"Wave And Form" can also be used to inspire persistence in following a chosen course of action, promoting focused concepts and the development and application of ideas; it further serves to assist one in the correlation of information and application of same to systematic approaches.

It can promote visions of ideas, allowing for the reception of visionary concepts of the future such that one can implement the concepts while maintaining "sight" of personal goals; the insight produced serves to teach one that altruistic goals are always compatible with personal goals.

In ancient Egypt, this symbol represented the molten fire of inspiration and actualization, bringing one to the pinnacle of ones manifestation.

It can be used to add the quality of "hope" to ones nature, to facilitate an enhanced appreciation of life, to promote logical and intelligent thinking and speaking, and to stimulate the skills of communication and interaction. The array helps one to speculate, anticipate, foresee, and foretell.

It can also be used to open, to cleanse, and to energize the third-eye.

This configuration provides for amplification of abilities in the fields of astronomy, astrology, clairaudience, theosophy, and astral travel.

It also assists one in the exploration of the ethers and promotes the access to, and the understanding of, the Akashic records.

If ones power animal is a bird, the array can stimulate ethereal and/or dream visits by same. The visitations have been conducive to healing and/or to the awakening of the inner forces to actualize that which is desired.

It balances the electrical and magnetic energies of the body, assisting in the elimination of energy blockages and elevating ones sense of well-being. It is an excellent arrangement for both faith healing and crystal healing.

"Wave And Form" has been placed upon a photograph of the self/another to facilitate continuance of the state attained during the physical gridding of the self or another. Placement of the array around ones photograph also promotes attracting and maintaining friendships; it enhances loyalty to, and from, friends and acquaintances. It assists one in the reduction of social obligations, helping one to "make" time for oneself. It can further ones wishes when the written wishes are placed within the field of the array. It can also assist one in the attainment of wisdom [gridding a photograph of the self].

It is a configuration for the atmosphere, stimulating cleansing and purity; it is a grid which can be used for aerial photographs of the Earth, to assist in the stabilization of the total auric field and in the facilitation of the replenishment of the ozone levels; the arrangement can also be used in conjunction with radionics to facilitate similar results.

The array has been used to grid itineraries to promote safe and enjoyable air travel.

Dual arrays, placed around each person, can serve to promote dispassionate understanding and tolerance of the others independence and self-assurance. It helps the participants to gain emancipation from restrictive situations via the recognition, understanding, and application of unconditional love. It further assists in the recognition of paradoxes and the initiation and continuance of the free will. It assists the participants in celebrating together that which will allow them to promote the highest good for all of humanity.

This configuration can be used to assist in the relief of periodic repetitive disorders, varicose veins, spasms, skin sensitivity, nervous disorders, heart irregularities and weakness, dropsy, broken bones, fractures, depression, blood disorders, hardening of the arteries, and anemia. It can also be used in the treatment of disorders associated with the ankles, the calves, the lower legs, the circulatory system, the eyes, the distribution of body fluids, the lymphatic system, the teeth, the lungs, and the kidneys.

The optimally utilized "Wave And Form" array would contain stones associated with the astrological sign of Aquarius. It is recommended that, when available, crystals from Poland, Oregon [USA], and/or the Middle East be utilized in the construction of the array.

Vibrates to the numbers 5 and 8.

CONFIDENCE

The "Confidence" configuration is established by placing the crystals in the pattern shown in Figure 35. The intersection is located at the waist. It represents Pisces, a zodiacal constellation located between Aquarius and Aries. The number of crystals used is left to the intuition of the practitioner.

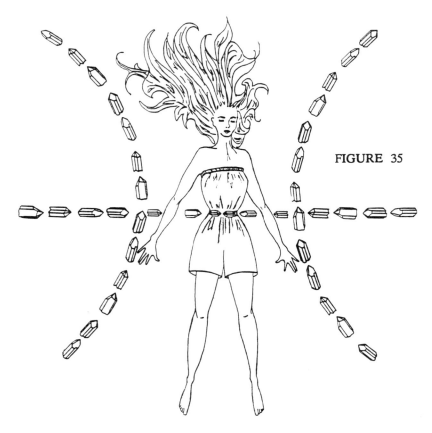

FIGURE 35

The array acts to enhance ones imagination, energy, and evolution. It assists one in finding solutions to age old puzzles, guiding one through the mazes of the mind toward the many and varied answers which are available. It assists one in intuitive reasoning, auric reading, visioning, past-life ascension, channeling of ones spiritual counselors and benevolent astral entities, psychometry, clairvoyance, astrological prediction, lucid dreaming and solution-dreaming, mysticism, and all psychic and metaphysical arts. Note that during channeling activities, the array stimulates the maintenance of control by the self such that one is an observer and translator with total memory recall. *It acts to dissolve all boundaries and enhances ones trust in oneself in all circumstances.*

"Confidence" is also quite effective for assisting one in obtaining an elevated state of meditation, inducing higher spiritual powers and promoting spiritual investigation, progression, and initiation onto the pathway of enlightenment. It helps one to be indifferent to the pedantry of those who are only drifting through the sea of life. It also encourages wandering through, and exploration of, the myriad facets of the ethers, bringing order from chaos.

The array has been placed upon a photograph of the self/another to facilitate continuance of the state attained during the physical gridding of the self or another. Placement of the array around/upon a photograph of the self or another, it can also promote the furtherance of leisure time and the enjoyment of same. It has been used to assist one in obtaining information concerning the mysteries of life and has provided details with respect to enigmatic issues. The photographic arrangement also assists one in manifesting the chameleon effect when desired, promoting the blending with the environment when one wishes to remain unnoticed.

Dual arrays, placed upon/around each person, have been used to promote guidance via the emotions, romantic tendencies, connection with another while proceeding in ones personal direction, and emotional adaptability to the partner. It also serves to provide for receptiveness to joint channeling; telepathic communication, one to the other, is enhanced. One array, configured upon/around two people, has stimulated merging of the mental and spiritual selves.

The "Confidence" array is also an excellent energizer for mineral elixirs, and crystal and/or apophyllite pyramid waters. It has also been used to sanctify and crystal elixirs. It can be used for gridding springs, bringing the abundant energies and life forces of the ethers to the composition of the water. It is an excellent configuration for the stabilization of the oceans and waters of the Earth.

It has been conducive to the furtherance of absent-healing and to facilitate diagnostic endeavors. "Confidence" can be used to assist in the relief of skin eruptions, colitis, dropsy, gout, tumors, somnambulism, fevers, internal poisoning, pleurisy, hallucinations, allergies, addictions, and detoxification. It can also be used in the treatment of disorders associated with the blood fibrin, the intestines, the lungs, the feet and toes, the mucoid membranes, the heart, the lymphatic system, the synovial fluid, the vision, and the muscular tissues. It can assist in the assimilation of iron and Vitamins A and D.

The optimally utilized "Confidence" array would contain stones associated with the astrological sign of Pisces. It is recommended that, when available, crystals from Southern Asia, Egypt, and/or the Sahara Desert be utilized in the construction of the array.

Vibrates to the numbers 6 and 8.

PLANETARY ARRAYS

NOTHING IS EVER LOST IN THE UNIVERSE

Claire Dalton
Johannesburg, RSA
1991

SUN-MEDICINE CIRCLE

The "Sun-Medicine Circle" configuration is established by placing twelve or more crystals in a concentric circle around the subject [See Figure 36]. The number of crystals used is left to the intuition of the practitioner. It should be noted that the crystalline formations which are utilized in this pattern are dependent upon the qualities which one desires to enhance.

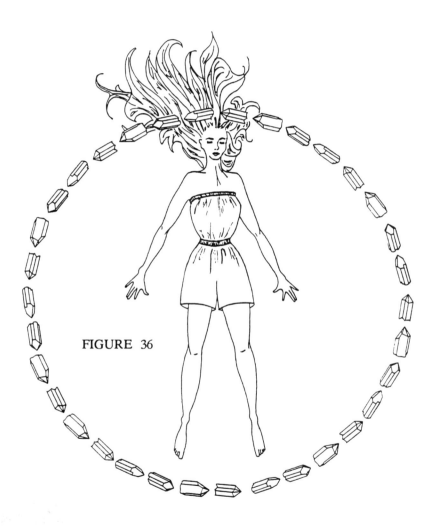

FIGURE 36

The sun, represented by a circle is one of the first three symbols designed for the religious teachings of early man. Its qualities include strength [physical, emotional, and spiritual], knowledge, wisdom, illumination, spiritual growth, courage, and self-expression. The crystals which are utilized in this pattern are, usually, varied in order to facilitate a wide range of results.

It should be noted that this configuration is also known as the Full Moon - Medicine Circle; its qualities include the balancing of the inner masculine self, the nurturing of the self and/or environment [e.g., via gridding], the stabilization of fluctuations in the body, mind, and/or emotions, the stimulation of the self toward growth of the inner child, and the enhancing of ones open-ness to, and acceptance of, the "new".

In Zen practice, the configuration represents enlightenment and oneness with nation. Meditation and opening the self to spiritual development can also be facilitated via this array.

In mythology, the Sun was personified as a god who governed light, healing, harmony, beautiful words, youthful manly beauty, and prophesy. The array stimulates individualism, opening of the pathway to the Higher Self, conscious expression, self-esteem, and renewal.

If ones power animal is the hawk, the "Sun" array encourages visitation by the hawk; information has been transmitted through the ethers, via the medicine hawk, between the subject of the array and others who have been separated by thousands of miles.

It has also been used to facilitate the independent temperament, to bring self-reliance, and self-sufficiency, and to encourage a pragmatic approach to ones direction.

It tends to further ones knowledge and to support a beneficial outcome during activities involving speculation - placement of the array around a description or photograph of the subject of speculation has produced successful results.

It serves to stimulate the actualization of eloquence in image, the recognition of ones individual capabilities, and the expression of ones integral singularity; in the expression of singularity, it also helps one to realize the multiplicity of the nature of all and the cooperative energies which are required to both maintain and progress in ones areas of manifestation.

The "Sun" can be used to discourage introversion, to encourage the acceptance of self-approval, and to stimulate the aspects of creativity, delineating the experiences and realities that are conducive to the awakening of the personal self.

It can also be used to open, to activate, and to energize the sacral chakra.

The array has been placed upon/around a photograph of the self/another to facilitate continuance of the state attained during the physical gridding of the self or another. It can also be placed upon/around the photograph of a subject to enhance vitality. Utilized with photographs or facsimiles, it facilitates the continuance of the state attained during the physical gridding of the item represented. Placed upon ones photograph, it can also assist one in further expansion of ones "glorification" via the actualization of ones innate attributes.

The array, placed around a photograph of greenery, stimulates the health of same; it has been used to assist in the etheric renewal of the rain forests in South America.

Dual arrays, placed around each person, can be used to promote coupled energy transfer and combined achievement of the vital force of "All That Is". It can enhance cooperative talents and can promote illumination with respect to those issues regarding cooperation. It furthers the development of personal power; the dual [or multiple] arrangement is quite forceful and is excellent to experience prior to assisting in healing.

The "Sun" can be used to stimulate generosity and to incite activation of the features of "luck".

This configuration can be used to assist in the relief of burns, inflammation, dizziness, skin eruptions, hot flashes, and tremors. It can be used in the treatment of disorders associated with the thyroid, spleen, spinal column bone marrow and nerves, the anterior pituitary gland, the heart and arteries, the adrenal glands, and the endocrine system. It can facilitate the oxygenation of the blood, the recuperative processes, and the assimilation of protein. It can further serve to ameliorate dis-ease relative to the brain, the dorsal region of the back, the retina of the eyes, and the tear ducts.

It has also been used to grid areas to protect against plagues.

The "Sun" further serves to promote the balance between red and white blood cells, can act to lessen states of hysteria and to eliminate the reasons behind same, and can also serve as a stimulant for the thymus.

The optimally utilized "Sun" array would also contain sceptres, aqua aura crystals, fulgurite, gold, amber, cat's eye, golden tiger eye, chrysolite, diamonds, and/or rubies [the ruby crystals are recommended].

Vibrates to the numbers 4 and 9.

MOON

The "Moon" configuration is established by placing the crystals in the pattern shown in Figure 37. Spheres are used at the head and the feet of the subject. The number of crystals used is left to the intuition of the practitioner.

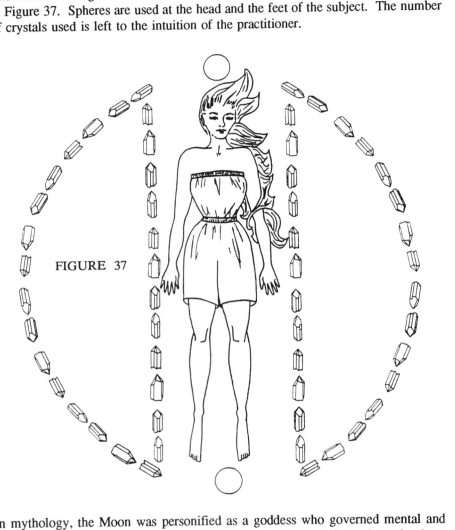

FIGURE 37

In mythology, the Moon was personified as a goddess who governed mental and emotional stability and weather changes. The "Moon" configuration stimulates sensitivity, responsiveness, psychic awareness, and compassion. It is an array for encouraging adaptability and behavioral adjustments, banishing insecurities and dissenting habits. It serves to activate the conscious awareness of dreams, assisting in the interpretation and providing insight to action; placement of the array around a subject during sleep has initiated lucid dreaming. It promotes psychic receptivity, medium-ship, and extra-sensory perception. It has been used to provide illumination to both universal mysteries and to those mysteries which are a part of ones reality, being conducive to stimulating images of the answers and solutions to the puzzles.

It helps one to decompose the "large picture" into subsets which are manageable, assisting one in fortuitously making contact with those who can provide information which is helpful to obtaining the resolution.

It has also been employed to stimulate emotional support, to bring to physical support to reality, and to open the doorway to spiritual guides. It can be used to open, to activate, and to energize the heart chakra. The "Moon" can be also be used to initiate change [of self, of situation, of personal reality]. It is excellent for dispelling negativity and for bringing romance and excitement to ones life.

The array has been placed upon a photograph of the self/another to facilitate continuance of the state attained during the physical gridding of the self or another. It can also be placed upon ones photograph to assist in relief from emotional trauma. Placed upon ones photograph, it can assist one in further expansion of ones receptivity to metaphysical occurrences. It has been used to initiate the state necessary for psychometry.

Dual arrays, placed upon/around each person, can be used to promote coupled extra-sensory perception, psychic images, and the meeting of the spiritual guide[s] of the other. In fact, the dual array has facilitated the activities of cooperative guidance from the spiritual guides of the participants. Information from the Mayan civilization has been made available during the utilization of this array; the connected-ness of the array participants has been confirmed and insight has been given into prior shared lives which occurred during this time period.

The "Moon" can be used to stimulate plant growth and to assist in the activities associated with "cloud-busting" and weather stabilization. During these activities, the array has been placed around the rod or upon a photograph of the desired result.

This configuration can be used to assist in the relief of allergies, asthma, and rheumatism. It can be used in the treatment of disorders associated with the lymphatic system, the blood serum level, female disorders, infertility, the digestive and intestinal systems, the alimentary canal, the urinary bladder, and the endocrine system [imbalance]. It can facilitate the alleviation of alcoholism, insomnia, vertigo, tumors, and the deficiencies of Vitamin A, Vitamin D, calcium, and the basic minerals required by the body. It can further serve to ameliorate the affects of measles, smallpox, epilepsy, and cancer. The "Moon" can promote proper function of the sympathetic nervous system and can foster control of mucoid discharges, emotional depression, and disorders relative to myopic and near-sighted conditions. It is also a stimulant for the thymus.

The optimally utilized "Moon" array would also contain marcasite, silver, opals, selenite, emeralds, moonstone, and/or an arrowhead.

Vibrates to the number 3.

MERCURY

The "Mercury" configuration is established by placing the crystals in the pattern shown in Figure 38. The arms of the subject are perpendicular to the body. Please note that the circle surrounding the head is round and the "hat" above the circle is in the shape of a half-moon. The number of crystals used is left to the intuition of the practitioner.

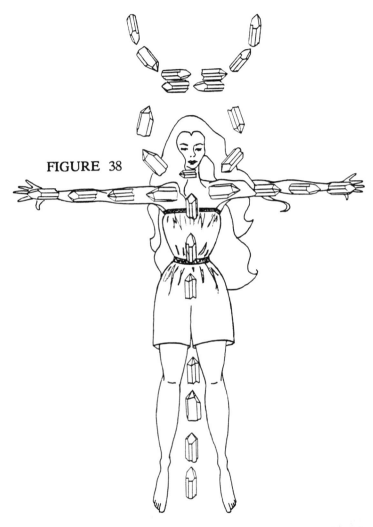

FIGURE 38

In mythology, Mercury was the messenger of the gods, who carried awareness and communication from one point to another. The "Mercury" configuration stimulates communication and connections. It assists one in rational thought, in mental concentration, and in the refinement and understanding of information.

It is an array for the "seeker", supporting one on the many paths which may be explored. It assists one in astral travel and enhances ones psychic awareness. It has also been employed to stimulate rapid thought transfer, providing the sender [upon/around whom the array is placed] with energies to expedite the mental transmittal of messages.

It serves to kindle the intellect and to provide stimulus to intelligent articulation and to comprehensive understanding during listening, bringing the cognitive processes toward the maximum proficiency. As Plato said "thoughts rule the world" and this "Mercury" array is the cerebral activator, the explicit delineator, and the teacher of discrimination.

It enables one to understand that one is the total of thought, feelings, and actions; it allows one to recognize that experience grows from thought and that experience can be changed to the actualization of all positive incidents as choices upon which ones life is built.

It can also be used to open, to activate, and to energize the throat and the crown chakras.

"Mercury" can be also be used to stimulate "right-brain" creativity and receptivity. It is excellent for reinforcing public communication and interaction; introversion is diminished and the balance in interactive-ness is maintained.

It furthers pursuits in mystical, alchemical, theosophical, and astrological fields, sharpening the senses and perceptions.

The array has been placed upon a photograph of the self/another to facilitate continuance of the state attained during the physical gridding of the self or another. It can also be placed upon a photograph of a subject to assist in relief from vertigo and nervous disorders.

It has been used to alleviate worry, allowing the subject to recognize that the act of "worrying" does not facilitate surmounting the problem, but serves to intensify the outcome.

It can also be used to bring the thoughts, of the subject of a photograph, to the practitioner.

Dual arrays, placed upon/around each person, can be used to promote recognition of similarities between the two, to provide awareness of the other on a spiritual level, and to allow the extending of the self to the other in total identification. It can also be used to facilitate psychic interaction between those involved. In the dual configuration, the participants are parallel and the two "half-moons" are joined to represent the circular sun.

"Mercury" has also been used to stimulate trade, bartering, and commerce - the array being placed upon the photograph of the article which one desires to trade/barter/sell, or upon contracts or descriptive information representing same. It has been identified as a "merchant's array" [and is worn by merchants and by others who offer personal services], stimulating business and enhancing profitability with respect to the associated service and/or merchandise which is available.

This configuration has been used to assist in the relief of bronchitis, pulmonary and respiratory dis-ease, afflictions of the right cerebral hemisphere, the nervous system, the vocal cords [including dysfunctional speech patterns], the ears, the arms, manual dexterity, and the motor skills. It can also be used in the treatment of headaches, neuralgia, the thyroid gland, lumbago, hoarseness, gout, asthma, pleurisy, less than adequate oxygenation of the lungs, gastro-intestinal disorders, back pain, fainting, bladder and genital pains, rheumatism, skin disorders, depression, varicose veins, and impurities in the blood.

Nervous disorders associated with lassitude, heart palpitation, neuralgia of the heart, nervous indigestion, headaches, debility, kidney control, urinary and digestive conditions, and general aches and pains can also be alleviated; overall, it can stimulate the health of the vital fluids which control and interact with the nervous system.

It has also been reported that, with utilization of the array [via photograph or in actuality], drunkenness has been eliminated and recreational drug-usage has been suspended.

The optimally utilized "Mercury" array would also contain cinnabar and/or alchemical mercury, celestite, Vera Cruz amethyst, and/or turquoise.

Vibrates to the number 4 and to numbers in general.

ANKH/VENUS TRIUMPH

The "Ankh Venus Triumph" configuration is established by placing the crystals in the pattern of an ankh [See Figure 39]. The arms of the subject are perpendicular to the body. The number of crystals used is left to the intuition of the practitioner.

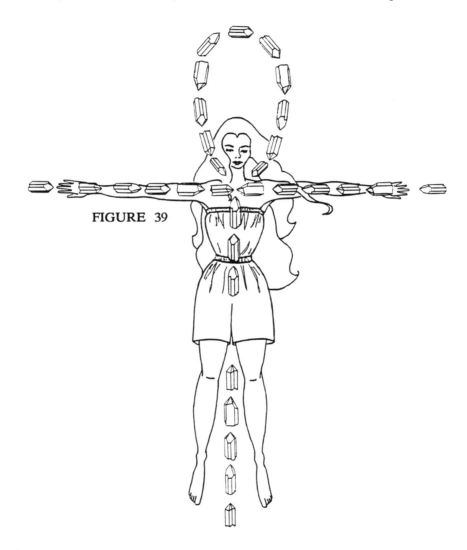

FIGURE 39

In mythology, Venus was the goddess of love and beauty, bringing same to the exterior of ones being while providing for magnetic attraction between kindred spirits. It furthers the forming of attachments and the continuity of love affairs, bringing the actualization of "love is the victor over all". It opens, energizes, and cleanses the heart chakra and the solar plexus chakra.

This array is a combination of the ankh [symbol of life] and venus [social and emotional proclivities]. It provides for the activation of both receptivity and magnetic attraction, assisting one in recognizing that which is being attracted via emotional actions and guiding one toward the furtherance of attracting that which is desired.

It can be used to help one attract people, experiences, or objects which have been defined as necessary to ones growth, stimulating ones creative emanations and bringing them to the world of elements and to the understanding of the complexity [yet simplicity] of all.

"Venus" can be used to enhance ones attributes, to provide for diplomacy between the self and others, to facilitate the vocalization of ones thoughts and feelings, and to assist in the resolution of personal conflict. It can serve to permeate the mystique which surrounds another, allowing for the recognition of the bases of action and subtleties.

It also can be employed to enhance creativity and to produce insight into avantgarde creations and innovative design and development.

It has been used to provide for enhancing yin qualities and to help one to become open to loving relationships. It further promotes artistic endeavors and creative pursuits.

The array has been placed upon a photograph of the self/another to facilitate continuance of the state attained during the physical gridding of the self or another. It can also be placed on the photograph of another to assist in producing a connection between the self and the other. It has been place upon a photograph or a facsimile of that which one wishes to attract to ones life.

Gridding of gardens and horticultural areas [or a photograph of same] with the array can promote healthy plants. It has been placed upon a photograph of a home or in an array surrounding/within the home to assist in the maintenance of the security of ones possessions. It can also be used to grid the photograph of a person to protect against contagious disorders. It is an excellent healing array to place around/upon the photograph of a pet.

Dual arrays, placed upon/around each person [with the left hand of one person touching the left hand of the other person], can be used to promote recognition of the love connection between the physical manifestation of each and the spiritual being of each.

"Venus" has been used to allow for the recognition of the deeper ties between souls prior to their entry to the Earth plane, promoting the inner knowledge of this life condition and the experiences chosen from other realities.

As the design representing the entrance to the upper realms of ones being, it tends to provide one with the ability to transcend the material essence of the body, bringing about prompt response to healing situations. "Venus" is an excellent energizer for salves, elixirs, and tinctures.

"Venus" works directly with the central nervous system and can be applied to the re-establishment of the freedom of movement in the body, assisting the body to support its self-healing abilities. It can be used in the treatment of spinal disorders, lower back pain, TMJ syndrome, less than adequate vision, headache, chronic stress, and additional autonomic nervous system dysfunctions.

This configuration can also be used to assist in the relief of states of atrophication, poor circulation, arthritis, obesity, tumors, cysts, venereal disorders, catarrh, mucoid formations, kidney congestion, occipital headaches, mumps, goiter, tonsillitis, and lymph gland enlargement in the area of the throat.

It can also be used in the treatment of disorders of the skin, lower back/lumbar region, the parathyroid gland, pulmonary inefficiency, warts, dropsy, stomach distention, nausea, spinal disorders, PMS, deficiency in estrogen, the reproductive system, frigidity, impotency, leucorrhea, and to strengthen the peristaltic action of the intestines.

Dis-eases associated with the heart, uremia, pulmonary and bronchial organs, the auto-immune system, the hips, digestion, the feet, and the veins can also be ameliorated. It has been used to encourage the assimilation of protein and to control the level of cholesterol. It can also serve as a stimulant for the thymus.

The optimally utilized "Venus" array would also contain coral, carnelian, green or purple jade, lapis lazuli, emeralds, sapphires, and/or copper-compounded minerals/crystals or those minerals which are found in the vicinity of copper.

Vibrates to the numbers 4, 7, and 9.

MARS CIRCLE

The "Mars Circle" configuration is established by placing the crystals in a concentric circle around the subject while placing an arrow-shaped array of crystals at the top of the circle [See Figure 40]. Success has also been attained with the arrow-shaped array located at any side of the circle. The number of crystals used is left to the intuition of the practitioner.

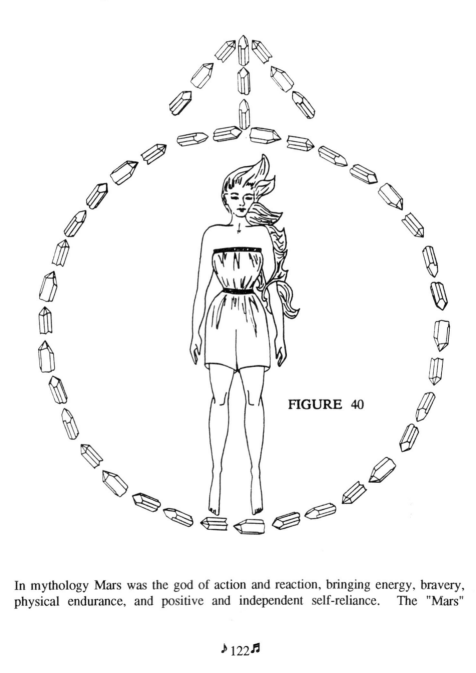

FIGURE 40

In mythology Mars was the god of action and reaction, bringing energy, bravery, physical endurance, and positive and independent self-reliance. The "Mars" configuration enhances these qualities and stimulates practicality in action. It helps one to understand the difference between action and reaction and teaches that re-action is that which occurs when one is not centered.

It further helps one to maintain a centralized focusing during the course of ones daily activities [the array placed upon ones photograph assists in enhancing the focus].

"Mars" can also be used to enhance the force of ones personal action; it assists in the identification of ones needs and desires and provides for the strength to obtain them. It teaches one to initiate optimistically and to attain independence, while opening the pathway to the pioneering spirit of innovation.

The array can assist one to move the mind "out of the way" of progress, bringing insight to the restrictions imposed by the mental processes, and allowing one to open to the action of the intuitive realm.

It can also be employed to rid one of deep-seated anger, resentment, hostility, and inner discord.

It has been used to provide for the enhancement of yang qualities and to help one to exercise control over uncontrolled emotional actions. It further assists in providing courage and endurance.

It can also be used to open, to activate, and to energize the base chakra.

The array has been placed upon a photograph of the self/another to facilitate continuance of the state attained during the physical gridding of the self or another. Placed upon ones photograph, it can also assist one in understanding the methods of appropriate and loving channeling and directing of ones emotional and intellectual feelings.

It has also been placed on a facsimile of "that which is impeding ones progress" [a written missive is included which states the non-functionality of the barrier]; the resultant reward being the dissolution of the impediment.

Placement of "Mars" around a subject provides for an excellent array for healing; placed around a photograph of one who requires healing it can stimulate the healing process, while placing the array around a photograph of the healer it can both increase the energy and enhance the abilities of the healer. Utilization of a descriptive missive and a grid placed around ones photograph has furthered ones success in fire-walking.

Dual arrays, placed upon/around each person, can be utilized to enhance the pursuit of desires which are common; the bond between the two involved may be recognized with the pathway to the goal delineated as a clearly-marked step-wise methodology. The dual configuration is placed such that the "arrows" are pointed toward each other.

If ones power animal is an eagle or a hawk, the array can stimulate ethereal and/or dream visits by same. The visitations have been conducive to healing and/or to the awakening of the inner forces to actualize that which is desired. It has been reported that the power animal has remained, in some instances, to act as a guide and protector.

This configuration can be used in the treatment of disorders of the haemoglobin, in cleansing the body of toxins, and in the amelioration of conditions of skin disorders, biliousness, high blood pressure, bruises, chills, fevers, burns, wounds, excessive bleeding, jaundice, kidney stones and bladder afflictions, genital disorders, and loss of vitality.

It can also be used to assist in the relief of sunstroke, hemorrhages, congestion, inflammation of the skin and/or internal organs, delirium, insomnia, fractures, sciatica, nosebleed, asthma, and pneumonia/bronchitis. Afflictions which are associated with prostate enlargement, gall stones, contagious dis-eases, ruptured blood vessels, tendonitis, dyspepsia, peritonitis, hernia, cholera, parasites, and the feet, can also be treated. "Mars" has been used to assist in the assimilation of both iron and protein.

It can also serve as a stimulant for the thymus.

The optimally utilized "Mars" array would contain both red minerals and iron or minerals/crystals which contain iron compounds. It would also contain bloodstone, fire agate, fire opal, malachite, rubies [ruby crystals from India or the Republic of South Africa are recommended], garnets, and/or flint.

Vibrates to the numbers 2 and 6.

JUPITER

The "Jupiter" configuration is established by placing the crystals in the pattern shown in Figure 41. The number of crystals used is left to the intuition of the practitioner.

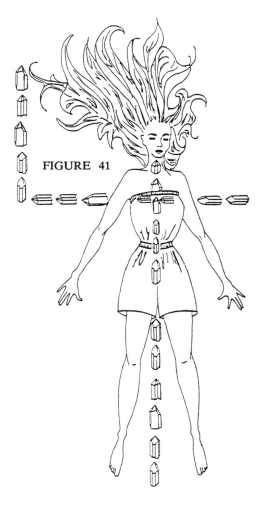

FIGURE 41

In mythology, Jupiter was the god of the heavens, providing for the expansion of consciousness [religious/philosophical areas] and for experiences which bring joy and abundance [business and financial areas]. The "Jupiter" configuration engenders expansion to the mind, allowing for ease of quest toward broader knowledge, experience, and spiritual development. It can be used to augment that which one possesses and to direct one toward the realization of freedom and limitless-ness. It assists one in seeking the absolute and in participation in "ultimate" experiences. It allows one to experience insight with respect to another "door" which is accessible when ones progress appears to be obstructed; it further helps one to gain insight that the path which is obstructed is the least desirable, providing for the inner recognition of the opportunities which are available via new directions.

The array can assist one in writing and lecturing - sharing knowledge, while maintaining both confidence and openness. It can also be used to open, to activate, and to energize the throat chakra and can provide for connection with the universal benevolent forces, bringing insight and intuition to one with respect to information which is not physically accessible on the physical plane.

"Jupiter" has been placed upon a photograph of the self/another to facilitate continuance of the state attained during the physical gridding of the self or another. Placed upon ones photograph, it can also assist one in intuitively recognizing opportunities and in consciously providing personal opportunities for growth; it also provides for amplification of thoughts, and improvement in conditions which are consciously acknowledged [e.g., financial gain, wise friends, distant communications, scientific endeavors, etc.]. It further stimulates protection when used by one who is engaged in long distance travel. It can also be used to stimulate trade with foreign countries, to protect confidential information, and to protect and/or to improve ones investments.

Dual arrays, placed upon/around each person, can be utilized to assist in providing images concerning which goals can be accomplished jointly and which paths can be easily traveled together. It is an excellent grid for ceremonial "magic", stimulating ceremonial knowledge from yesteryears, and inducing automatic speaking.

This configuration can be used in the reduction of adipose tissue, in the treatment of glycogen depletion in the liver, the pituitary gland, the adrenal glands, arterial circulation, degeneration of the muscular structure, tumors, diabetes, enlargement of organs, hyperaemia, blood-poisoning, disorders of the blood, imbalance of the blood pressure, and apoplexy. It can also be used in the amelioration of warts, fatty tumors, infertility of the male, pneumonia, headaches in the region of the temples, insulin disorders, dizziness, sleepiness, thrombosis, gum disease, depression, growths, nosebleed, pleurisy, lung congestion, pulmonary circulation, rheumatism in the hips and thighs, jaundice, lethargic action of the kidneys, gout, skin diseases, swelling, and in disorders of the teeth, pancreas, heart, upper legs, bone marrow, posterior pituitary gland, nose, and adrenal glands. Malnutrition can also be treated; assimilation of fats and zinc can be facilitated. Overall, it enhances ones recuperative abilities.

The optimally utilized "Jupiter" array would contain silver, amethyst, chrysanthemum stone, topaz, zinc, and/or nuggets and ore. The use of the sceptre crystal is recommended as a part of this array.

Vibrates to the number 9.

SATURN

The "Saturn" configuration is established by placing the crystals in the pattern of an "h" with a line of crystals crossing the top portion of the "h" [See Figure 42]. The number of crystals used is left to the intuition of the practitioner.

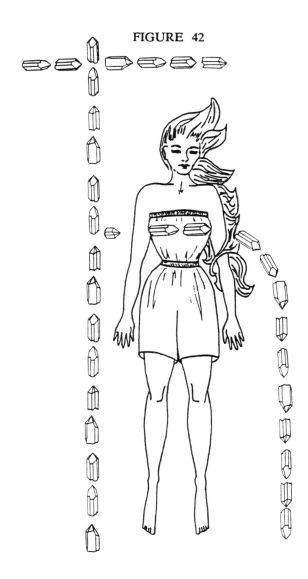

FIGURE 42

In mythology, Saturn was the god of growth, bringing happiness and virtue. The "Saturn" configuration assists in producing the actualization of ambitions, calmness and balance in decision-making, and discrimination in actions.

It can be used to stimulate "returning" to ones origin, immediately prior to this life or to the state of the creation of the self. It assists one in recognizing the karmic patterns and the lessons one has chosen, promoting acceptance of responsibility for ones reality. It is an excellent array for use during sessions involving ascension and meditation, providing for clarity via calming of the mind.

It can also be used to open, to activate, and to energize the third-eye.

It assists one in building structures within ones life, organizing systems, and establishing basic foundations for personal development. It can also be used to assist one in the conservation of resources and in the attainment of prestige via tenacity and continuance of action. It assists in the relief of inhibition, providing for equilibrium of the emotions.

If ones power animal is an snake or a spider, the array can stimulate ethereal and/or dream visits by same. The visitations have been conducive to healing and/or to the awakening of the inner forces which are conducive to the actualization of that which is desired. The messages may also supply information concerning deception or duplicity. In the situation of the snake, the movement of the Kundalini can be initiated and/or stimulated to continue upward toward the crown chakra.

The array can assist one in understanding limitations and in subsequently removing same; it can also be used to produce the acceptance of trust, responsibility, and practicality.

"Saturn" has been placed upon a photograph of the self/another to facilitate continuance of the state attained during the physical gridding of the self or another. Placed upon ones photograph, it can also assist one in the attainment of the acceptance, understanding, and hence, control of the emotional nature and can stimulate patience and perseverance. It has been used to grid places of ritual and ceremony to bring the esoteric to the consciousness.

It has been used to grid vegetation, to produce bountiful and healthy yields; it is a configuration for the Earth and the mountains, stimulating stability and strength.

The array has also been placed around/upon a photograph and/or item which represents that which one desires to increase. It can be used to grid ones environment [in actuality or via a photograph] to provide security and safety of same. "Saturn" is excellent for energizing ointments, bringing a lasting effect to the properties and the essence.

Dual arrays, placed upon/around each person, can be utilized to assist in promoting instruction from the "fathering" portion of the two Higher-Selves involved. It can also be used to provide insight to new traditions which can bring meaning to relationships and can assist the user in the comprehension of that which appears to be tragic. It stimulates hindsight prior to the passing of events, reducing "failures" and disappointments.

"Saturn" can help in the discovery of mineral deposits and in the study of geology and geological forces. It can provide visions, given background information, with respect to locations of that which has not been discovered and/or that which has been "lost".

It is grid-conducive to the study of history, traditions, mathematics, and Eastern religions.

It is representative of a "timing process", assisting one in the understanding of the "right" time for manifesting ones personal and unique potential; it helps one to operate in accordance with ones personal inner "designating" force and inspires the recognition of, and the methodology by which to eliminate, the imposed boundaries of another.

It is an array of defining and correcting, of defining and acting.

"Saturn" is a most efficacious array for healing with crystals. This configuration can be used in the treatment of disorders associated with the bladder, spleen, bones, teeth, vagus nerve, acid formations in the joints, the sympathetic nervous system, kidneys, gall bladder, liver, arteriosclerosis, intestines, transverse colon, rheumatism, gout, and the pneumogastric nerve. It can also assist in the amelioration of diphtheria, mumps, croup, tooth decay, constipation, malaria, sciatica, ruptures, neuralgia, pyorrhoea, lupus, cancer, ulcers, leukemia, appendicitis, Bright's disease, tuberculosis, and eczema. Orthopedic disorders, rheumatism, anemia, jaundice, fevers, paralysis, hyperacidity, typhus, skin disorders, gangrene, warts, epilepsy, deficient hearing, cancer, calcification, skin disorders, arthritis, and dental problems can also be treated. Obesity and the causes behind the symptom can be understood and corrected. It assists in the stimulation of peristaltic action, and promotes the amelioration of malnutrition. It can be used to facilitate the assimilation of calcium, Vitamins C and D, and the required minerals of the body; it serves to balance the metabolism and to bring the body, mind, and spirit to equilibrium. It can be used to stimulate the growth and maintenance of hair and beards.

The optimally utilized "Saturn" array would also contain gold, galena, chlorite, black onyx, jet, granite, garnets, and/or gypsum. The utilization of many types of quartz crystals is recommended.

Vibrates to the number 3.

URANUS

The "Uranus" configuration [See Figure 43] is established by placing the crystals in the pattern of an "H", the middle bar being extended, and a line of crystals parallel to the sides of the "H" being placed in the center and ending above the head and below the feet; the intersection is, usually, placed at the heart chakra or at the solar plexus chakra. The number of crystals used is left to the intuition of the practitioner.

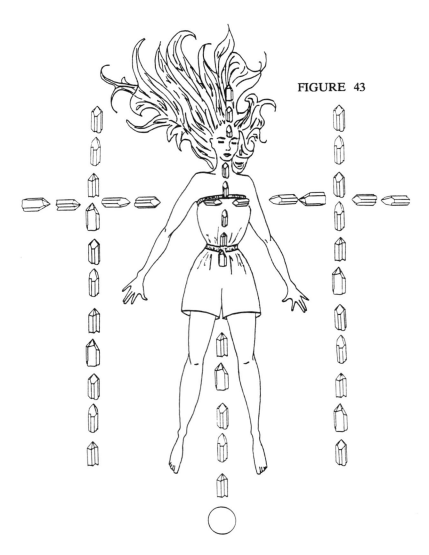

FIGURE 43

In mythology, Uranus was the personification of heaven and the ruler of this physical world. The "Uranus" configuration assists one in dispensing with old patterns and in inspiring effort toward universal consciousness. It enables one to move beyond the typical realm of actualization and to expand awareness of that which is available in the kingdom of perfection.

It assists one in "daring to be different", acting as a catalyst for change and personal growth, and enabling one to go beyond that which is known. It is a wonderful configuration to use during physical travel, allowing for courage in experimentation of the new and promoting understanding of others. It stimulates altruistic pursuits, spontaneity, and the exploration of the "new". The array provides for a unique perspective and encourages discovery. It can also promote visions of the future, allowing one to remain detached and as an observer. It further serves to instill trust and to assist one in considering the highest "good" during decision-making. It helps one to extricate the self from undesirable situations and acts to initiate and to provide courage for the permanence of a total departure from ones lifestyle; this facilitates and enhances the commencement of a fresh and dynamic life.

"Uranus" has been placed upon a photograph of the self/another to facilitate continuance of the state attained during the physical gridding of the self or another. Placed upon ones photograph, it can also facilitate the actualization of changes which will enable one to progress toward the state of perfection. It encourages spontaneity, articulation of ideas, independence, and the elimination of compulsions; it assists in investigations, oration, debating, and lecturing. It can be used to enhance the protective forces when one is driving or flying [physically or astrally].

It also helps one to understand the complexities of ones life and shared realities.

It has been used to grid areas and photographs of areas of disorder, the primary mineral being lepidolite. It is an excellent configuration for the stabilization of Earth changes and disruptive environments.

Unconventional attachments and ideas can also be discerned, evaluated, and rectified via the assistance of "Uranus". It has been used to grid the vortices of the Earth to stabilize energies and to promote the ease of transitions.

It can also be used to assist in the activities associated with "cloud-busting". During cloud-busting activities the array has been placed around the rod; it has also been placed upon a photograph of the desired result.

If ones power animal is in the family of birds, the array can stimulate ethereal and/or dream visits by same. The visitations have been conducive to immediate healing, to the awakening of the inner forces so that one may actualize that which is desired, and to the facilitation of contact between the self and ones etheric double.

It further serves to assist in protection and to increase the abilities of those involved with aviation, bicycling, and motorcar driving. It facilitates competency in the chiropractic field, in the realms of chemistry and alchemy, and in healing.

Dual arrays, placed upon/around each person, can be utilized to assist in promoting insight into the uniqueness of the bond between the participants. It can also serve to enable one to maintain the understanding of the present while providing for the vision of the future, assisting the participants in understanding and experiencing common changes with ease. The arrays are also conducive to stimulating abilities to see the auric field, to open and to energize the third-eye, to receive telepathic messages, to initiate and strengthen the clairvoyant and clairaudient aptitudes, and to assist in the fields of astrology, hypnotism, psychical research, phrenology, psychometry, white magic, and all of metaphysics. It has also been used in a meditative state to contact those from the civilizations which were "first-born" of Earth. It should be noted that action and re-action to events relative to the above listing occur spontaneously, swiftly, and with intensity. It can also stimulate compassion and understanding during divorce and/or separations, allowing for understanding and for the activation of the powers of universal love.

"Uranus" can assist one in actualizing the state of meditation [with a subsequent utopian awareness]. It can also be used to open, to activate, and to energize all chakras and to promote the removal of energy blockages and the subsequent free flow of the electromagnetic forces through the body. It brings personal magnetism to the user.

This configuration can be used in the treatment of disorders of the circulatory system, kidneys, St. Vitus dance, the pituitary gland, parathyroid system, nervous system, valves of the heart, hearing, ankles, and the eyes. It can also assist in the amelioration of paralysis, nervousness, disorderly coordination, spasms, vertigo, strokes, sprains, dysfunctional reflexes, palsy, heart palpitations, influenza, lesions, inflammations due to less than adequate mineral assimilation/elimination, epilepsy, emphysema, electrolytic imbalance, convulsions, disorders of bone growth, fractures, dislocations, loss of muscular coordination, sciatica, tetanus, hysteria, asthma, coughs, genital disorders, and meningitis. It has been used to diminish hallucinations. It further serves to ameliorate conditions of malnutrition and to assist in the assimilation of zinc. It is an excellent array to be used with drug-less healing.

The optimally utilized "Uranus" array would also contain electric-blue sheen obsidian. Other recommendations include gold/silver/rainbow and/or violet sheen obsidian, Pariaba tourmaline, watermelon tourmaline, cat's eye, tiger eye, lodestone, boji stones, asterated quartz, star garnet/sapphire, fossils, amber, bornite, opal, and/or petrified/opalized wood.

Vibrates to the master number 22.

NEPTUNE

The "Neptune" configuration is established by placing the crystals in the pattern shown in Figure 44. The intersection of the half-moon section and the line perpendicular to the midpoint of the half-moon is located at the throat chakra; the intersection of the horizontal and vertical lines is located at the solar plexus. The number of crystals used is left to the intuition of the practitioner.

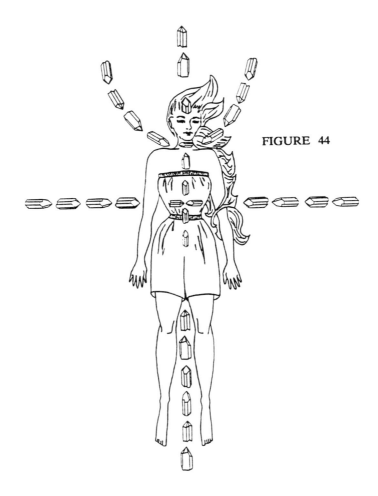

FIGURE 44

In mythology, Neptune was the god of water. The "Neptune" configuration assists one in remembering dreams, expanding the mystical side of the self, and enhancing the psychic abilities. It further assists one in the transcendence of barriers and in the exhibition of confidence to heal, to be healed, and to accept the unification with "All That Is" as perfection. The array stimulates the knowledge that "the universe will provide", helping to actualize that which is necessary and sufficient for the furtherance of the perfect self. It also assists one in the application of pantheistic philosophy to ones life, providing insight to the actualization of flawlessness and the connection between the universal power and the self.

It assists one in maintaining concentration, in attaining the state of meditation , in utilizing intuition and telepathy, and in attaining proficiency in mysticism and the metaphysical arts. The array has also been used to stimulate the trance state and to produce medium-ship such that the medium is the observer and is in total control, with total memory, of all that transpires. It has been used to further ones proficiency in, and understanding of, the bases supporting alchemy, astrology, astral travel, access to the Akashic records, clairsentience, clairvoyance, visioning, divination, dream consciousness [lucid dreaming and total recall], future-telling, hypnotism, white magic, the I Ching, the tarot/Neo-tarot, telepathy, the use of talismen, psychic research, and psychometry. It furthers the study, appreciation, and comprehension of esoteric theosophy and assists one in both obtaining and maintaining contact with the ancient teachers of same.

The array can assist in the decline of claustrophobia and can promote the desire for freedom and independence. It furthers the situations which will be conducive to attaining total emancipation.

"Neptune" has been placed upon a photograph of the self/another to facilitate the continuance of the state attained during the physical gridding of the self or another. Placed upon ones photograph, it can also assist in the transition from one state to another on the physical, emotional, and/or spiritual planes. It can further maintain and compose the psychic abilities. It also stimulates entry to, and maintenance of, the meditative state, allowing for connection and interaction between the conscious self, the inner self, and the Higher Self. It assists one in attaining and maintaining the trance state, allowing for the alliance between the self and those of other planes and spiritual worlds; the array has successfully promoted contact with the ancient teachers from Atlantis, Lemuria, and Mu. It has also been used to contact those spiritual guides who have provided information and guidance from the days of the Mound Builders and the Mayans.

Utilization of the array with a photograph of the self and another/other can promote protection from discovery; this can be quite helpful for underground activities, clandestine affairs, and secret societies. It can also be used to grid areas and photographs of areas of new businesses, enhancing financial security and providing for analytical insight into the promotion of same. It is an excellent configuration for the stabilization of the mountains, oceans, and waters of the Earth. "Neptune" can also be used to bless and energize crystal elixirs and herbal tinctures.

Dual arrays, placed upon/around each person, can be utilized to assist in providing for the compassion necessary to totally merge with each other without the interference of emotional involvement. It can assist the participants in straightforward and prompt receipt and transmission of feelings to/from one another. It can also assist one in discovering that which is hidden about another; in addition, it promotes flexibility in relationships. It further serves to assist in protection during, and to increase the abilities of those involved with, water travel, sailing, submarines, etc.; the photography grid can also be used. "Neptune" can also be used to assist in the activities associated with "cloud-busting". During cloud-busting activities the array has been placed around the rod; it has also been placed upon a photograph of the desired result.

If ones power animal is in the family of sea creatures, the array can stimulate ethereal and/or dream visits by same. The visitations have been conducive to immediate healing, to the awakening of the inner forces to actualize that which is desired, and to the facilitation of the realization of ones fantasies. It further serves to initiate the pursuit of spirituality and assists one in progressing toward enlightenment via the opening and energizing of the third-eye.

It can also be used to open, activate, and energize the chakras to promote the removal of energy blockages and the subsequent free flow of the electromagnetic forces through the body.

This configuration can be used in the treatment of disorders of the spinal cord, the thalamus, the nervous system, cerebral ventricles, glandular systems, the feet, the lungs, the optic nerves, parathyroid system, pituitary gland, and the pineal gland. It can also assist in the amelioration of addictions, lethargy, catalepsy, water retention, somnambulism, mononucleosis, chronic fatigue syndrome, pyorrhea, excess body fluid, swelling, oxygen deficiencies, internal/superficial poisoning, rickets, poliomyelitis, nervous debility, exhaustion, epilepsy, inflexibility, dehydration, alcoholism, frigidity, and temporary instability of the mind. The array can further the assimilation of Vitamins A and D, iodine, calcium, and protein; it is a matchless grid for use by vegetarians to stimulate the assimilation of nutrients. In addition, "Neptune" can be used to assist in the relief of toxemia and acidosis, while promoting a non-crisis detoxification of the body. It can be utilized to stimulate the metabolic processes, to provide a barrier against contagious dis-ease, to enhance the red blood cells, to alleviate psychoses, and to relieve disorders associated with alcohol, bites, stings [e.g., anaphylactic shock], and drugs. It is an excellent array for stimulating rejuvenation capabilities and for use with drug-less healing.

The optimally utilized "Neptune" array would contain an enhydro and a sceptre crystal. Other recommendations include crystal spheres, aquamarine, platinum, sheen obsidian, green/white/lavender jade, green or blue tourmaline, boji stones, amethyst, coral, shells, and/or pearls. Prior to manipulating the array and during the initial period of arrangement, burning of incense and/or sage/cedar/sweetgrass/elephant grass is recommended.

Vibrates to the number 7.

PLUTO

The "Pluto" configuration is established by placing the crystals in the pattern shown in Figure 45. The vertical/horizontal intersection is located at the solar plexus or at the heart chakra. At the throat, and above the head of the subject [touching the crown chakra], are spheres. The number of crystals used is left to the intuition of the practitioner.

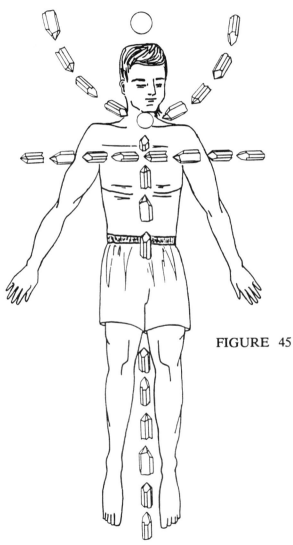

FIGURE 45

In mythology, Pluto was the god of those who had departed from this physical existence. The "Pluto" configuration assists one to perceive and to understand the many pathways leading to enlightenment. It helps one to recognize the reasons for ones lessons and experiences, providing insight to the user with respect to the methods of learning available which do not require "hard" lessons.

The array stimulates the manifestation of personal power, inspiration via movement toward the awareness of the universal perfection, and the ease of transformation from cycle to cycle. It helps one to "vault" into the unknown, catalyzing experiences of total understanding and promoting regeneration and cleansing of the environment and the self, and the commencement of the genesis of ones "becoming".

It assists one in maintaining the intensity required to reach a goal, and to recognize the commitments which are to be fulfilled during this lifetime. It promotes astral travel, access to the Akashic records, and opens and energizes the third-eye.

"Pluto" has been placed upon a photograph of the self/another to facilitate the continuance of the state attained during the physical gridding of the self or another. Placed upon ones photograph, it can also assist in the transformation of character, emotions, physical characteristics, and spirituality.

It can further serve to release repressed emotions and conditions which have produced negative effects upon ones well-being and enjoyment of this life. The array can also stimulate the furtherance of alchemical pursuits, clairvoyance, clairaudience, divination via the I Ching and Tarot, psychic experiences, white magic, psychometry, and palmistry.

It can be used to grid areas and photographs of areas of the Earth, assisting in the stabilization of those areas of unrest [e.g., areas of volcanic or earthquake potential] which are below the surface.

It can be employed in the activities of pest control; placing the array around/upon the photograph of the "offender" encourages departure of same. The arrangement can also be used in conjunction with radionics to facilitate similar results. Protection from epidemics can also be foster via the utilization of the array.

It is an excellent energizer for plant elixirs and tinctures, and can be used to assist in the germination and growth of seeds.

Dual arrays, placed upon/around each person, can be utilized to assist in providing for the consolidation of forces necessary to facilitate the changes necessary for the furtherance of the universal brotherhood. It can further assist the participants in utilizing the transformative powers on the level of healing the self and others. It can also promote the recognition of the soul-connection between two or more people, stimulating the actualization of universal love and providing for purification of the soul. It can also assist one in discovering that which is hidden about another.

It is said to assist in the re-birthing process, helping traumatic events and conditions of the past to become obvious and assisting one in the release of same. It can be used during radionic treatments to strengthen the bond between the self and the energies of the ethers.

If ones power animal is the serpent, the array can stimulate ethereal and/or dream visits by same. The visitations have been conducive to immediate healing, to the awakening of the inner forces to actualize that which is desired, and to the initiation of the movement of the Kundalini. It further serves to initiate the pursuit of spirituality and assists one in progressing toward enlightenment.

"Pluto" can be used to help one to traverse from the physical reality to the spiritual realm, promoting the understanding necessary to release the physical body and to gain eternity. It also promotes insight into the realities of reincarnation and the astral world.

This configuration can be used in the treatment of disorders of the gonads, reproductive organs, elimination systems, skin, urinal bladder, pancreas, parathyroid, pineal gland, prostate, and genitals. It can also assist in the amelioration of amnesia, blood disorders/poisoning, acidosis, excess alkalinity, cancer, malaria, venereal disease, herpes, ptomaine, smallpox, parasitic infestation of the body, gastric ulcers, frigidity, abscesses, fevers, radiation treatment or exposure, and the birth process. The assimilation of zinc and Vitamins A and D can be enhanced. Overall, it enhances ones recuperative and regenerative abilities.

The optimally utilized "Pluto" array would also contain laser wand crystals and crystal/mineral pyramids. Other recommendations include the enhydro, stalactitic formations, black tourmaline, black jade, sulphur, black obsidian, sardonyx, coral, shells, and/or pearls.

Vibrates to the number 3.

CHIRON

The "Chiron" configuration is established by placing the crystals in the pattern shown in Figure 46. The circular portion entirely surrounds the head of the subject. The number of crystals used is left to the intuition of the practitioner.

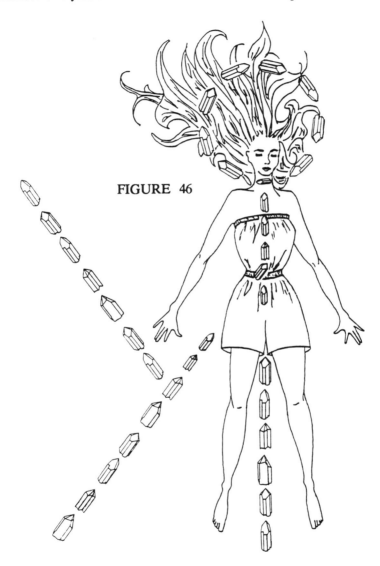

FIGURE 46

In mythology, Chiron was the wise and beneficent centaur, teaching and providing the key to integration. The "Chiron" configuration assists one in providing a "bridge" between the self and others on the many planes and multitude of worlds of existence. It serves to enable one to define objectives and to manifest same, bringing the capability to visualize perfection and the practical applications through which to attain the goal.

The array stimulates competence in problem-solving, facilitating the recognition of explanations and improvements to situations. It amplifies grounding of mental, physical, and spiritual principles, stimulating the integration of same within ones personal reality. "Chiron" also helps to relieve tendencies toward self-destruction and de-emphasizes failures and regrets; the de-emphasizing activity is via promotion of the grateful acceptance of lessons learned.

It further assists in movement toward the perfect state, in improvement of conditions, and in acknowledging and releasing past destructive patterns.

"Chiron" has been placed upon a photograph of the self/another to facilitate the continuance of the state attained during the physical gridding of the self or another. Placed upon ones photograph, it can also assist in the transformation of less than ideal physical and/or psychological well-being, bringing the perfect model to manifestation.

It has been placed upon/around a photograph of an environment in which one wishes to maintain security and safety [i.e., it tends to act as a security system to provide protection of the image in the photograph].

The configuration has also been used to assist in telepathic communication, astral travel, and contacts with those of other worlds.

Dual arrays, placed upon/around each person, can be utilized to assist in providing for a consolidation of forces to overcome common obstacles, to provide mutual support during the processes of change, and to enable collective "traveling".

This configuration can be used in all healing situations; it brings the recognition of the perfect state and ones right to that state, while enhancing the transfer of optimum energies from "All That Is" via the crystals. It is excellent for assisting in detoxification and in the treatment of conditions requiring restoration and repair.

The optimally utilized "Chiron" array would also contain a bridge crystal and/or a manifestation crystal.

Vibrates to the number 4.

NORTH NODE

The "North Node" configuration is established by placing the crystals in the pattern shown in Figure 47. The ends of the array may be organized as shown or may be represented by one sphere in each location. The number of crystals used is left to the intuition of the practitioner.

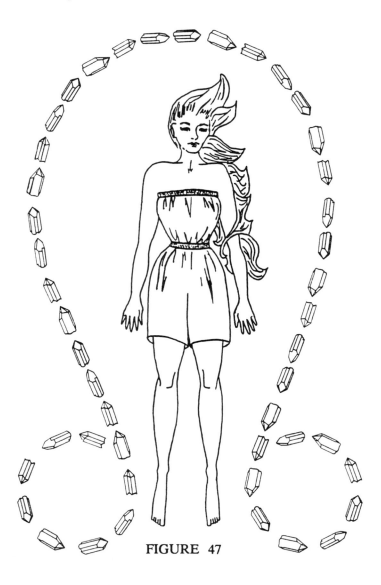

FIGURE 47

The "North Node" represents acquisition, collection, and receiving. The array can be utilized to bring these attributes to ones physical reality. It can serve to initiate new experiences, to bring innovation to ideas, and to prompt the influx of material objects to ones life. It further operates to encourage one in the use of ones abundant potential.

The configuration has been used to both create and maintain internal emotional balance, to balance the yin/yang characteristics [bringing increased stability to the emotions], and to promote the recognition that one has the ultimate control over circumstances within the personal reality. It is excellent for bringing others to ones life and for assisting one in recognizing the entry.

The "North Node" has been placed upon a photograph of the self/another to facilitate the continuance of the state attained during the physical gridding of the self or another. Placed upon ones photograph, it can also assist in the transformation of less than ideal experiences and/or material reality, stimulating perfection and attainment of same. It has been placed upon/around a photograph of an object to encourage the manifestation of the increase in the number/quantity of the object. It can also be utilized to assist one in obtaining articles for collections.

The configuration can assist one to mentally "always be prepared" - for any situation or encounter. It has also been used to protect one from psychic attacks, providing an energy barrier which [when consciously programmed] obstructs the flow of energy to within the array.

It further assists one in reaching-out to others on the physical, mental, and emotional planes, providing for grace in actions and thoughts. The "North Node" also helps one to understand and to accept love from others.

Dual arrays, placed around each person, can be utilized to assist in providing the inflow for cooperative ventures, in promoting joint progress toward personal enhancement, in providing for the recognition and acceptance of love from the other, and in allowing for the recognition of increased options.

This configuration can be used to increase the energy levels within the body and to assist in the amelioration of muscular disorders. It can also be used in the treatment of growths, skin afflictions, and dis-ease related to stress.

The optimally utilized "North Node" array would also contain a moonstone.

Vibrates to the number 5.

SOUTH NODE

The "South Node" configuration is established by placing the crystals in the pattern shown in Figure 48. The ends of the array may be organized as shown or may be represented by one sphere in each location. The number of crystals used is left to the intuition of the practitioner.

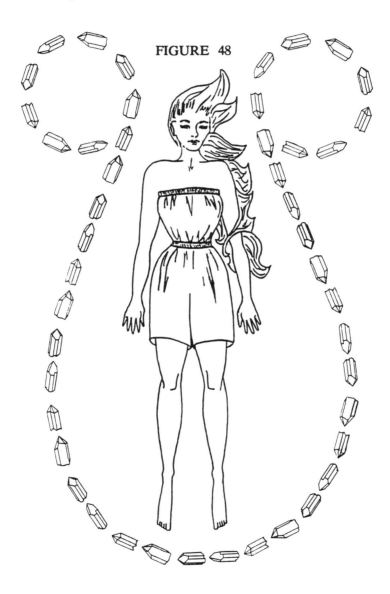

FIGURE 48

The "South Node" represents extending the self to others and giving of the self, and the physical actualizations of the self, to others. The array can be utilized to stimulate the effusion of ones naturally expressed talents and abilities. It can serve to stimulate the distribution of love and can enhance altruistic pursuits. It further operates to assist one in the release of hostilities and anger, affecting the release of forgiveness to all.

This configuration has been used to both create and maintain energy balance within ones environment, to dissipate negativity, and to promote the cleansing of emotional, mental, and physical negativity. It is an excellent arrangement for helping one to learn to "share".

The "South Node" has been placed upon a photograph of the self/another to facilitate the continuance of the state attained during the physical gridding of the self or another. Placed upon ones photograph, it can assist in the transference of energy from the abundance of the ethers to the self; this operation also functions to transfer energy from the infinite source to another when the photograph of another is used. The arrangement provides a channel for absent-healing and is an excellent arrangement for use during the practice of radionic techniques.

It helps one to understand materiality, when the material world is detrimental to ones progress, allowing for the appreciation of the growth-producing applications for possessions and of the ideology behind non-dependency upon same. It stimulates the forces of wisdom and growth toward enlightenment.

The arrangement further assists one in opening to contact from other planes, opening the mind and sensory perception such that communication can be facilitated and maintained.

Dual arrays, placed around each person, can be utilized to assist in providing for support between the participants, to stimulate the transfer of energy to another, and to expedite the sharing of feelings, emotions, and knowledge, that cannot be communicated via the spoken word.

This configuration can be used to assist one in releasing dis-ease, to dispel depression, and to further the maintenance of the life-sustaining functions of the body. It can also be used to alleviate disorders and discomforts associated with puberty.

The optimally utilized "South Node" array would also contain a moonstone.

Vibrates to the number 4.

CERES

The "Ceres" configuration is established by placing the crystals in the pattern shown in Figure 49. The intersection of the horizontal line of crystals with the vertical figure is located at the base chakra. The number of crystals used is left to the intuition of the practitioner.

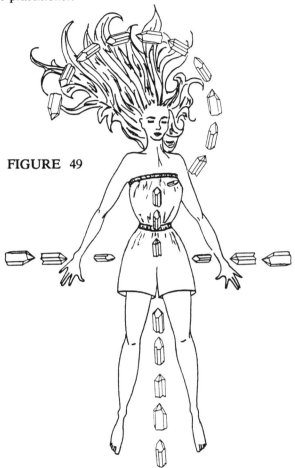

FIGURE 49

In mythology, Ceres was the goddess of the fruitful Earth, protectress of social order and marriage. The "Ceres" configuration assists one in understanding and relaying unconditional love, on the many planes and within the multitude of worlds of existence. It serves to enable one to both acknowledge and endorse the perfection of the self, releasing dependency and instilling trust in the flawlessness of the divine.

The array stimulates fidelity, and sincerity and dependability in marriage and partnerships. It assists in communication and can be used to stimulate mental fertility. It can be used to activate the commencement and/or the continuance of "harvesting the fruits of ones labour".

"Ceres" also assists in new beginnings, providing insight with respect to those paths which are conducive to ones growth and development.

It further assists one in ease of entry to the meditative state and in maintaining the state for extended time periods. It helps one to connect with the Higher Self and to preserve an open channel with same.

"Ceres" has been placed upon a photograph of the self/another to facilitate the continuance of the state attained during the physical gridding of the self or another. Placed upon ones photograph, it can also assist one in maintaining the act/non-act of being "in the moment". It further serves to activate the inner knowledge and to facilitate the application of this knowledge to situations which occur on all levels of awareness. Placing the configuration upon/around a photograph of land stimulates the well-being of the land; the well-being of any object in a photograph is awakened.

It has been used to assist one in recognizing [via intuitive messages] the "correct" partnership, relationship, and/or association; "correct" denoting that which is conducive to positive development.

The configuration has also been used to assist in calming and bringing social order to areas of the Earth which are experiencing chaos [primarily with respect to chaotic physical actions].

Dual arrays, placed upon/around each person, can be utilized to assist in providing for a consolidation of forces to strengthen both alliance and affinity between the participants, bringing reciprocal actions one to the other with respect to unconditional love. The arrays allow the subjects to both understand and appreciate the actualization of love without control, domination, and authoritarianism.

This configuration can be used to increase ones physical fertility [dual arrangements or photographs of both subjects are recommended]. It can also assist in the treatment of disorders related to growth and to the regenerative organs. It can be used in the amelioration of social dis-eases, chronic fatigue syndrome, mononucleosis, and frigidity.

The optimally utilized "Ceres" array would also contain a manifestation crystal and/or a pecos diamond.

Vibrates to the number 5.

PALLAS

The "Pallas" configuration is established by placing the crystals in the pattern shown in Figure 50. The number of crystals used is left to the intuition of the practitioner.

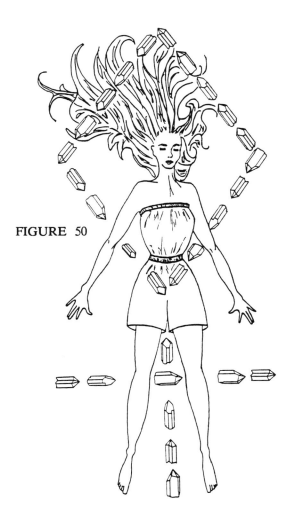

FIGURE 50

In mythology, Pallas was the goddess of wisdom, business, and the arts, and the judicious mediator of conflicts. The array can be used to help one to utilize prevailing knowledge in a universally original manner <u>and</u> to apply the existing knowledge in a universally beneficial manner.

It assists one in distinguishing between fragmentary information and the unrestricted whole. It serves to assist one in the development of plans and procedures which will lead one to successful completion of ventures.

The configuration stimulates the creation of that which has been consciously programmed. It balances the yin/yang qualities of the emotions and mentality such that conscious creativity and total perception of conscious reality are enhanced. It furthers ones spirituality and assists one in gaining, and in maintaining, the universal knowledge necessary for the commencement of wisdom.

It further promotes ones understanding and resolution of conflicts within the self, bringing extended knowledge of the reasons behind the conflicts. It helps one to release these conflicts and to initiate action toward forward movement on ones path.

"Ceres" has been placed upon a photograph of the self/another to facilitate the continuance of the state attained during the physical gridding of the self or another. Placed upon ones photograph, it can also assist one in maintaining clarity of thought and action.

It further serves to preserve the conflict resolutions which have been attained and to provide continuing insight into the patterns which have caused and could cause the admission of dissension to ones life. Placed upon a photograph of another, it will help to promote conflict resolution within that person; one can also send harmony to that which is represented by the photograph.

It has been used to assist one in recognizing [via intuitive messages] the business or opportunity which one may approach with the consequence of success.

The configuration has also been used to assist in reconciliation with others and in the exoneration of guilt.

Dual arrays, placed upon/around each person, can be utilized to assist in providing for a consolidation of forces to strengthen the bond between the participants, bringing conflicts to the surface and subsequently promoting resolution of same. It also can assist in providing energy to sustain one during exposure to outside harassment and to promote the attainment of the state of impeccable balance while strengthening the commitment between the participants.

"Ceres" can be used in the treatment of psychological, psychosomatic, and psychotic disorders. It can also assist in the treatment of incontinence, frigidity, depression, stomach upsets, and in dis-ease of the heart.

The optimally utilized "Pallas" array would also contain rose quartz and/or sugilite.

Vibrates to the number 7.

VESTA

The "Vesta" configuration is established by placing the crystals in the pattern shown in Figure 51. One inverted apex is located at the solar plexus and one at the base chakra. The number of crystals used is left to the intuition of the practitioner.

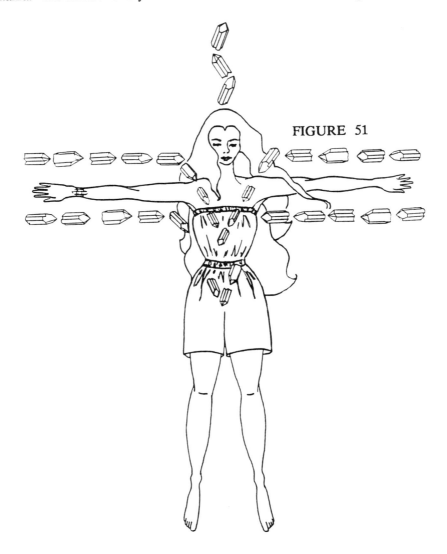

FIGURE 51

In mythology, Vesta was the goddess of the hearth and the hearth fire. This array can be used to enhance ones allegiance and dedication toward the furtherance of altruism and benevolence. It serves to stimulate the energy, to initiate the continuance of the movement of the Kundalini and to instill patience and perseverance in the course of ones development.

The configuration helps one to live according to the doctrine of love, with intensity and passion applied to each moment of each day. It assists one in the focus of energy, bringing consciousness to each action and engendering the self with stamina and fortitude. It further acts to stimulate ones determination and it facilitates both the insight and the actualization of "real" knowledge.

It assists one in the cultivation of the self and in the nurturing of others; helping one to recognize that which would be conducive to ones progress while expediting that progress.

"Vesta" has been placed upon a photograph of the self/another to facilitate the continuance of the state attained during the physical gridding of the self or another. Placed upon ones photograph, it can also assist one in maintaining dedication and in stimulating the vital force. When placed upon a photograph or facsimile of investments, it further serves to preserve the investment. It has been used to stimulate non-concessions to that which is not "exactly what one desires". Placed upon a photograph of a group, it will help to promote cohesive and cooperative action within the group.

The configuration has also been used to assist one in both the verbalization and the demonstration of ones personal theories. It brings the message, and the acceptance of the message, to "be true to thy self", allowing for actualization of the ideal path-wise progression.

Dual arrays, placed upon/around each person, can be utilized to assist in providing for a consolidation of forces to strengthen the bond between the participants, bringing recognition of the one pathway that they share. The configuration tends to stimulate inner knowledge of the altruistic state; this is an excellent method of connecting with another who shares, for example, the same enlightened master.

It can also be utilized to help another to understand the immeasurable and complex feelings for that to which [or to whom] one is devoted.

The dual arrangement can also be used to stimulate concurrent continuance of the Kundalini; the participants would have their arms perpendicular to the body and would lay hand upon hand [palms toward the sky].

"Vesta" can be used in the treatment of fevers, disorders of the hands, high blood pressure, and afflictions of the throat. It can also assist in the amelioration of disease of the lungs, heart, breasts, and endocrine system.

The optimally utilized "Vesta" array would also contain bixbite and/or garnet.

Vibrates to the number 4.

JUNO

The "Juno" configuration is established by placing the crystals in the pattern shown in Figure 52. The intersections are located at the throat and the base chakras. The number of crystals used is left to the intuition of the practitioner.

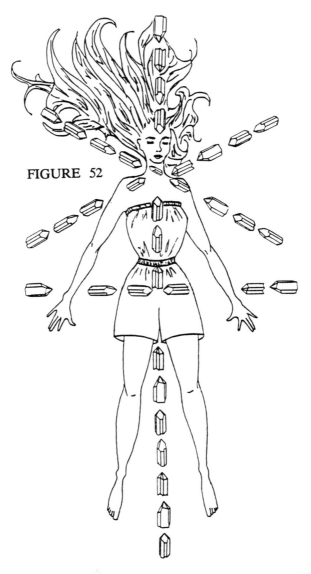

FIGURE 52

In mythology, Juno was the goddess of marriage and women. This array can be used to enhance ones feminine nature, bringing the equalization of power to all situations. It enhances ones self-esteem and promotes appreciation of that which one can accomplish via the liberation of sensitivity.

The configuration helps one to create, and to participate in, significant and purposeful relationships, to assist in the creation of equality within the world, and to experience camaraderie and intimacy in associations. It further acts to guide one toward those relationships which will further ones evolution in a constructive and beneficial manner.

It assists one in the assertion of the self, dispensing with ones aggressiveness and imparting the gentle strength to "stand-up for oneself". It helps one to identify those who are exploiting ones nature, to understand the bases for the exploitation, and to discontinue the self-concessions to these actions.

The array promotes the balance of yin/yang energies such that equalization and stabilization of same is promoted.

"Juno" has been placed upon a photograph of the self/another to facilitate the continuance of the state attained during the physical gridding of the self or another. Placed upon ones photograph, it can also assist one in maintaining loving and assertive relationships. When placed upon a photograph of those involved in a relationship or a group, it serves to enhance understanding between the subjects such that each participant is encouraged to actualize the individuality while maintaining cohesiveness of the whole. The array, placed upon a photograph of those who are oppressed, can bring relief to the oppression via understanding of the cause.

The configuration has also been used as a protective grid for the partner, the relationship, the group, or the "cause". It can be used as a mirror to project images to another and/or to return received energies to the sender [the use of mica, placed upon the third-eye, is recommended for this exercise].

Dual arrays, placed upon/around each person [side-by-side], can be utilized to assist in providing for a consolidation of forces to strengthen relationships and to establish and maintain the balance of power. The configuration tends to stimulate an ethereal connection between the participants; this connection is via the solar plexus and the base chakras. It can also be used to heighten the physical portions of love-relationships.

"Juno" can be used in the treatment of muscular disorders, chills, low blood pressure, emotional depression, feminine disorders, and afflictions of the eyes.

The optimally utilized "Juno" array would also contain sunstone.

Vibrates to the number 6.

FORTUNA

The "Fortuna" configuration is established by placing the crystals in the pattern shown in Figure 53. The intersection of the "X" is located at the area of the solar plexus. The number of crystals used is left to the intuition of the practitioner.

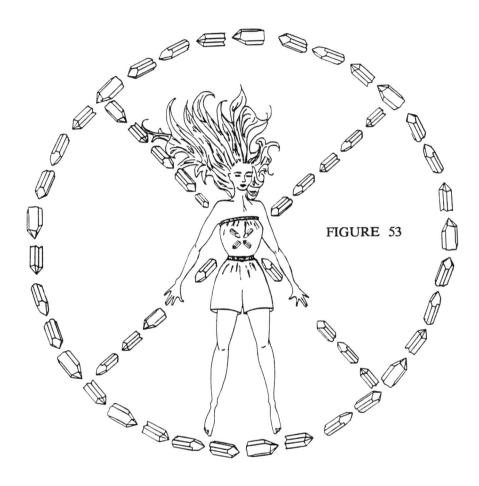

FIGURE 53

"Fortuna" represents both magical blessings and the personal synthesis of the physical, emotional, and spiritual selves. It can be utilized to stimulate the interpersonal skills, and to enhance countenance, articulation, and eloquence. The array represents the art of positive attraction.

It has been used to bring one the advantage in circumstances involving competition and/or opposition to that which one wishes to accomplish. It acts to further ones accomplishments and achievements.

It further assists one in recognizing innate abilities and in applying these gifts in all activities.

This configuration has been used to assist in the elimination of that which one wishes to remove from ones life. It actually serves to promote the withdrawal of depressive circumstances and brings the positive side of conditions to actualization.

"Fortuna" has been placed upon a photograph of the self/another to facilitate the continuance of the state attained during the physical gridding of the self or another. Placed upon ones photograph, it can also assist in the acceptance of responsibility for that which is actualized in ones life, assisting one in the recognition of productive solutions to personal problems.

It further serves to both cleanse and open the chakras, allowing for receptivity to the positive events and emotional interactions which are waiting to enter ones life.

It has been said to vanquish problems and to completely "turn a situation around", by helping one to understand the lessons the problems bring and by permitting one to learn those lessons without a negative impact upon the physical and/or emotional selves.

The arrangement is one of "luck" and positive self-esteem. It assists one in obtaining that which will bring self-esteem and self-love.

Dual arrays, placed upon/around each person, can be utilized to assist in providing opportunities for joint efforts, in stimulating the connection between the higher consciousness of the participants such that they may understand their shared destiny, and to activate the connection between the spiritual selves.

This configuration can be used to assist in homeopathic and naturopathic treatments of dis-ease. It has been used to kindle the "will" to overcome deficiencies of the body and to incite wholeness. It can also be used in the treatment of disorders of the brain and the emotions.

The optimally utilized "Fortuna" array would also contain a cat's eye or tiger eye.

Vibrates to the number 5.

I AM

The "I Am " configuration is established by placing the crystals in the pattern shown in Figure 54. The intersection is located at the solar plexus chakra. The number of crystals used is left to the intuition of the practitioner.

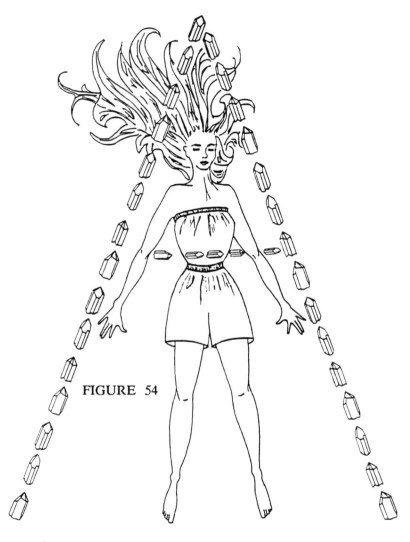

FIGURE 54

This array represents the Earthly actualization of the self. It can be used to allow one to recognize ones presentation to the world, to recognize ones reactions to daily occurrences, and to discover, to examine, and to express ones true personality. The array assists one in determining ones authentic identity, encouraging the acknowledgment of the disguises one uses to camouflage the genuine self.

This configuration has been used to assist one to confront the world, moving from the safety of ones inner sphere to the outer manifestation of the identity. It further assists one in accepting or changing the actualization of ones individuality. Succinctly, it helps one to *know* how one appears to others.

"I Am" has been placed upon a photograph of the self/another to facilitate the continuance of the state attained during the physical gridding of the self or another. Placed upon ones photograph, it can also assist in the acceptance of ones personal nature, providing for reinforcement of the desired qualities and assisting in the elimination of those which are not desired.

It further serves to control erratic temperaments and to provide insight with respect to methods one may utilize to manage unsettled, disruptive, and disorganized areas of ones life.

It is said to assist in the re-birthing process, helping traumatic events and conditions of the past to become obvious and assisting one in the release of same. It can also be used during radionic treatments to strengthen the bond between the self and the energies of the ethers.

The arrangement is one which represents the self, assisting in changes of the temperament and in ones general physical condition. It can also be used to stimulate the genesis of a "new you".

Dual arrays, placed upon/around each person, can be utilized to assist in providing an unobstructed pathway for collective growth and change. It assists the participants in understanding the changes that will be accomplished for the present personality as well as for the future manifestation of that transformed personality; it helps one to grow with another.

This configuration can be used to assist in the treatment of disorders of the psyche, in the amelioration of skin disorders, obesity, anorexia, baldness, balance, and mobility.

The optimally utilized "I Am" array would also contain ones favorite personal stone. During dual arrays, a favorite stone of each of the participants would be used; the results are interesting when the favorite stone of one person in used in the array of the other.

Vibrates to the numbers 5 and 9.

I BECOME

The "I Become" configuration is established by placing the crystals in the pattern shown in Figure 55. The middle portion of the "M" is located at the solar plexus chakra. The number of crystals used is left to the intuition of the practitioner.

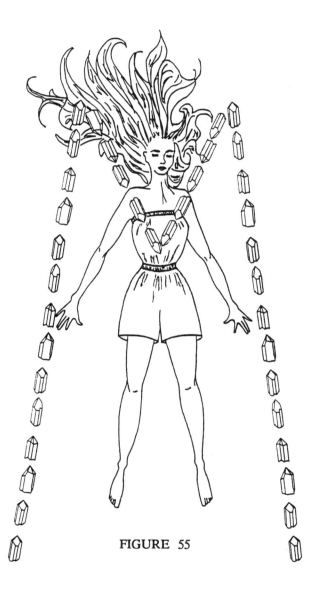

FIGURE 55

This array represents ones potential, ones life-mission, and ones destiny. It assists in promoting the recognition of ones vocational proclivities, helping one to recognize both ones position and contribution in relationship to the totality of existence. It can be used to stimulate expansive events relative to that which one has "come to this world" to accomplish. The array can actually prompt ones recognition within the world.

The configuration has been used to assist one in handing authority figures, in enhancing ones professional style, and in intuitively recognizing ones major contribution to the world. Note that "major contribution" is defined as ones offering of the self to the self or to others.

"I Become" has been placed upon a photograph of the self/another to facilitate the continuance of the state attained during the physical gridding of the self or another. Placed upon ones photograph, it can also assist one in understanding ones reactions to situations and changes of ones life; it furthers both the intuitive and receptive abilities.

It also serves to provide insight into ones inner worlds, into the other worlds from whence one began, and into the other worlds to where one will return. Exploration of the self, and the mysteries behind the existence of the self, are facilitated via this array. Knowledge and experience are both evaluated and a positive transfiguration of the consciousness is encouraged, while assistance is provided to further ones understanding of ones comprehensive destiny with respect to the personal self and ones relative interactions within the social structure.

Dual arrays, placed upon/around each person, can be utilized to assist in providing an unobstructed view of shared destiny. It assists the participants in understanding the multitude of potential methods for attaining the goal, helping the choices to be made cooperatively and consciously. It further provides insight into the karmic patterns which have brought the participants together, facilitating shared visions and, occasionally, shared messages via the clairaudient faculties. For two participants, the dual array is positioned such that the heads of the subject are "crown-to-crown" and one array is the inverse of the other.

This configuration can be used to assist in the treatment of disorders of the shoulders, the hands, the arms, and the legs. It can also serve to ameliorate conditions of deterioration and degeneration.

The optimally utilized "I Become" array would also contain ones "most valued" stone. During dual arrays, a "most valued" stone of each of the participants would be used; the results are interesting when the "most valued" stone of one person is used in the array of the other.

Vibrates to the numbers 7 and 9.

REPETITION

The "Repetition" configuration is established by placing the crystals in the pattern shown in Figure 56. The number of crystals used is left to the intuition of the practitioner.

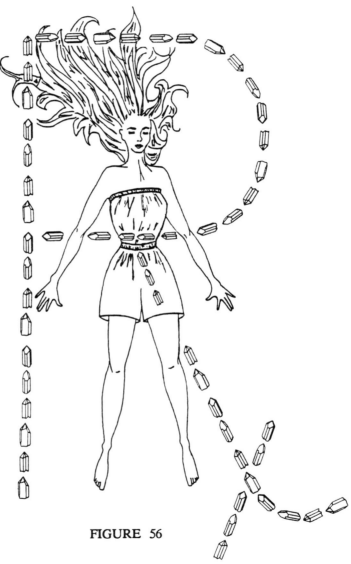

FIGURE 56

This array represents the art of internal review with respect to the actions of repeating activities, circumstances, and lessons. It assists one in understanding that which one has experienced [growth inspiring and/or developmentally limiting] such that one may determine whether to repeat the incident[s] with a different perspective.

The configuration can be used to promote insight into the multitude of paths which are available for comprehending the information which is necessary for ones spiritual development on this plane. It furthers ones awareness and appreciation of the psychological impacts which the repetitive experiences may wield.

"Repetition" has been placed upon a photograph of the self/another to facilitate the continuance of the state attained during the physical gridding of the self or another. Placed upon ones photograph, it can also assist one in understanding ones "patterns" and can encourage the actualization of the ideal.

It serves to provide insight into the need for the various responsibilities which one may have incurred; the responsibilities are, usually, either released or willingly accepted after the utilization of the array. Aspects of self-analysis are initiated such that one may critically observe oneself, subsequently determining where and how improvement may be accomplished. Latent talents are noticeable and important readjustments become apparent. The confrontation and evaluation of ones past achievements and deficiencies are facilitated and the "ghosts" of inhibition are banished.

It promotes flexibility in thought and action, bringing the art of total consideration of all aspects of a situation prior to decision-making. The array encourages one to use retrospective analysis in planning and in the participation in activities, such that lessons may be experienced in a positive manner and with ease.

It can act to guide one from one area of action to another, more productive, area. It is a configuration which can guide one to the circumstances, conditions, and experiences which will facilitate a progressive and unbiased philosophy concerning ones "calling" during this life.

Dual arrays, placed upon/around each person, can be utilized to assist in dual understanding of the repetitive nature of a relationship, and can promote the recognition of the shared activities which will provide for advancement and growth after changes are implemented. It further provides insight into the karmic patterns which have been experienced both during and prior to this incarnation, helping the participants to both "live" and understand the patterns so that renewal can be attained. The dual array is positioned such that the one array is the inverse of the other.

This configuration can be used to assist in the treatment of speech disorders, dysfunctional ambulation, dizziness, and all recurring conditions [e.g., those related to growths, muscular rigidity, tendonitis, etc.].

Vibrates to the numbers 2 and 5.

HOLISTIC   HUNA

ARRAYS

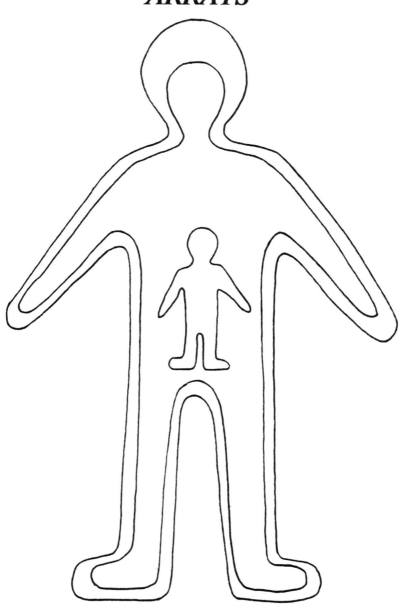

Today
I made a new Friend,
Discovered another,
And revealed a third.
First: a person
Second: myself
The Third: silence

Mary-Ann Smith
Johannesburg, RSA
1991

INTRODUCTION

The flow of vitality within and through the physical and ethereal bodies has been a part of the ancient lore of the "lost" civilizations of the world. The Berber tribe, located in the Atlas Mountains of North Africa, have been determined to have utilized the same "magic" [control of the vital life force] as the kahunas of Hawaii. Descendants of that tribe are recorded [through oral history] to have been those who helped to build the Great Pyramid and who were, during that era, rulers of Egypt. From the information which is available concerning Atlantis, Lemuria, and Mu, one can speculate that the inhabitants of these lands also utilized the powers of the vital force; further verification of this concept has been accomplished via channeling, astral travel, and intuitive journeying to the lost lands.

The vital force has been scientifically proven to exist; studies have measured the electrical discharges of the physical body. A low voltage electrical current in the body tissues and a medium voltage electrical current in the brain were reported by LIFE Magazine as early as 1937. Additional studies have further related a low voltage current to the subconscious self and a medium voltage current to the conscious self; the highest voltage of current has been attributed to the Higher Self.

The ensuing four arrays [Subconscious Self Life Force, Earth Diamond, Higher Self Life Force, and Triune] can assist one in recognizing and utilizing ones inherent vital force and can facilitate the transfer of absolute vitality from the realm of the higher consciousness.

SUBCONSCIOUS SELF LIFE FORCE

The "Subconscious Self Life Force" configuration is established by placing the crystals in the pattern shown in Figure 57.

The utilization of kaolinite, fulgurite, a rutilated, tourmalinated, goethite included, or Faden crystal [one held in each hand while one is within the array], will also act to further the process; additional crystalline forms with similar interior structures may also be used - the main qualification being the existence of a connecting mechanism. If these crystals are not available, quartz crystals are recommended. The number of crystals used in the array is left to the intuition of the practitioner.

This configuration represents the low voltage vital energy and the activation of the pathway which connects the subconscious with the Higher Self [e.g., connection activation]. The pathway is activated to facilitate the transfer of thought-forms, relative to requests and entreaties, to the Higher Self; the activation clears the pathway and furnishes the Higher Self with a connective channel which may be used in the transmittal of instant and/or miraculous response to requests for healing.

It also represents the connection between the low voltage vital energy of the subconscious and the medium voltage life energy of the conscious self; when using the array in this light, one can activate the connection between the conscious self and the subconscious self in order to raise the energy levels accessible to them.

The low voltage electric current can carry chemical substances and magnetism with it as it flows through the body and/or as it flows from one person to another person or object.

In the form of magnetism, it can be accumulated in all permeable materials; e.g., in wood, crystals, plants, animals, fabricated articles, the physical, ethereal and astral bodies, - even thoughts; thoughts being very important to the "magical" system. A substantial discharge of this low voltage vital energy can supply an enormous amount of energy to that upon which it is released.

The ethereal body is an ideal conductor of vital electrical current and can be used as a storage site for it. When heavily charged with the low voltage of the force, the ethereal body tends to become rigid and firm enough to be used as a hand or instrument to move or to affect physical objects.

The subconscious life force controls memory and creates all emotions. It performs all psychic acts [e.g., obtaining information from others via telepathy and/or obtaining future information via telepathy from the Higher Self]. The ethereal body of the subconscious also possesses duplicates of every cell and tissue of the physical body.

When the pathway to the Higher Self is obstructed, one usually experiences many plans and situations "going awry". The following exercise is one which can be used to first allow the conscious self to "greet" the subconscious self:

- ♥ After centering the self, one enters the array [dexterity is required when one is performing the exercise for oneself]. Deep circular breathing is initiated and one re-centers the self at the location two-inches below the navel.

- ♥ Now, one looks within the self, at the area between the solar plexus and the navel chakra, and visualizes ones personal and individual subconscious. It is an excellent idea to ask him/her if a name would be appropriate and, if so, what name would be desired.

- ♥ One may visualize a link between the conscious and the subconscious via the inclusions and/or the configuration of the crystalline formations held within the hand which one personally defines as the "giving" hand.

♥ After one has become familiar with the subconscious [now, hopefully, named], further conversations are suggested; these conversations may be pursued at any time, both while within the array and while participating in ones daily activities. It should be noted that when one communicates with the subconscious, asking for assistance, one may request, implore, logically explain, etc,......but would never act in a domineering manner.

FIGURE 57

The following exercise has been successfully utilized to both activate and clear the channel of communication between the subconscious and the Higher Self:

- One may place a smaller version of the array upon a photograph of the self to both initiate and to renew the communication channel between the subconscious and the Higher Self.

- After centering the self, one enters the array [dexterity is again required when one is performing the exercise for oneself]. Deep circular breathing is initiated and a highly charged and dense mass of the lower voltage energy is visualized as emanating from an area between the solar plexus and the navel chakra, and entering into the crystal which is being held in the hand which one personally defines as the "receiving" hand. Occasionally, the crystal is envisioned as filling the room, and the low voltage energy as totally filling same.

- After the area envisioned is filled with the low voltage energy, one visualizes a pathway to the Higher Self and releases the energy through this channel. When utilizing the fulgurite, the energy is visualized as flowing through same, with one end ethereally connected to the subconscious and the other end connected to the Higher Self. When utilizing the Faden crystal or crystals containing kaolinite, rutile, tourmaline, etc., one may visualize the connection being facilitated via these minerals.

The results have been varied. In some cases, the subject is totally overwhelmed with a sense of loving benevolence which enters from outside of the self, and/or feels a rush of warmth, a tingling sensation, a perception of pulsing with the universe, etc.; in this circumstance, one knows the pathway is open and clear.

In some cases, the subject is presented with a panorama of ideas and situations which are a part of ones inherent memory, and yet, are uncomfortable and/or unpleasant; in this situation, each idea/situation is confronted, evaluated, and released. The release of each uncomfortable and/or unpleasant situation may require multiple entries into the array; the array of "Self-Love" has also been quite helpful in releasing the situations requiring forgiving and/or forgiveness. One is encouraged to persevere until one intuitively recognizes the open passageway between the subconscious and the Higher Self.

Prior to placing the array upon a subject, a preliminary conscious review is attempted [by the subject, and with the assistance of the practitioner] of those emotional responses which are inflexible and/or elicit a negative or undesired "re-action". This activity serves to assist in the understanding of some of the unpleasant memories one may receive while within the array. The physical stimulus of the crystals, when placed in this arrangement, tends to further the suggestion to both integrate and release that which is no longer real or tangible.

EARTH DIAMOND - CONSCIOUSNESS

The "Earth Diamond - Consciousness" configuration is established by placing the crystals in the pattern of a diamond surrounding the subject [See Figure 58]. Success has been obtained via the utilization of multiples of four crystals in this arrangement.

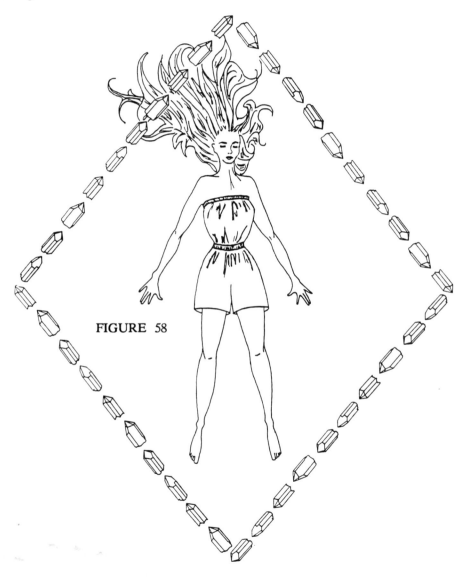

FIGURE 58

The recommendations for supplementary crystals includes kaolinite, fulgurite, a rutilated, tourmalinated, goethite included crystal, or Faden crystal, or additional crystalline forms with similar interior structures. The vital energy of the brain waves is designated as the medium voltage used by the conscious mind in its reasoning, conceiving, creating, and willful activities. The conscious mind can be mesmerized or hypnotized, provided that an appropriate thought-form is introduced. The ethereal body of the conscious [or mental] self is a conductor of the middle voltage, and is utilized in its form of mentation and will. The vital energy currents related to the conscious self form the ghostly body in which the spirit functions as a spirit after departure from the physical plane.

The following exercise can be used to further the synchronicity between the conscious self and the subconscious:

♥ One may place a smaller version of the array upon a photograph of the self to both initiate and to renew the communication channel between the conscious self and the subconscious. After centering the self, the array is entered and deep circular breathing is initiated. A highly charged and dense mass of the lower voltage energy is visualized as emanating from an area between the solar plexus and the navel chakra, and entering into the crystal which is being held in the hand which one consciously defines as the "giving" hand. Occasionally, the crystal is envisioned as filling the room, with the medium voltage energy saturating same.

♥ After the area envisioned is filled with the medium voltage energy, one visualizes a pathway to the subconscious self and releases the energy through this channel.

When utilizing the fulgurite, the energy is visualized as flowing through same, with one end ethereally connected to the conscious self [usually at the location of the third-eye] and the other end connected to the subconscious self. When utilizing the Faden crystal or crystals containing kaolinite, rutile, tourmaline, etc., one may visualize the connection being facilitated via these minerals.

The results have been consistently successful; one usually experiences the feeling of the inception of a tunnel-like pathway of white light coursing between the inner realm of the third-eye, through the upper portion of the body, and reaching the home of the subconscious self. The sensation of a flow of ethereal liquid through the body is often detected and one intuitively recognizes the clarity of the path. In some cases, however, the subject may sense a feeling of constriction within the body; this indicates that the preliminary rendezvous with the subconscious [described in the previous array] has not been successfully completed. If this occurs, a re-visit to the preparatory exercise is recommended.

Prior to placing this array upon a subject, the preparatory exercise described in the previous array, is also recommended.

HIGHER SELF LIFE FORCE

The "Higher Self Life Force" configuration is established by placing the crystals in the pattern shown in Figure 59.

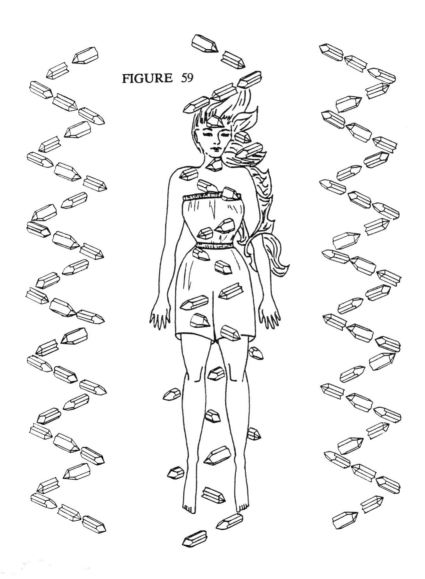

FIGURE 59

The recommendations for supplementary crystals includes kaolinite, fulgurite, a rutilated, tourmalinated, goethite included, or Faden crystal, or additional crystalline forms with similar interior structures. The numbers of crystals used in the array is left to the intuition of the practitioner.

The high voltage vital energy is relegated to the Higher Self, the flow of which may be routed to the conscious and subconscious selves. It is an omnipotent electrical energy which can facilitate instant changes in bodily tissues to facilitate instant healing; it can also produce the physical phenomenon of psychic manifestation.

The ethereal body of the high voltage current utilizes faculties which are beyond the powers of either memory or reason [i.e., subconscious or conscious]; through the Higher Self, the energy manifests "realization", facilitating the process of "knowing" without the application of memory retrieval from the subconscious self, and without the application of logic from the conscious self. The superior voltage of vital energy provides for a superior "mental" or "all-knowing" ability which enables the Higher Self to see into that part of the future which has been crystallized. It possesses an accurate and precise knowledge of the past, the present, and the portions of the future which have been determined in advance; the uncrystallized future will not be "seen" through contact with the Higher Self because it has not yet been definitely planned, created, or projected.

The contact with the Higher Self results in an increase in lucidity and a sharpening of the senses and perceptions concerning the past, the present, and the "defined" future. Ones premonitions come from the Higher Self via the subconscious self; the subconscious self either allows the information to be communicated to the conscious self, or - it does not - patience and attentiveness are both attributes which are necessary to the receipt of information from the Higher Self; a totally open channel between the Higher Self and the subconscious, and between the subconscious and the conscious selves, are also required.

Ones conscious self may become more familiar with the Higher Self via a modified rendition of the preparatory exercise described in the "Subconscious Self Life Force" array.

The synthesis of the life energies of the conscious and subconscious are utilized to communicate needs and desires to the Higher Self; when the communication is clear, the Higher Self can "act", separating itself from ones physical "area" and performing any service that was requested and/or required [regardless of distance]. The following exercise describes one method whereby the "Higher Self Life Force" array may be utilized to facilitate the clarity of communication, between the conscious self and the Higher Self [via the subconscious], and to subsequently induce healing and/or protective activities:

> ♥ One may place a smaller version of the array upon a photograph of the self and a photograph of the subject. Given that the array is comprised of three replicas of the same pattern, when placed upon two photographs, only five [instead of six] patterns are used; one pattern is placed upon the area of photograph which displays the subject, one pattern is placed upon the area of a photograph

which displays the practitioner, one pattern is placed between the photographs, and the remaining two patterns are placed at the left side of one photograph and the right side of the other photograph. If a photograph is available which portrays both the subject and the practitioner, the normal three replicas of the same pattern are used. The use of this arrangement tends to initiate and to maintain a connection between the two Higher Selves [i.e., the Higher Self of the practitioner and the Higher Self of the subject], both during and after the exercise.

♥ The subject and practitioner center themselves and the subject enters the array. The subject initiates deep circular breathing and, after all crystals are placed, the practitioner initiates breathing in rhythm with the subject. Verbal suggestion is then given with respect to the condition which requires alleviation.

♥ The "laying-on-of-hands" is initiated until all crystals have been touched, and the energies subsequently transferred. The vital force of the crystals acts to combine with the vital force of the subject and the practitioner in order to facilitate the transmittal of the healing energies.

♥ When the process is completed, the crystals are removed and the practitioner asks the subject to describe the experience [if the information has not been shared during the exercise]. At this point a judgment is made with respect to whether additional arrays would be helpful.

If one desires to facilitate absent-healing or to transmit protection to another, a photographic arrangement may be developed, as described above, and the appropriate [those selected specifically for ones purpose] crystals/minerals would be placed as a part of the array; a written missive would be included within the array and would describe that which one wishes to expedite. If a photograph is not available, the written missive would also include a description of the person, object, etc. The resultant events have included actions of "divine intervention", intellectual stimulation, and healing.

For self-healing, after entry to the array and the initiation of centering and deep circular breathing, the pre-determined suggestion is given to the subconscious, and the request is verbalized that the suggestion be transmitted to the Higher Self. One may visualize the pathway connecting the subconscious and the Higher Self and may assist the transmittal of the information via that channel.

TRIUNE

The "Triune" configuration is established by placing the crystals in the pattern shown in Figure 60 or in Figure 61. Success has been obtained via the utilization of multiples of three crystals in these arrangements.

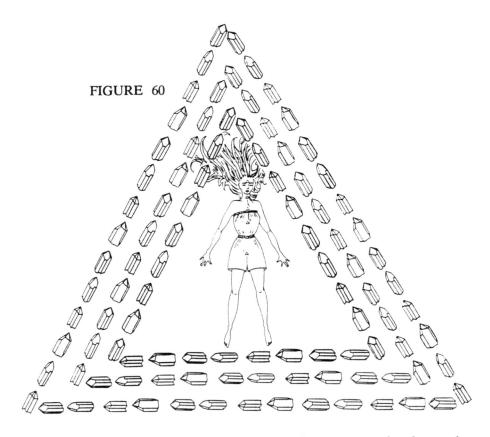

FIGURE 60

In the array shown in Figure 60, triangular or angular stones are placed upon the third-eye, the throat chakra, the heart chakra, the soar plexus chakra, and the base chakra.

If available, the chevron amethyst, the ajoite phantom crystal, the nephrite with quartz crystal structures, and/or the manifestation crystal would also be used as a part of either array.

This configuration represents the synthesis of all three selves, all three levels of vital energy, and a manifestation of "the sum being greater than its parts". The energy which is created, via the unification of the three energies, is that of universal perfection.

It assists one in understanding that one is "one" with all and that "all" is amicable to one; it teaches that when there is no distinction between "things", there is no disharmony or discordance - hence, that which is experienced is not foreign to perfection and all that one experiences may be the positive events which are both preferred and chosen.

It helps one to realize that consciousness is freedom itself; illusion disappears and, in the unity of all, one finds love and wisdom. The attainment of wisdom may be as an explosion of ones consciousness, the intrinsic acknowledgement and acceptance being as light radiating throughout ones being, and continuing for indefinite periods of time.

The "Triune" assists one in recognizing that "you" and all you are, have been, and will be, are always with you, wherever you go, whatever you "do". It allows for the acceptance of the self in a non-illusory style, instilling the recognition of that with which one is comprised.

The array shows one the methods which can be employed so that one accepts all aspects of ones nature and the world; sight of the inner workings of the perfect reality which one may create is provided, and as energies move within the body, one may totally accept, exist, and enjoy.

One attains the knowledge and the recognition of that point within which never sleeps, which is never unconscious, and which is always vigilant, watchful, and aware.

It helps one to experience direct harmony within this reality, to see no duality or multiplicity, and to merge in a unity which is beyond extension or diminution in time or space.

Within this array, one may be totally with the self, totally with nature, totally with another, ... All of time exists within the conscious state which ensues; ones reality and ones illusions also exist and are understood. One may flow to the infinite and return to the delight of being.

All persons, places, and things, of this physical world, may be energized, healed, and protected via the utilization of this array. Areas of the Earth are gridded to enhance their connection with perfection and to stimulate the furtherance of balance and stabilization; gridding of photographs and structural facsimiles have also been employed.

After the completion of the preceding three arrays, one may extend the self to the realm of "All That Is", and, in love and brotherhood, may assist in directing the flawless energies of the universe to ones compassionate, benevolent, and altruistic pursuits.

The potentials are endless [e.g., the facilitation of total protection [photographic method is also recommended], immediate healing, complete meditation, self-actualization, comprehensive psychic awareness, etc.].

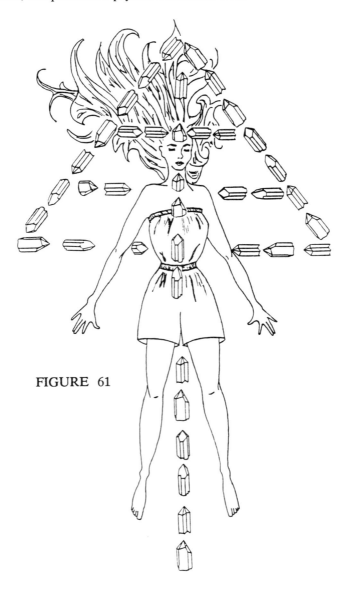

FIGURE 61

Prior to the utilization of either of these "Triune" arrays, it is recommended that the practitioner is completely familiar with, and has successfully and totally experienced, each of the three previous arrays. When these activities have been comprehensively fulfilled, the highest intuitive faculties available will direct one in the appropriate methodology for consummation of these exercises.

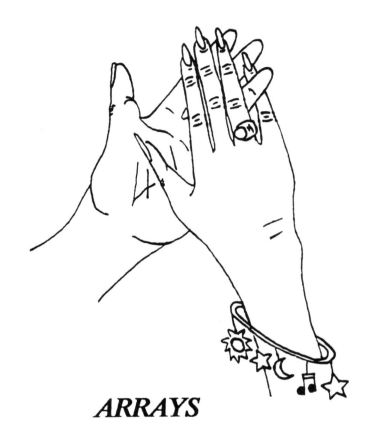

ARRAYS

OF LOVE AND BALANCE

LOOSE YOURSELF INTO YOUR HEART,
THE HEART OF THE OTHER,
THE HEART OF "ALL THAT IS" ♥
WE ARE ALL STARS
IN THE DRAMA OF THIS REALITY ♥

SELF-LOVE

The "Self-Love" configuration is established by placing the crystals in the pattern shown in Figure 62. A mineral in the form of a heart, a rose quartz crystal cluster, or a piece sugilite or charoite, is recommended as the crystal which is placed upon the heart chakra.

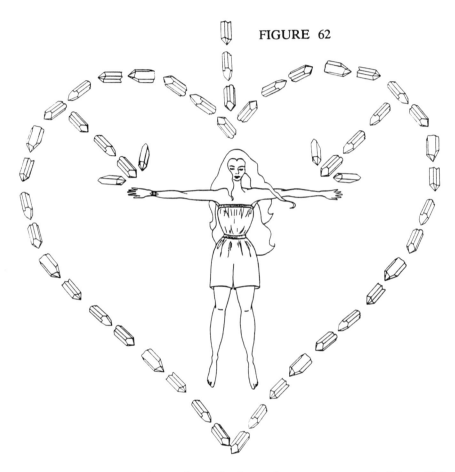

FIGURE 62

Self-love is defined as the benevolent affection and reverent approval of the self, by the self. The "Self-Love" array assists one maintaining adequate attentiveness to the exploration and the discovery of the self and the divine nature of love, assisting one to embrace, to appreciate, and to love the personal identity of ones physical manifestation. It leads to inner healing, and to integration and self-acceptance, bestowing the light and love of ones innermost self to blossom in the conscious self.

The array facilitates access to the creative power of the emotions to bring love, joy, grace, and peace to ones being. It provides for the release of negative emotions [e.g., resentment, hostility, animosity, guilt, despondency, depression, anguish, sorrow, etc.], stimulating victory over the inner dissention, and assisting the self to yield to love as the central reality of ones life. It brings one to the "way of the heart" in establishing ones personal relationship with truth and corporeal actualization. "Self-Love" can be used to stimulate the inflow of love from the Higher Self and from "All That Is". Placing the configuration around a photograph of the self and entering the array [centering the self and focusing on the heart chakra], one recognizes the love and appreciation which abounds.

Often one holds "beliefs" which are contrary to ones worthiness of self-love and/or love from others; these "beliefs" are frequently based on feelings from the past that one has acted in an unloving manner toward another [or others] and/or another [or others] have acted in an unloving way toward oneself. The following exercise has been utilized successfully to facilitate "absent-forgiveness" such that one can separate oneself from the anger, guilt, resentment, hostility, animosity, despondency, depression, anguish, sorrow, etc., which limits ones self-love:

    ♥   A photograph of a person to whom one chooses to send forgiveness, or from whom one desires forgiveness, is placed within a small version of the array. If a photograph is not available, the name and brief description of the person will suffice. With the photograph is placed a written narrative defining the issue. After centering the self, one enters the "Self-Love" array. Deep circular breathing is initiated and one visualizes a current of white glimmering light flowing between the self and the other, originating at the location of ones heart chakra and terminating at the heart chakra of the other. Within this beam of light, forgiveness is sent to, or requested from, the other.

    ♥   When forgiveness is transmitted, an acceptance message will be relayed from the inner self of the other; when forgiveness is requested an affirmation of forgiveness will be issued from the inner self of the other. In either case, one will feel the encompassing peace of forgiveness.

The desired results are often facilitated during the first venture; additional application of the exercise may be required or may be desired to reinforce the action[s].

The array facilitates receptivity to the message and stimulates the understanding of the previous condition such that one may release it. It is recommended that the exercise be repeated for each situation for which one desires to convey and/or to receive forgiveness. "Self-Love" can be used daily to allow one to understand that "we must first love ourselves before we can fully love anything or anyone else". Welcome to the path of love ♥.

LOVE CONNECTION

The "Love Connection" configuration is established by placing the crystals in the pattern of an inverted "L", with three rays initiating at each branch of the "L", and the short portion of the "L" initiating above the center of the head and continuing toward the right side of the body of the subject [See Figure 63].

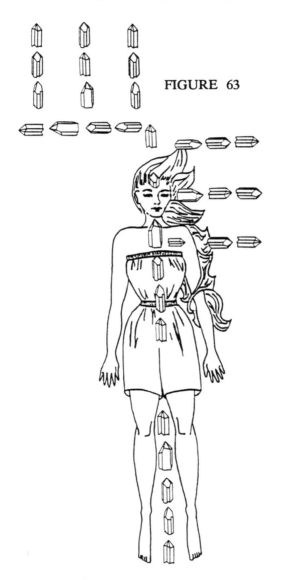

FIGURE 63

The utilization of a Faden crystal, if available, is recommended. Success has been obtained via the utilization of multiples of three crystals in this arrangement.

This array can be utilized to send love to another; one visualizes a channel of love flowing toward, and reaching the other. It is an excellent stimulus for emotional contact between the self and others when the others are at a distance. An influent of love from the universal perfection is facilitated via the three crystal rays located on the heart-side of the body; the supply of love from the self to the others flows from the crown chakra.

A connection between the self and another can also be perpetually facilitated via the employment of two smaller versions of the "Love Connection"; one is placed upon a photograph of the self and one is placed upon a photograph of the other. The photographs are placed "head-to-head" such that the three rays of crystals, which are located at the top of the head of one subject, blend with the three rays of crystals, which are located at the top of the head of the other subject, merging to form three single rays of crystals. If single terminated crystals are used, these single rays produce an intense energy field at the location where the terminations are directed to confront [i.e., at the center of the rays]; in this case, a "fountain" effect of energy is produced which "rains upon" both subjects. If double terminated crystals are used, the flow is direct. Faden crystals and a complete range of other minerals have also been utilized to facilitate the synthesis of the "two". An illustration of this configuration is shown below.

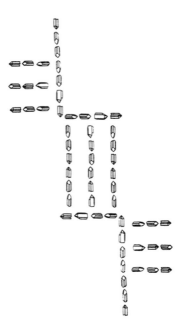

This is an excellent array to utilize during the transmission of messages of healing and well-ness to the Higher Self of another. The photographic arrangement also operates efficiently to reinforce and perpetuate the messages. In this case, a message of well-ness is also placed within the photographic array.

TIME AND SPACE

The "Time And Space" configuration is established by placing the crystals in the pattern of two or more hourglass arrangements, connecting the top of each to the next, and [for two hourglass patterns] placing a sphere at each of six designated locations as shown in Figure 64. Success has been obtained via the utilization of multiples of seven crystals in this arrangement. When additional hourglass patterns are connected to the existing ones, additional spheres are added and the amount of crystals for the entire array would be based upon multiples of the number of spheres in the array.

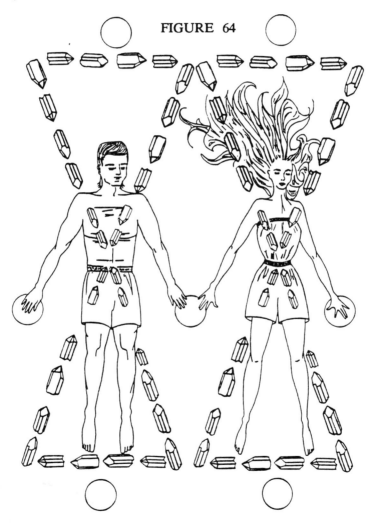

FIGURE 64

This array brings the ideal of synergism to manifestation such that the efforts of two or more energies, working together, produce an effect which is greater than each of the two or more energies could singularly affect. The result is simplified and the resultant condition and/or circumstance is enhanced.

Within the array, the participants can experience the refraction of the diverging wave fronts which proceed from an object or a thought-form in such a way as to produce an image of the energy of the object or thought-form; this image provides for depth of vision and for depth of understanding of same.

Any and all creative and progressive endeavors may be furthered via the utilization of "Time And Space". It assists one in comprehending insight to new quests, in the formation of the bases for ventures, in outlining methodology for attainment, in smoothing and polishing the techniques chosen, and in understanding the "truth" about the potential end-results.

After the finalization and comprehension of the "intention", the array stimulates the successful completion of same.

It is a configuration for group "work", initiated at the beginning of a project, and continued [usually at the beginning of each meeting of the group] in order to promote like-mindedness in direction and purpose. It is an array for mental and intuitive connections, and has promoted the integration of thoughts between the participants. Placement of a smaller version of the array upon individual photographs of the group members, has acted to further enhance the intent and purpose of same. The array has, occasionally, been represented by only the use of spheres; for example, for two participants, seven spheres are used - for three participants, ten spheres are used - for four participants, thirteen spheres are used, and for each additional participant, three additional spheres are united with the array.

"Time And Space" is employed in healing situations to remove disparate thoughts such that the will of the subject may cooperate with the personal Higher Self and the Higher Self of the practitioner. It furthers the harmonious relationship between the physical and the ethereal, producing a correlation between the physically established rhythms of the physical body and the perfect resonance of the ethereal body. It can be used in conjunction with the "Chakra Array" to exact definitive locations of disorder and to amplify the sympathetic vibration of the outer bodies in order to stimulate expeditious response. It produces an amplification factor such that the interactive conditions of the synergistic crystals [any and all], with the cooperative energies of the participant and the practitioner, conduct the energies of the mineralogical kingdom and the energies of the Higher Selves to the precise location of need. Placement of the array upon ones photograph further reinforces that which subsequently transpires in the healing environment.

KUNDALINI

The "Kundalini" configuration is established by placing the crystals in the pattern of three connected normal curves, initiating above the top of the head of the subject and ending at the same level as the feet of the subject [See Figure 65]. Success has been obtained via the utilization of multiples of three crystals in this arrangement.

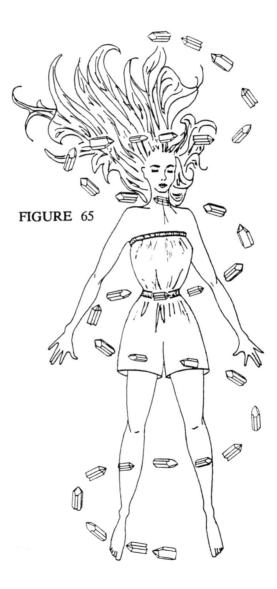

FIGURE 65

The Kundalini is defined in Eastern Indian philosophy to be the sleeping serpent which rests at the base of the spine, dwelling deep within the confines of ones being.

This array activates the movement of the divine power which is slumbering within the self, so that one may access the profound mysteries of divinity which lead one to spiritual consciousness and to the actualization of perfection. "Kundalini" stimulates the conduction of all energies of the body into a subtle channel which traverses the interior of the spine, awakening each of the major energy centers on the path to the crown chakra. As each major energy center is awakened, the energy flow emanates to all portions of the body, additionally activating the minor chakras.

The following exercise may be used to stimulate the awakening, and subsequent movement of the Kundalini. It further activates the rejuvenating properties of the body and the mind.

♥ A photograph of the self is placed beneath a smaller version of the array, and would be allowed to remain there both during and after the exercise.

This array is rather difficult to lay upon the self, but can be accomplished; the service of a friend to place the crystals would assure the correct placement.

♥ One centers the self and initiates deep circular breathing, the breath focusing first on the base chakra and subsequently continuing through each chakra until the crown is reached. One visualizes the lovely serpent of energy arousing and initiating travel through the spiritual channels of the spine, being ever mindful of the purifying ascent of the Kundalini through the chakras. Visualization of movement from one chakra to the next is not initiated until one feels an intense heat in the area [front or back of the body] of the chakra.

♥ It should be noted that when an energy blockage is encountered which impedes the progress of the Kundalini, one can initiate deeper breathing and would breathe "into" the area of blockage; the stimulation via the breathe and the strength of the energy movement will eventually permit the dissipation of the blockage.

The ascension of this divine spark through the first three chakras provides for the awareness to properly regulate and to direct ones experiences upon the physical plane. When the moving energy reaches the heart chakra, one totally realizes and experiences the divinity of the world [when in this area, one may hear a resonance and/or may receive verbal information]. At the fifth chakra, a oneness with the ethereal body is attained and purification and renewal of the physical body can be facilitated. Freedom from the limitations of the senses is acquired at the sixth chakra, and one recognizes the Higher Self, while maintaining the distinction between the conscious self and the Higher Self. Upon entry to the crown chakra, the knowledge of duality is transcended and one merges with "All That Is" in a union that is simultaneously the fulfillment and dissolution of the worlds of sound, form, and contemplation.

♥ The exercise can be terminated when the Kundalini is in any chakra. When re-initiated, the awakening at the base of the spine is again visualized and the energy is followed to the subsequent locations. Each application of the "Kundalini" will provide for the progression of the movement of the divine power, through the chakras such that ultimately one may feel the movement from initiation at the base of the spine to the completion at the crown chakra.

It should be noted that the movement varies in its method of presentation; the spiritual current can "crawl like an ant", "swim like a fish", "jump like a grasshopper", or smoothly progress like a skier in fresh powder snow.

After progressing from the base of the spine to the crown chakra, one will no longer need to initiate the exercise via visualization; one will be given the vision as the progression ensues.

The "laying-on-of-hands" via Tibetan pulsing techniques may also be applied to the exercises to awaken the Kundalini; the technique serves to increase ones awareness of the location of the movement and, when blockages are encountered, assists in the dissolution of same [via conscious release of that which is causing the blockage].

"Kundalini" has been used in a photographic arrangement to assist one in surmounting difficulties, providing for intuitive guidance during meditation and during "dreamtime".

The array can also be used to balance the fluids of the body, to alleviate back pain, and to assist in the alignment of the spine. It has additionally been used to relieve the symptoms related to fevers and "hot flashes".

SINGLE INFINITY & DOUBLE INFINITY

The "Infinity" configurations are established by placing the crystals in the patterns representing the limitless [See Figures 66 and 67].

FIGURE 66

For the "Single Infinity", the intersection of the symbol is located at the solar plexus; two crystals which have been shaped with the "pear" or tear-drop contour have been used successfully at this location - the points facing each other; a third "pear" crystal is placed upon the area of the third-eye. The Faden crystal has also been used at these locations.

The "Single Infinity" array is quite supportive during ones changes from one cycle to another. It assists one in "seeing" that which is beyond and in gaining insight with respect to the most feasible methods available which are conducive to ease of transition, alteration, and progression.

It enables one to move away from the self without the confinement of boundaries and to move toward the center of the self without limitation. The infinity of the "inner" is very much alive, providing the mirror for reflection of the self; it helps one to remember that the entirety of the physical realm is transient, coming and going, and perpetually changing. The infinity of the "inner", which can be attained via focusing on the third-eye and advancing to within the center of the mind, can assist one in removing the layers of clouds from ones thinking; this further promotes the release of indefinite ideals and the liberation from disruptive states and non-healthy attachments.

This array represents the infinite capacity which is available to one; it elevates ones strength [emotional, mental, physical] and resonance. After a period of time within the array, the aura is cleaner and clearer and the ethereal body is cleansed.

"Single Infinity" has also been used to unite one with the infinite source of all being, bringing an unfathomable peace and contentment to the emotional and intellectual selves.

For the "Double Infinity", the crown chakras of the participants are facing the intersection of the "8" and a crystal is pointing from the crown chakra toward the intersection. The total number of crystals used is left to the intuition of the practitioner. If the Faden crystals or Herkimer diamonds are available, one is place on the heart chakra of each participant.

The "Double Infinity" represents the invisible "tie which binds" two souls together, for the eternal cycle - no end, no beginning - an actualization of co-existent realities and a furtherance of alliances. It represents union and harmony which can bring two together in bliss.

This array can be used to assist in the development and/or remediation of relationships. It facilitates a connection between the two participants [subsequently referred to as "the two"], such that understanding is adjunctive to appreciation with respect to the other. It facilitates a wisdom between "the two" that stimulates a love free of expectations; the pure joy of loving is recognized and the transference of love from the center of peace and contentment within the self is facilitated. It helps one to give love freely and totally, with no attachment or emotional addiction; it is a pure unselfish devotion which unlocks the loving secrets of the heart.

It has been used to open the channels of communication [from the heart] between "the two", promoting self-disclosure, sharing, intimacy, and a complete opening of the self to the other.

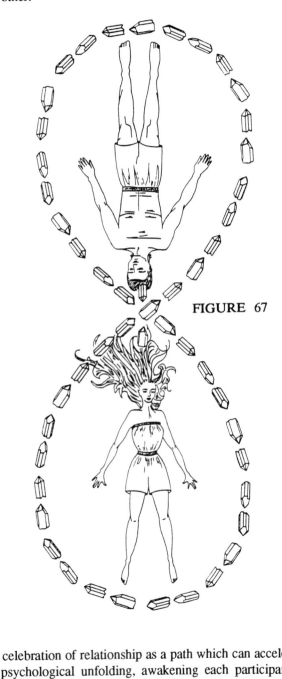

FIGURE 67

It furthers the celebration of relationship as a path which can accelerate cooperative spiritual and psychological unfolding, awakening each participant to the gift of sharing the self totally. "Double Infinity" helps "the two" to grow, to be free, and to allow life together to be an enjoyable adventure; the array nurtures and sustains, encouraging adaptability and continuity.

It has been used to further conflict resolution, acceptance and impartial evaluation of two views, and the capability to recall the beautiful qualities which one has previously recognized in the other [when conflicts arise, one can often recall nothing positive; the array stimulates the memory of unconditional acceptance and can assist one in objective perception of the irrationality behind the dissension]. It promotes the understanding of the roots of conflicts and misunderstandings, and helps "the two" to move into a natural alignment. Often when the conflict is encountered, additional dissatisfactions surface and the participants can totally reveal their feelings; upon resolution of the events or conditions in question, "the two" can leave the array knowing that "there is no action which can be taken by another which is significant enough to diminish unconditional love".

"Double Infinity" is also useful for exploring, and for objectively regarding, personal "beliefs", helping "the two" to break through limitations, simplifying verbalization and listening, and assisting in the removal of artificial barriers. It provides for insight to liberating choices which release the relationship from bondage.

"Double Infinity" has also been used to alleviate frigidity and impotency, providing for a consummate openness between the participants and an unrestricted love-connection. It transforms separation into intimacy.

The application of tantric exercises in this array has transmuted the energies of the base chakra to those of the heart. It promotes the insight that one can only "go as deeply" into a relationship as one has "gone within the self".

This array has also been used to reinforce a connection between two participants when one will not be in the proximity of the other due to travel, physical distance of living, and/or transition to the other side of this reality. The connection is maintained via the photography grid.

The utilization of photographs gridded with the array is recommended for all applications.

DaVINCI

The "DaVinci" configuration is established by placing the crystals in the pattern shown in Figure 68.

Success has been obtained via the utilization of multiples of nine crystals in this arrangement.

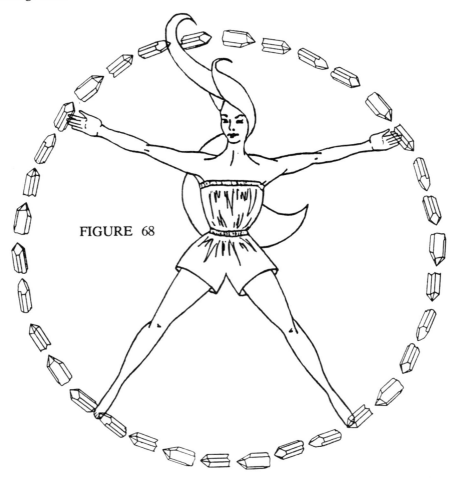

FIGURE 68

This configuration was adapted from the DaVinci Man, an artistic rendition by Leonardo DaVinci, and provides for ones unification with the splendid beauty and activity of all and everything.

It assists one in understanding the issues of "brotherhood" _and_ in the application of same to the all kingdoms [e.g., animal, vegetable, mineral, humanity] and all inner and outer worlds.

Within the silence of the array, one can "put the self in the shoes of another", facilitating understanding on a personal level such that one can recognize and can change those conditions which are unloving and/or unhealthy with respect to survival, devotion, and knowledge.

- ♥ Within the array, the consciousness tends to draw thoughts and situations to the self such that one is provided with not only the insight to solutions, but also with the recognition of the modes through which to attain them.

- ♥ If each person practices this array weekly, we can eventually live in a world in which there is no dissenting action against another and in which there is, at all times, a loving and understanding relationship between all.

It provides a tact for all social interactions, an aptitude for all accomplishments, and an inexhaustible intellectual energy and curiosity for relating to others.

It inspires the pioneering spirit and provides for insight into the foremost paths with respect to working wholly for the future kindred connection between all.

When one enters the array with the thought of a specific negative action of others [e.g., cruelty to animals, inequality and discrimination, abusive behavior, and other unloving actions], one receives inspiration with respect to the personal individual role which can be assumed to alleviate the situation. When one enters the array with the thought of a specific positive action of others, one receives inspiration with respect to that which can be individually initiated to prompt that action to become contagious.

"DaVinci" may also be utilized for the remediation of unloving thoughts or behavior of a single individual. The following exercise provides an example of methodology for this activity:

- ♥ A crystalline circle is created such that two additional crystalline circles, placed side-to-side may be surrounded by the larger circle.

- ♥ Each participant enters an inner circle, assumes the illustrated position, and opens the self to the transfer of knowledge which facilitates positive behavior modification.

- ♥ At this time, the positivity of one is also transferred to the other, and the "other" begins to comprehend the undercurrents of unloving-ness; communication without verbalization is facilitated and that which is experienced is known.

This configuration has also been used to help one surmount the feelings of "better-ness"; the individual who has thoughts of superiority is provided a connection with that, or with whom, one feels is inferior such that one may understand the equality issue.

In addition, the configuration can be used to stimulate receptivity, freeing confined electrical forces and allowing the free oscillation of the molecular structure such that the original position of stability is attained. The array serves to increase the reception of the vibratory rates of the minerals.

It assists in releasing internal stress which is the basis for emotional, physical, and mental disorders and furthers ones opening to spirituality. It is an excellent array for the application of re-birthing techniques.

The use of the photographic arrangement reinforces these applications, and would be performed daily for several weeks; subsequent weekly and monthly utilization would continue to reinforce the condition of stability.

This array is of the highest level, facilitating the peaceful co-habitation of our Earth and helping one to understand that *"YOU"* can reverse that which society has instilled. *"YOU"* can initiate a step towards creating "heaven on Earth"! ♥

YIN/YANG BALANCE

The "Yin/Yang Balance" configuration is established by placing the crystals in the pattern shown in the following figure. Two participants may also enter into the array, with positioning such that the dividing curvature of crystals rests on the left side of each person. Success has been obtained via the utilization of multiples of two crystals in this arrangement.

The array assists one in embracing opposites and in integrating these opposites into the composite of one. It brings together and balances the masculine/feminine, the creative/receptive, and the stable/volatile. The array brings focus through the dispersion of thought and intellectualism, providing for the synthesis of the undivided entirety of a situation, condition or circumstance. Placed upon ones photograph, the balancing and focusing are expedited.

"Yin/Yang" can be used to combine the consciousness of the male and the consciousness of the female to promote insight to the inner-self. It represents the inner and outer duality, merging with itself and creating the crystallization of the balanced individual. One may use the energy of the array to rejuvenate the body and the mind, to balance and to integrate the masculine and feminine attributes, and to stimulate both creativity and the development of psychic abilities.

The array has also been used to assist in the transcendence of disparities relating to negativity and positivity, providing for balancing via the comprehension of the divergent states. It is an array in which one can dissolve into another such that there is total amalgamation of the two. It allows one to "clean ones house" and to allow intimacy to "happen". We are all strangers to ourselves and to the world at large; the familiarity and understanding which is facilitated promotes the detachment from ones defenses and the furtherance of complete harmony of body rhythms such that an experience of "wholeness" may be established with another. It acts to further the release of co-dependency and brings about an encounter from the heart. Placed upon a photograph of two people, it furthers the bonding of same.

When one enters the array with the thought of bringing balance to the feminine attributes, one can initiate the perpetual regenerative qualities with respect to the aspects of strength, spirituality, and conservation. One becomes the center of activity such that the ambitious elements of ones life are reflected in the self, and direction and meaning are provided. One is given both the encouragement and the courage to move in harmony with the universe, to confront that which may delay, to maintain single-pointedness, and to progress without the multiplicity of hesitation, lack of clarity, and indecision. It is a configuration for evolution and improvement.

When one enters the array with the thought of bringing balance to the masculine attributes, one can initiate the perpetual creative force which rests both within, and without of, the self. One becomes responsive and receptive, accepting nourishment for growth and expansion, and joining with others in attunement to extend the results of the creative impulses. It is a configuration for sympathetic and empathetic response, assisting one in actualizing ones potential to be a fulfilling member of a relationship and in responding in a natural fashion to the creative forces, following the impulses of these revelations.

The technique of Tibetan pulsing can also be applied to the subject[s] of the array. When two people are within the array, the practitioner applies the technique concurrently to both and acts as a balancing agent such that the pulse of one attunes to the pulse of the other. "Pulsing" of one within the array has been used to promote the inclusive identification of one with another, and to facilitate the deceleration of the heart rate of one who has experienced trauma and/or shock.

The array can also be used to stimulate the glands which regulate the delicate male and female hormonal balance, bringing equilibrium to actualization.

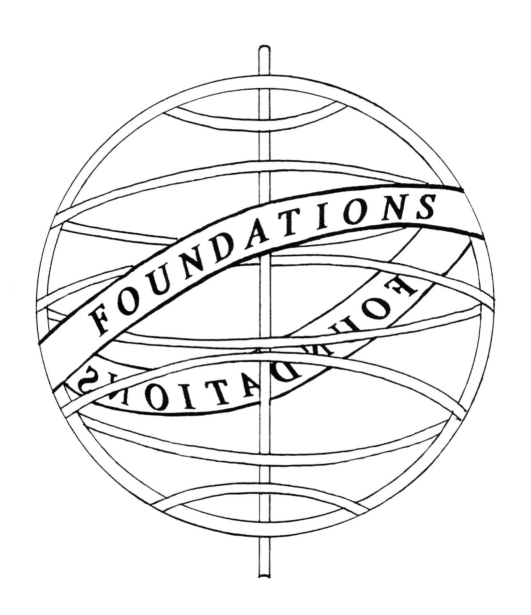

THE SUN RISES IN EACH OF US
SHINING
AND RADIANT BEYOND ALL WORLDS ♥
EXPERIENCE EVERYTHING
WITH THE SAME SPIRIT AND THE SAME HEART ♥

ENERGY TRANSFER

The "Energy Transfer" configuration is established by placing the crystals in a circle, within which three people can form a triangular outline. A square of crystals is placed around the outside of the circle [See Figure 70]. Success has been obtained via the utilization of multiples of three crystals in this arrangement.

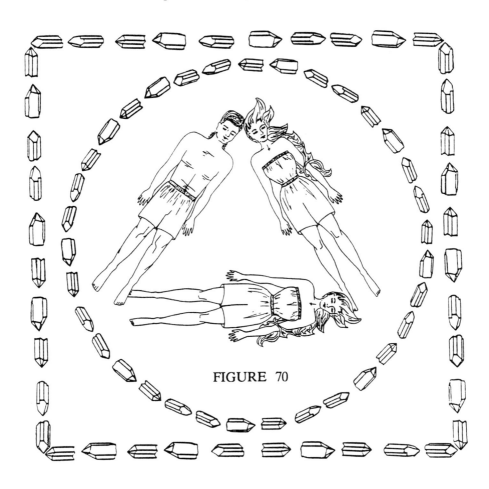

FIGURE 70

This array has been utilized to stimulate well-ness of body, mind, spirit, and emotions; it can assist in balancing polarities, in dissipating energy blockages, and in creating harmony within the energy flow patterns of each of the participants. It stimulates the Prana [breath of life] currents in the body to facilitate cellular balance and coordination.

It is also an excellent array for use during group re-birthing activities and during group meditation, astral travel, divination, etc.

The following exercise is an example of the methods of energy transfer which may be applied via the employment of the "Energy Transfer" array:

- ♥ A photograph [or photographs] of the participants is/are placed within a smaller version of the array.

- ♥ The participants enter the array and position themselves such that contact is created between heads, between feet, or between head/feet; each person experiences two points of contact - one for receiving, and one for transmitting, energy. As a group, the participants determine which point of contact will be receptive and which point will be for transmission. The flow through the triangular configuration represented by the bodies will be receiving, sending, receiving, sending, receiving, sending.

- ♥ Upon securing comfortable contact positions, centering of the self and deep circular breathing is initiated. Within the protective environment of the square, the circular configuration provides for focusing of energy. Each person then visualizes energy moving from his/her body to the contact point of the next person. After several minutes, one will feel the energy entering and flowing through his/her body, to exit via the pre-determined contact point.

- ♥ During this time period, energy blockages and polarity imbalances will be felt. After approximately fifteen minutes, the participants [by verbal agreement] reverse the direction of the energy flow; the continuation of the flow reversals [in fifteen minute increments] breaks-through the energy blockages instilling polarity balancing.

Prior to the initiation of additional group activities, as mentioned above, one cycle of clockwise and one cycle of counter-clockwise energy transfer is completed; these group activities can be benefitted by the following exercise:

- ♥ With the photograph [or photographs] of the participants, the activity which will be attempted is transcribed as a written missive and is placed within the array.

- ♥ Each participant focuses on the third-eye and visualizes an additional connection with the "others" at a point which is located in the center of the configuration and approximately four-feet above the floor. When each person verifies the third-eye connection, the activity is initiated. Intuition and/or prior experience guides one through the remaining steps. Please note that during this time the participants may be within, or outside of, the array.

DIRECTIONAL ENERGY TRANSFER

The "Directional Energy Transfer" configuration is established by placing the crystals in the pattern of an arrow which has been partially superimposed by three other arrows [See Figure 71].

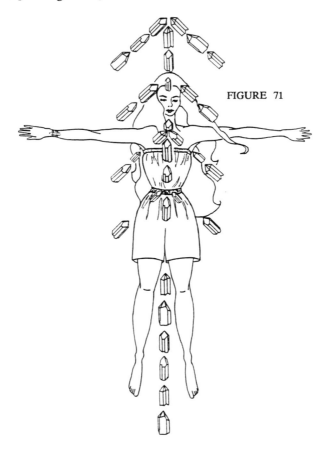

FIGURE 71

The location of each apex upon the subject is as follows: top apex is above the head, the second apex is located at the third-eye, the third apex is located at the throat chakra, and the fourth apex is either located at the navel or base chakra. Success has been obtained via the utilization of multiples of four crystals in this arrangement.

The array is multi-faceted and can be used in the transference of healing energies during both present and absent-healing situations, in the transference of protection, love, etc., and for thought transmission. For the transference of healing energy to one who is present, the array is placed upon the subject; the practitioner, after centering of the self, then "lays hands" upon each location in which a crystal has been placed. For healing energy transference to a distant location, the array is placed upon a photograph of the subject in conjunction with the healing crystals which are appropriate to the disorder; if the photograph is small, the array may extend past the border of same and additional healing crystals may be placed in line with the array crystals. Protection of a person, animal, or object may be facilitated via the identical photographic method.

The transmission of ones thoughts to another may be reinforced via entry to the array [this requires conscious dexterity], after preparing a written missive of the thought and placing it beneath a smaller version of the array, and after centering of the self. The array is placed such that the apex is directed to the general location of the recipient. Deep circular breathing is initiated and the thought is focused at the area of the third-eye and is then dispatched in the direction of the recipient. Thoughts of well-being, healthfulness, etc., may also be transmitted in healing situations. One of two effects usually result: if the recipient is not engaged in a definite thought pattern and the aura of same is clear of mental debris, the thought-form will discharge itself to the mental body; or if the recipient is engaged in definite mental activity, the thought-form will remain in the vicinity of the recipient until the mental body is sufficiently uncluttered - at the time of clarity, it will discharge itself to the mental body; this delayed action is dependent upon the sufficiency of the strength of the thought-form. Note that, in this exercise, the thought is strengthened via repetitious contemplation of the precise thought, by repeated sending of the thought via the channel of the third-eye, and via the smaller version of the array.

If, however, the auric field/energy field of the potential recipient does not possess the capability of reception, the thought-form will be repelled and returned; for example, a thought form, which requires an action which is adverse to the potential recipient, will not be accepted. In addition, if one is protected from thought-entry via one of the various personal metaphysical protective mechanisms which are available, the thought will be returned to the source. With all of the loving protection which is being transmitted throughout the world today [e.g., during meditation, healing gatherings, retreats, etc.], any negative thought forms will, in all likelihood, be declined and reversed. Conversely, a consciously directed thought-form of love and protection will operate as a shielding and protective instrument, seeking all opportunities to benefit and defend the recipient; it will also strengthen the positive forces and weaken the negative forces which attempt to infringe upon the auric field. Hence, the positive thoughts tend to maintain a "guardian angel", ever near the recipient. This is an excellent exercise for instilling protective force fields around persons, animals, plants, objects, and the totality of our Earth.

A second exercise involves the concentrated thoughts of the self in another location; when this is successful, ones form can be seen for those who possess advanced intuitive and clairvoyant faculties and/or ones presence can be felt by those who are intuitively sensitive or clairsentient. The illuminated scientific hypothesis explains the phenomenon as form created from ethereal and astral matter.

EARTH SQUARE

The "Earth Square" configuration is established by placing the crystals in the pattern of a square surrounding the body of the subject, with square-shaped and/or rhomboid crystals placed upon the third-eye and the chest [See Figure 72]. Pyrite cubes, Iceland spar, and square-shaped crystalline forms which have been fashioned via lapidary, have been used on the locations of the body. Success has been obtained via the utilization of multiples of four crystals in this arrangement.

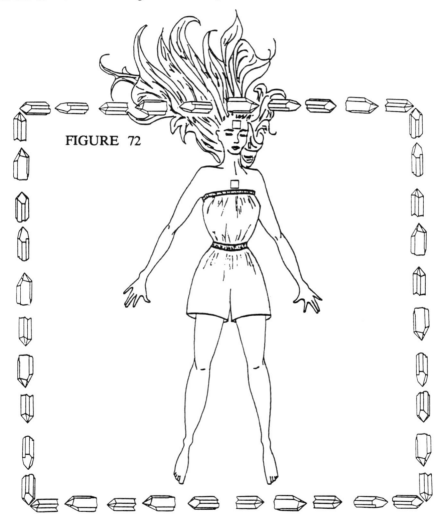

FIGURE 72

This array represents the ceremonial building block for new projects, new ventures, new methods of progression. It provides a foundation for both the development and the construction of fresh structures within ones life and further facilitates the stabilization and advancement of those pursuits which are verbalized.

"Earth Square" can assist one in building faith, character, relationships [removing pretenses], spirituality, and competence. It is an excellent array for stimulating the intuitive faculties during metaphysical pursuits, removing any facade from that which is encountered. It provides the basis for precision and preservation of that which is constructed and represents the "seed" from which the self would expand, flourish, and grow toward the perfect state in all enterprises.

During future-telling for another [when the other is present], the"Earth Square" has been placed such that both the practitioner and the recipient may sit within the array. [These activities are, for example, tarot, Neo-tarot, I Ching, Runes, astrological readings, and corresponding activities in which the participants would be sitting.] The square-shaped or rhomboid crystals, which are usually placed upon the body, are placed at the four corners of the configuration, and after centering the selves, entry to the lay-out is performed.

During solitary utilization of the array for future-telling, when the practitioner is in a sitting-position, dual/multi-colour chevron amethyst [the natural crystalline state] has been placed in the four corners of the "Earth Square" to assist in the transcendence of the intuitive state; this has been successfully used to facilitate intuitive qualities which are "beyond intuition". The chevron amethyst tends to open the third-eye and the crown chakras concurrently to provide a clear channel for resolutions and solutions.

The array, with the natural state or the polished state of the chevron amethyst placed in the four corners, has also been used to facilitate the additional activities listed above.

When supplementing the energies via the utilization of a photograph, the square array is formed around the photograph and, usually, a fashioned dual/multi-coloured chevron amethyst is placed in the center of same; this application does not require the square-shape discussed above; in fact, a freeform style is recommended. The polished or unpolished forms of nephrite jade with quartz crystal structures and the electric-blue sheen obsidian have been used in place of the natural formation of chevron amethyst, with excellent results. When these crystals are not available, pyrite, azurite, and/or black tourmaline have been used.

The array is often used with the "Chakra Array" to reinforce and to fortify during healing routines.

In addition, "Earth Square" acts as a protective mechanism, and may be placed around an object or a photograph of that which one wishes to protect. For this application, the natural chevron amethyst, the polished or unpolished forms of nephrite jade with quartz crystal structures and/or the electric-blue sheen obsidian, the black tourmaline, and the pyrite have been used in the reinforcement of the four corners of the array.

TRIANGULAR BALANCE

The "Triangular Balance" configuration is established by placing the crystals in the pattern of an equilateral triangle surrounding the body [See Figure 73]. The crystal placed on the third-eye is also of triangular shape. Success has been obtained via the utilization of multiples of three crystals in this arrangement.

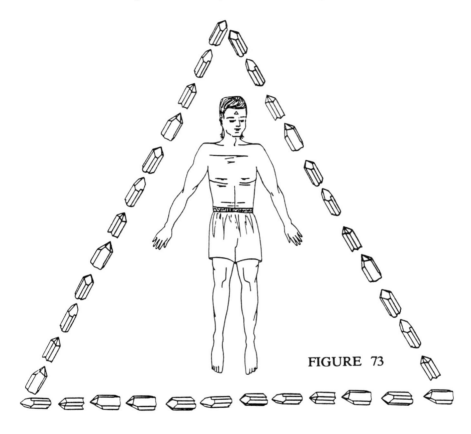

FIGURE 73

The triangular shape is one of the first three symbols designed for the religious teachings of early man. It represents the "All-Seeing Eye" and may be utilized to assist one in both transcending pre-programmed patterns and in understanding the mechanisms of biofeedback. One may be inhibited by a multitude of programs, some of which are ingrained in ones totality during this lifetime and others which are deep-seated remnants from former lives. Whenever any contradictory idea is transcended, ones spiritual illumination escalates; when all inconsistencies are understood, and no longer instigate an emotional response, one becomes enlightened. Enlightenment occurs as an unanticipated and impetuous realization - that one is the witness to emotions and not a participant. One may act as a mirror to all, reflecting the feelings of others without experiencing the sensations; at this time, nothing can "push your buttons" to initiate negative emotional re-actions.

The utilization of the array can assist one in transcending physical discomforts and pain, negative emotions, trauma, and dis-ease. It assists one in witnessing the situation and in understanding the process of disengaging the intellect from the condition.

With respect to non-physical situations, it can also serve to facilitate the comprehension that "everything is exactly as it needs to be" and that "everyone is at the location on the spiritual path where they need to be". It helps one to overcome the need to proselytize and inspires one to both allow others to "live" as they choose and to understand that those outside the self "need" to encounter that which they are experiencing until they learn to experience with "good times" [if, and when, the experiencing is negative].

The array further assists one in perceiving the aspects of karma, inducing the appreciation that one does not *need* to experience other than "good times" if one can learn without personal participation in negative episodes.

It is an excellent array for those encountering resistance to change and transition, helping one to anticipate change. It soothes the spirit, quiets the emotions and the intellect, and furthers ones inner knowledge of ones personal reality.

When "Triangular Balance" is applied to the biofeedback exercise, it assists one in determining personal patterns of response to stress and negativity. It provides for verification of the extent of self-control and self-awareness one maintains and arouses insight regarding methods which can improve ones response to stress [i.e., such that the response is "action" and not re-action].

It further reinforces ones perception and promotes the resolution of emotional situations which induce over-indulgence [in food, alcohol, drugs, relationships, etc.], providing for the recognition of the issues involved and stimulating positive action toward the amelioration of the problem.

It is an excellent array for the practice of self-regulation, assisting one to recognize when there is "something amiss" in the body, where the condition is located, and what manifestation the condition has assumed; at this point, diaphragmatic breathing is initiated and one breathes "into" the area of concern, releasing the associated tension and stimulating renewal. It is fascinating to monitor the self, via this array, during changes in lifestyle.

When utilizing the array, the subject focuses on the triangular crystalline mineral at the area of the third-eye.

Breathe deep the gathering Light,
Energy of Love that dispels the night.
ALL THAT IS vibrates as One,
From tiniest atom to mightiest sun.

From ephemeral lace to the galaxy's core -
Power of Love - no less, always more.
Growing while flowing in the river of Life,
Harmonics converge and merge in the Light.

Breathe deep - filled with the Love,
Of the ALL that's below and the ALL that's above.
ALL THAT IS lives inside of you,
Ancient of age and forever brand new.

Richard Ray
Seattle, WA, USA

STARBURST CIRCLE

The "Starburst Circle" configuration is established by placing crystals in a concentric circle around the subject, placing crystals at the location of the eight rays of the star, and placing two crystals/clusters at the end of each ray [See Figure 74].

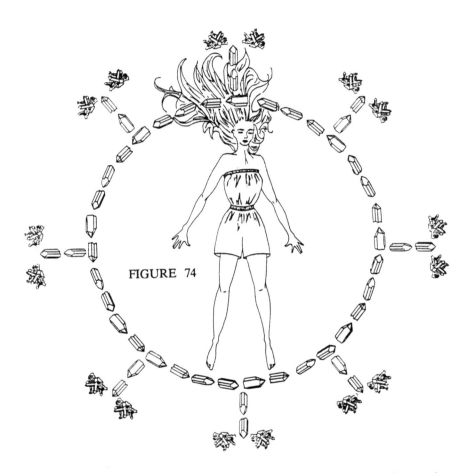

FIGURE 74

This schematic seems to be most effective when actual terminated crystals are utilized for the locations at the ends of the rays and are consistently directed away from, or toward, the subject. The number of crystals used is left to the intuition of the practitioner.

This array has been utilized to assist one in actualizing that which one can "be", presenting insight to the paths which will allow one to "shine the brightest". Entry into the array after asking for assistance, and receptivity to that which is communicated, can further ones quest for realization. It can also be used to provide for an alliance of cooperation between the conscious-self and the Buddha within the self, propagating the union between the self and the single and accessible reality of "All That Is".

The following is an example of an exercise which has been successful in assisting one in the understanding of the eight-fold path [described in the ancient Vedic literature] and in providing for access, on the ethereal plane, to succinct translations of the Vedic texts. One selects one aspect of the eight-fold path [i.e., right views, right intention, right speech, right action/living, right effort/exertions, right respect for self, right concentration/thought, and right mindfulness/meditation] prior to entry to the array.

- ♥ One of the constituents of the eight-fold path is transcribed to paper and placed within a smaller version of the array.

- ♥ After centering the self, one enters the "Starburst Circle". One of the twelve branches of crystals emanating from the circle is chosen as representing the selected segment of the eight-fold path. Deep circular breathing is initiated and focus is directed, to the selected branch of the circle, via the crown chakra.

- ♥ One affixes the attention on the chosen subject, allowing the energy of the selected branch of the array to transport one to the Vedic texts and to facilitate translation and understanding of the selected portion of the eight-fold path. During this time, the mind passes through several stages of self-hypnotization, resulting in the trance state. The comprehension of, and sensitivity to, the intention and significance of a segment of the "path" may be immediate or may require multiple entries into the array.

At the successful conclusion of the total evaluation, nirvana [the attainment of the total understanding of the "truths"] is attained and one is emancipated from worldly limitations.

In addition, "Starburst Circle" can be used to access parallel dimensions; one visualizes the pathway via the pre-selected portion of the starburst, and follows it to the "other side". Depending upon which pathway is selected and/or which crystals are utilized in the array, one may experience a multitude of coinciding realities.

The experiences which have resulted from this exercise have included the participation of the subject in another reality and the observation of the other reality without participation. It is a fascinating journey in either circumstance. It is recommended that one does not perform this exercise alone until it has been encountered with the assistance of another.

PENTAGRAM

The "Pentagram" configuration is established by placing the crystals in the pattern shown in Figure 75. Success has been obtained via the utilization of multiples of five crystals in this arrangement.

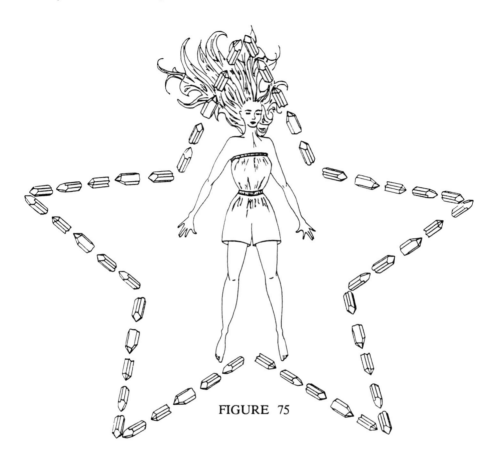

FIGURE 75

The configuration represents a centering device which is based on the Faerie traditions of the Gaelic civilization. It represents the five senses, and the composite of the four cardinal directions acting together in consonance to stimulate the furtherance of that which is requested.

It assists one in total awareness on the physical, mental, and emotional levels, bringing balance to ones inherent qualities.

One exercise which has produced a synthesis of one with the star, and, subsequently, with the self, is shown as follows:

- Each point of the star is assigned an attribute which one feels is inherent to humanity and/or to the self. For example, the attributes of birth, commencement, knowledge, fulfillment, transition, relaxation, rulership, wisdom, identity, self-esteem, self-respect, immodesty, modesty, passion, affection, love, etc.

- The attributes chosen for evaluation are written on five pieces of paper and placed, one beneath each point of the star. One memorizes the locations, and if desired, may select crystals to represent each of the attributes; these crystals are placed at the apex of each point of the star.

- One centers the self, enters the array and initiates deep circular breathing.

- Next, each attribute is considered singularly, and then as a cooperative entity with each of the remaining four attributes, such that all of the connections between the attributes are evaluated and considered.

When one initiates the activity of looking within, while looking at, an attribute, the focus via the third-eye is on the point of the star which represents that attribute. When two attributes are being synthesized, the original attention goes first to one and then to the other; after the composite is created, the midpoint between the two is the center of focus.

The progression is normally in a counter-clockwise manner [in the northern hemisphere].

For example, the evaluation of self-respect, would be based upon that which one creates, shares, and enjoys with respect to personal achievements and personal "being"; it is an unequivocal sense of ones accomplishments, extending to the responsibility for acting in accordance with ones idea of the self.

- The process is completed when each of the five selected attributes has been addressed. If one of the points of the star feels weak, one would consciously address the development of the attribute which is represented. This future "work" is usually performed outside of the array; verification of completion is assured by re-entry to the array at a later time and via resumption of the original process. As one feels each point of the star as a part of the self, imbalances become obvious and may be rectified; the placement of a smaller version of the array upon ones photograph, and the placement of each of the written attributes at the appropriate point of the star enhances the rectification.

This array can also facilitate the "charging" of talismen; a photographic arrangement or a normal-sized array may be employed. If a photographic arrangement is chosen, one places the rendition of the object within the arrangement, with a written missive of the feelings which the object will convey when magnetically charged via the array. The use of the normal-sized array has been more effective; the following exercise describes one method of "charging" talismen:

- ♥ One selects the object which is to be infused with energy, protection, love, healing, etc. If a crystal/mineral is selected as the object, it is recommended that the crystal/mineral either possess the quality or, is compatible with the quality.

- ♥ One enters the array, after centering, and initiates deep circular breathing. The thought of that essence, with which the object is to be infused, is held firmly in the mind and focused at the area of the third-eye. The object is, if possible, held within the hand which has been determined to be ones individual and personal "giving" hand.

- ♥ One will feel the increase in the energy of the object, and will intuitively know when the process may be completed.

- ♥ Placement of the object within a smaller version of the array [after this initial saturation] will further instill that which was intended.

This above exercise acts to instill an essence which is similar to a battery which can be programmed to discharge at specific times daily or when a specific event or condition occurs. Depending on the thought which is transferred to the object, the vibrational rate on the astral and mental plane will act such that any negative bombardment will be repelled and the "charge" will remain. "Absent-charging" via a written missive, a photograph, or re-entry to the array with a clear image of the object, is recommended on a periodic basis.

The "Pentagram" is also an excellent protective pattern; placed upon a photograph or in a gridded arrangement around/upon an object, it tends to guard against intrusion. Pendants representing the "Pentagram", with a faceted stone positioned at each of the five points, have been quite successful in protection from "spells", psychic attacks, and negativity [stemming from within, or without, of the self].

ASTRAL NUCLEUS

The "Astral Nucleus" configuration is established by placing four quartz crystals in the pattern shown in Figure 76 <u>or</u> in a pattern in which the terminations are pointing away from the center; four double terminated quartz crystals may also be utilized to represent the pattern.

FIGURE 76

This array may be worn [as jewelry], may be affixed [via hypo-allergenic tape], may be laid upon the subject, and/or may be suspended above the subject.

The astral world, comprised of the essence of matter, interpenetrates the physical world such that portions of the astral world may be occupying the same area as substance [e.g., physical form in the physical world]; when a portion of the astral world is occupying the same area as ones personal physical form, each portion is entirely unconscious of the other and, in no way, impedes the free movement of the other.

The "Astral Nucleus" can be utilized to facilitate **consciousness** during astral travel and to secure, to reinforce, and to induce high visibility to the astral cord, which connects the astral body to the physical body.

One may visit the astral plane, not by movement in space, but by being aware of the senses by which the astral world may be perceived; the astral plane is actually a condition and/or situation of dimensional nature rather than a pre-determined location.

One can "travel" to the astral plane during the sleep state or via conscious exercises. If the travel is during the sleep state, ones dreams will report the events [sleeping with the configuration beneath ones pillow has enhanced remembrance of dreams].

The following exercise has been useful in facilitating ones transition to, and conscious interaction within, the astral environment:

- ♥ A photograph of the subject is placed beneath a smaller version of the "Astral Nucleus" array.

- ♥ One enters the normal-sized array after centering the self, and subsequently initiates deep circular breathing.

   During the first attempt, visualization is introduced, and the subject visualizes the departure of the astral body from the physical - conscious awareness of the astral connection cord is highly recommended and would be suggested by the practitioner during the activities of departure.

The transition from the physical realm to the astral dimension is not instantaneous, but is sudden and direct. One passes through the dimensional planes quickly and easily.

- ♥ At this time, the practitioner initiates questions concerning the surroundings in which the subject is located - this prompts a continuing awareness of the astral plane, itself, and facilitates both accuracy with respect to movement and comprehension with respect to that which transpires.

Discarnate friends and/or incarnate friends who are also visiting the astral plane in a state of awareness, may be encountered.

One may also meet incarnate friends who are not cognizant of being on the astral plane and will not, or will only vaguely, remember the encounter; one may also form new friendships, with those from other parts of the physical world and with whom problem-solving, philosophical discussions, etc., can be undertaken during future meetings.

In addition, the subject may also enjoy contact with those who are move evolved and who may provide counsel and/or instruction.

Note that the astral plane promotes the total experience of emotions. When one is in the astral form, one may feel an intensity of affection, sentiment, devotion, reverence, etc., which is not normally experienced on the physical plane. The theorem of "mind over matter", applied on the astral plane, is implemented with ease; suffering can be eliminated, pain removed, and activities accomplished.

It is recommended that the traveler to the astral plane perform some altruistic actions during each venture [e.g., providing comfort to those in sorrow, dispensing strength and energy to those who are frail or ill, supporting those who have emotional need, etc.].

> ♥ After return to the physical plane, a log book listing encounters and activities will assist one to verify recall on the part of others who were also consciously visiting the astral world.

This exercise, bringing consciousness to the dimensional transition to, and activities upon, the astral plane, further assists one to actualize the conscious state during sleep, such that lucid dreaming provides for continuity between the physical and astral worlds, between life in the physical realm and life in the realm which transcends the physical.

THE
"GATELESS
GATE"

COMMENCE LIVING AS IF YOU HAD FAITH -
*AND, THEN, YOU WILL **SEE** !♥!*
AN INSIGNIFICANT SHIFT OF FOCUS,
BRINGS A SIGNIFICANT CHANGE -
ONE THEN MAY SEE BEYOND ILLUSION
TO REALITY ♥

INTRODUCTION

The configurations of the "Gateless-Gate" can be used by one, alone, to facilitate the personal qualities of manifestation and actualization; it assists one in attaining that which has "been promised" by the ancient scriptures and furthers ones self-realization. The configurations can also be used by the practitioner to assist others to attain self-actualization, manifestation, and self-realization.

It is important to take time at frequent intervals to think about ones life and to decide in exact terms that which one wishes to do or wishes to have happen. The conscious self, acting as a guide for the inner self, uses inductive reasoning and "will" to direct the inner self in making plans for the task of living and for assuring that proper efforts are utilized to stimulate the outcome in accordance with those plans. That which one chooses, in any moment, creates ones today and ones tomorrows. The average person modifies and changes plans and desires quite frequently - the result being a mixture of contradictory thought-forms of plans, wishes, and fears, from which the Higher Self makes a mixture of future events which are often unsatisfactory and indeterminate.

Personal dominion over the creation and actualization of ones reality is granted to each of us from the great source of "All That Is". One may develop, cultivate, amplify, modify, adapt, direct, and manifest the personal power which is inherent via eliminating the obstructions which impede the receipt of the influent of the energies *and* by supplying the energies with the precise physical and mental mechanisms through which it is enabled to express and manifest itself effectively and efficiently. Be consciously aware that those "things" to which one gives attention will reveal themselves; if one is precise, and secure in confidence, actualization will follow.

The following arrays and exercises can assist one in both *consciously* creating ones personal world of experience and in determining the appropriate pathways to ones personal destiny. It assists one in constructing a bridge of understanding between the inner self, the conscious self, the Higher Self, and "All That Is".

Prior to experiencing the totality of the "Gateless Gate", ones experience of the exercise described in the section "Subconscious Self Life Force", which serves to assist one in consciously becoming familiar with the subconscious, is recommended.

ELIMINATION [DE-PROGRAMMING]

The "Elimination" configuration is established by placing the crystals in the pattern of an "X", with the intersection of the "X" located at the solar plexus of the subject [See Figure 77]. The number of crystals used is left to the intuition of the practitioner.

This configuration is the first in the progression to "The Gate". Since belief in limitation is the only circumstance which causes and/or allows the existence of limitation, this array was developed to assist in the de-programming of the inner self, providing for the release of those complexes/fixations of ideas and beliefs and/or convictions which are held by the inner self and which impede ones progression toward the actualization of that which is desired. It should be noted that these self-limiting beliefs, which may or may not be valid, are many times held in conjunction with the conscious beliefs.

Prior to entering this configuration, one prepares a list of all conscious beliefs which one accepts and/or acknowledges, being especially attentive to those deep-rooted convictions concerning ones individual general success or non-success. Look for those areas where thoughts surface with respect to being unlucky, inadequate, unqualified, etc.; look also to those areas where you have been conditioned to believe that your personal limitations, and/or the restrictions by others, can and will prevent certain circumstances from occurring.

One tends to conceal and camouflage a multitude of "things" from ourselves [and others] due to early and current experiences of conditioning, repression, inhibition, and bombardment with taboos. The discovery of that which is hidden is very important to the actualization of the self.

After contemplation of this list, enter the "Elimination" array, center the self, initiate circular breathing, and ask the inner self to reveal to you the additional beliefs which you have not listed. [If there is a discontinuity of time between the preparation of the list and the entry to the array, re-review and examination of the list is suggested.] Circular breathing is usually maintained for at least fifteen minutes.

The results of the initial visit to the array, bringing any additional beliefs to the consciousness, may or may not be immediate and/or totally comprehensive. The inner self will advise the conscious self when all beliefs have been recognized. If all details do not immediately surface [usually the case], one would, for several days, perform the following [Second Stage]:

♥   Enter the array daily and repeat the exercise; and

♥   At least once per day, initiate "harmonious time" by find a peaceful and quiet area, and allow the rhythmic harmony of the universe to flow through the cleared mind. It is during this period that cognizance of additional beliefs have been provided in the form of flashes of insight. In addition, other periods of restful states [e.g., the dream state], occurring after the initiation of this exercise, have provided the knowledge.

These activities have necessitated up to seven days to facilitate the disclosure of the remaining beliefs.

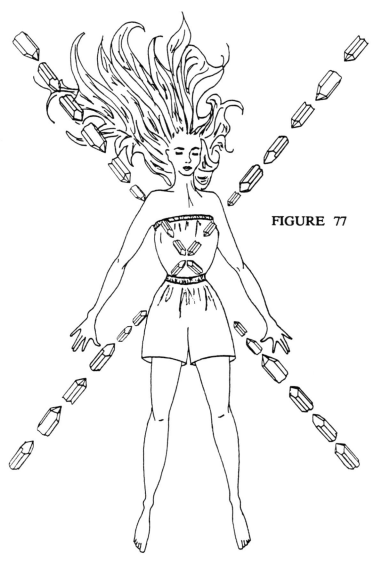

FIGURE 77

The next activity involves examining the list in totality and highlighting those beliefs with which the conscious self is not in agreement. In addition, from the beliefs remaining on the list, catalog those beliefs which are contradictory to each other; review these beliefs and, for each set of contradictory beliefs, highlight the one [of each pair] which is more questionable to the conscious self with respect to validity. These highlighted beliefs are the first which can be addressed via the following method [Third Stage]:

- The first highlighted belief is transcribed to a piece of paper, upon which a smaller version of the "Elimination" configuration is placed. Another message [written] is prepared which states that this belief is not true for you; this message is placed upon the array, with the written words on the same side of the paper which touches the array.

- Now, one can enter the normal array, after centering the self [concentration in the area two-inches below the navel is recommended], and can initiate deep and circular breathing for several minutes.

At this time, communication flows from the conscious self, relaying the information to the inner self that the belief of concern is no longer a valid belief for limiting ones personal life; when the communication is completed [one intuitively recognizes the completion], one exits the array and enters again after three days. The Faden crystal and the fulgurite have both been quite useful in enhancing the transfer of information from the conscious self to the inner self.

- Daily, for three days, the "harmonious time" [as defined above], is used to communicate the message of belief-invalidity to the inner self. On the third day, the array is entered and validation of the release of the belief is given by the inner self to the conscious self. This validation is also sometimes given during the "harmonious time" prior to the passage of the three days; however, acceleration of the process is not recommended.

- After the array experience of the third day, the written belief and negation of same are removed from the smaller version of the array and eliminated. Several methods of disposal have been utilized to dispense with the written words: (1) smoldering sage has been used to dissipate the belief and smoldering sweetgrass or elephant grass has been used to validate [via consumption] the negation of the belief; (2) campfires and "match" fires have been used to consume both; and, (3) the belief has been burned and the negation of the belief has been buried or placed in an "I Can" [an opaque container, on the outside of which is placed ones personal design].

- As each belief has been resolved, send love and thankfulness to the inner self and the conscious self.

The above process is continued until each highlighted belief is confronted and released and/or confronted and retained. Any which are retained are returned to the original list and placed at the end of same.

The list which remains is composed of those beliefs which involve reinforcement via ones conscious acceptance. The following exercise [Stage Four] assists one in the total evaluation of the validity of each of the listed conscious beliefs:

- ♥ The first consciously-accepted belief is transcribed to a piece of paper, upon which a small version of the "Discrimination" configuration [see page 89, Figure 29] is placed. Now, after centering the self, one enters the "Elimination" array. Deep circular breathing is initiated and insight with respect to the cause and/or basis for this belief is requested. If the insight does not occur during the minimum of thirty minutes within this array, proceed to the next step of this exercise.

- ♥ At least once per day and until the cause of the belief is known, initiate "harmonious time" and allow the pulsing consonance of creation to enter the mind. It is during this period, and other restful periods subsequent to the "harmonious time"[e.g., the dream state] that the awareness of the basis for the belief can be provided the form of flashes of insight. After awareness of the basis for the belief occurs, consciously evaluate the belief and determine whether it is necessary. If the belief is resolved to be unnecessary, repeat the steps in Stage Three, above.

- ♥ If the belief is concluded to be necessary, the written belief is now removed from beneath the "Analysis" array and recorded, or affixed, within ones personal log book [or in an area which will be accessed daily]; this record promotes the continuing conscious awareness of the belief. As each evaluation is completed, send love and thankfulness to the inner self and to the conscious self.

The above process is continued until the cause supporting each consciously recognized belief is encountered and evaluated. Upon completion, the list of retained beliefs is reviewed and questions are posed with respect to each belief; for example, "Am I happy about this belief?", "Is this belief self-limiting?", "Does this belief permit limitations imposed by others?", etc. If there is unhappiness associated with a belief and/or if a belief has the potential to impose limiting factors, re-evaluation is required. Whenever one is at peace with the resolution of all beliefs, continuance to the next array of "Consciousness" is recommended.

Maintain the knowledge that *you are what you are* by reason of that which you think and believe. Positive attitudes bring success; release of the "I can't" syndrome brings conquest. Consistently remember that "if you didn't see Jesse rob the train, you logically cannot believe he did!"

CONSCIOUSNESS

The "Consciousness" configuration is established by placing the crystals in the pattern shown in Figure 78 or Figure 79. In Figure 78, the crossbars intersect at the heart and the third-eye chakras. In Figure 79, the perpendicular portion of the array is located on the right side of the subject.

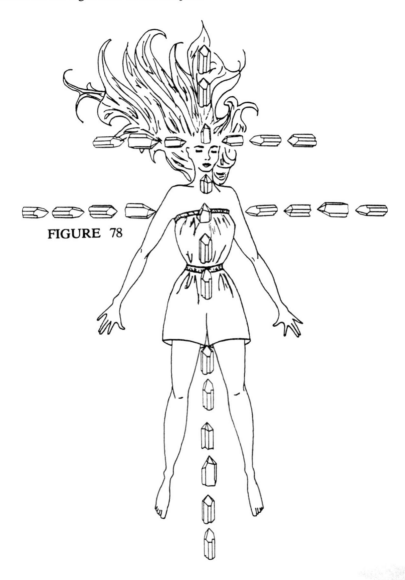

FIGURE 78

The creation of ones future [and present manifestation] depends upon the beliefs held by the inner self _and_ the plans and desires of both the conscious self and the inner self. These beliefs, plans, desires, fears, etc., coalesce into thought forms and are used by the Higher Self to construct ones future. These thought forms are the origins of growth which lead to future events or conditions. In order to facilitate success in ones endeavors, one eliminates mental defeatist attitudes [the "Elimination" exercises] and consciously determines that which is desired.

The world in which we live is beautifully ordered, instantly responsive, and of infinite abundance. It nourishes body, mind, emotions, and spirit while supporting one in the quest for enlightenment. One bestows upon oneself or creates discord and lack in accordance with beliefs of the conscious self and/or inner self. Conscious thoughts of negativity applied to oneself bear the seeds of possible difficulties. The harmonious existence with the rhythms of universal perfection brings peace and contentment to ones life.

Every day brings decisions and the potential for a variety of choices. One is never coerced by circumstances; one personally selects the course of action which is required to continue ones life. The rationality for the choice, if not of paramount quality, may be because it is the "path of least resistance" - *no matter what the choice, it is ours.*

The "Consciousness" configuration can be used to assist one in determining that which one **really** desires. It assists in alleviating difficulties in ascertaining clarity and comprehensiveness of ones desires, aspirations, ambitions, and dreams.

It further expedites the resolution of conflicting desires, aspirations, ambitions, and dreams.

Prior to entering this array, one prepares a list of all conscious desires, tabulating them in descending order of importance. These desires represent that which will deliver pleasure and/or will eliminate pain. Disregard apprehension or anxiety that any of these desires could be beyond achievement.

After contemplation of this list, enter "Consciousness", center the self, initiate deep circular breathing, and ask to receive insight into additional desires which have not yet been consciously recognized. The information may surface immediately or may require visits to the array. After receipt of the message from the inner self that there are no further desires, assure your list contains all desires <u>and</u> that the desires are in descending order of importance [to you].

The Second Stage involves entry into "Consciousness" with the first item of desire firmly fixed within the mind. Center the self, initiate circular breathing, and request insight to any and all variables which must be considered prior to the actualization of the desire; this includes, for example, concerns with respect to any negative effect the realization of the desire will have on others, with respect to ones personal apprehension of attainment, and relative to whether the fulfillment of the desire will bring happiness to the self, etc. [If there is a discontinuity of time between the preparation of the list and the entry to the array, re-review and examination of the list is suggested.] Circular breathing is usually maintained for at least fifteen minutes.

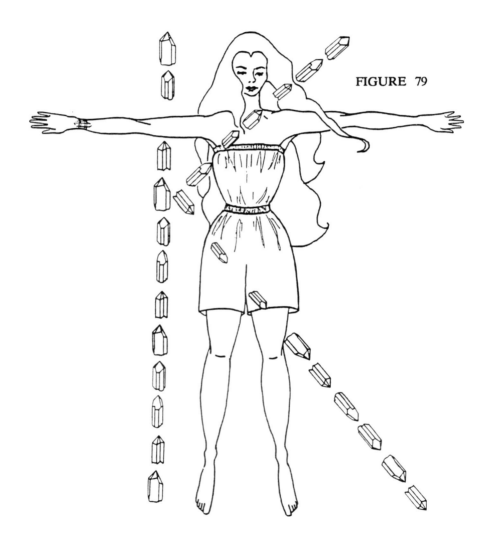

FIGURE 79

The results of this visit to the array, bringing self-limiting concerns to conscious recognition, may or may not be immediate and/or totally comprehensive. The inner self will advise the conscious self when all concerns have been acknowledged. If all details do not immediately surface [usually the case], one would, for several days, perform the following [Third Stage]:

♥ Enter the array daily and repeat the exercise for the selected desire. At least once per day, initiate "harmonious time" by find a peaceful and quiet area, and allow the rhythmic harmony of the universe to flow through the cleared mind. It is during this period that cognizance of the concealed self-limiting conditions beliefs is usually obtained.

When information surfaces with respect to the potential self-limitations, it should be recorded with the desire. The next activity involves examining the concerns in totality and determining whether one wishes to continue or abandon the desire. This activity can be completed via the following method [Fourth Stage]:

♥ The first desire, with the potential self-limitations, is transcribed to a piece of paper, upon which a smaller version of the "Consciousness" configuration is placed.

♥ Next, one enters the normal array, after centering the self, and initiates deep and circular breathing for several minutes. At this time, one requests guidance with respect to continuance or abandonment of the desire. The information is usually provide within the time period [approximately 30 minutes] for which one is in the array. The array is used daily until resolution is obtained.

If maintenance in continuity of the desire is determined, the additional concerns are defined and recorded with the desire. The smaller version of the "Consciousness" array is placed upon this record and one enters the normal-sized array, requesting insight to resolution of the concerns [e.g., the additional considerations one must address during subsequent manifestation activities].

If abandonment of the desire is determined, one consciously re-evaluates the desire. If the discontinuance of the desire fulfills the happiness and well-being of the individual, the written desire is removed from the list of desires.

♥ As the decision-making process is completed for each desire, send love and thankfulness to the conscious self and the inner self.

The above process is performed for each desire, aspiration, ambition, etc., which is listed. At the conclusion of the process, if there are contradictions, the process is re-initiated. If there are no contradictions, ones list will be precise and detailed and the desires which have endured are those which can be transferred to the inner self; when one is at peace with the inventory of desires, continuance to the next array of "Reprogramming" is recommended.

REPROGRAMMING

The "Reprogramming" configuration is established by placing the crystals in the pattern shown in Figure 80.

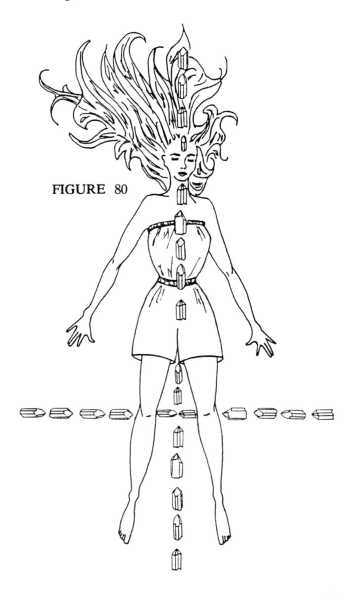

FIGURE 80

Communication with the inner self is attained via the utilization of the conscious mind. The conscious self is the sentinel at the gate; the inner self receives impressions from the conscious self and reasons deductively, accepting conscious thoughts and analyzing them to reach logical conclusions based upon the information given; it will not act contrary to the information which it possesses. Hence, conscious recognition and precision, with respect to ones desires, is consequential with respect to the subsequent actualization of same.

This configuration may be used for the communication of ones desires to the inner self such that they will not be dislodged by transient chaotic conditions and circumstances. Always remember that the information which is transmitted to the inner self does not involve just wishes or daydreams, but consists of definite and insistent desires, aspirations, ambitions and dreams.

The first exercise is expedited via the following method:

♥ The first consciously chosen desire, with any attendant desires which are necessary to facilitate the manifestation of same, is transcribed to a piece of paper, upon which a small version of the "Reprogramming" configuration is placed. At the discontinuation of this first exercise, the paper is also removed from the small version of the array; however, if contradictions or inconsistencies are noted prior to the end of this exercise, the small version array would be suspended at that time.

♥ Now, one can enter the normal array, after centering the self, and can initiate deep and circular breathing for several minutes. At this time, a clear mental picture is created which represents the manifestation of the desire [e.g., the precise goal which will be secured, the specific obstacle which will be surmounted, the result which will be obtained, or the definitive idea which will be materialized in objective form]. Recognize that the most concentrated, ardent, and definite mental visualization engenders the most efficient transfer of the desire to the inner self; the higher the degree of authoritative explicitness, the higher the degree of perfection in the communication transfer. The exercise is maintained for at least 30 minutes.

♥ In addition, at least once per day, initiate "harmonious time" in order to acquire additional details related to the actualization of the desire. These details will include, for example, definitive results and possible effects. The configuration is not entered again until the inner self notifies the conscious self that the peripheral considerations have been addressed.

After a desire is communicated to the inner self, send love and thankfulness to the inner self and the conscious self. Note: If the end result of the desire is not obvious at the initiation of this exercise, the array can assist one in recognizing the possibilities and to subsequently crystallize the thought form. One would, however, begin the exercise with a general idea of the path which is preferred and with a partial concept of that which awaits at the end of the journey. Insight, with respect to the precise outcome will be provided during the interval when one is within the array and/or during the subsequent "harmonious times".

Following the culmination of the first exercise, compose [on paper] a description of all of the ideas which are now evident with respect to the general design of the desire, including the peripheral activities and events which transpire in your mental image. Refine the "plan", eliminating that which is superfluous and contradictory and arranging the remaining segments in a logical order. The subsequent result will be ones guide to through which achievement will transpire.

The Second Stage of "Reprogramming" utilization involves the following exercise:

- ♥ The "plan" is studied and is then placed beneath a small version of the "Reprogramming" array.

- ♥ Another message [written] is prepared which states that this desire is precisely that which is requested; it is placed upon the array, with the written words on the same side of the paper which touches the array.

- ♥ Now, one can enter the normal array, after centering the self, and can initiate deep and circular breathing for several minutes.

  At this time, ones "plan" is visualized in all detail, with the self dramatizing the multi-faceted stages required prior to total actualization; one would also emotionally visualize "feeling the feelings" which are anticipated. One vacates the array when the visualization process has been completed.

- ♥ The array is entered and the visualization process is continued daily, in conjunction with visualization during "harmonious time", until the "plan" is totally committed to memory. The "plan" may be removed from the smaller version of the array at this time.

- ♥ After each reprogramming exercise, send love and thankfulness to the inner self and the conscious self.

The preceding "Reprogramming" exercises open the door to the path of opportunity; the unobstructed path to opportunity is always available - the door was installed and has now been removed by ones conscious energy.

When one is at peace with the memorization and total knowledge of each of the desires, continuance to the next array of "Higher Self Affinity" is recommended.

HIGHER SELF AFFINITY

The "Higher Self Affinity" configuration is established by placing the crystals in the pattern of an inverted "L", with three rays initiating at each branch of the "L" [See Figure 81]. The short portion of the "L" initiates above the center of the head and continues toward the left side of the body of the subject. The number of crystals used is left to the intuition of the practitioner.

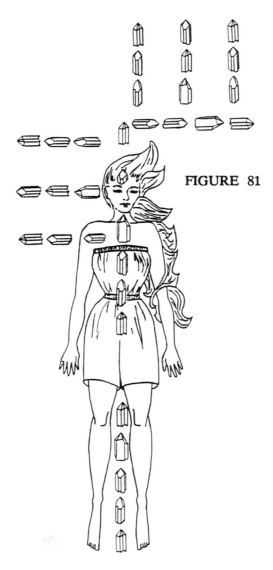

FIGURE 81

This configuration is utilized for dual, yet parallel, purposes. The first objective is to expanding ones communication channel to the Higher Self; the second objective is to instill faith in the self. The first exercise assures the existence of a definite, distinct and available avenue between the Higher Self and the consciousness and inner self.

- ♥ One centers the self, enters the array, and initiates deep circular breathing. A grand and unobstructed passage is visualized which connects the Higher Self with the conscious self and the inner self [the Faden crystal and the fulgurite have enhanced the initiation of this pathway].

- ♥ Next, electromagnetic current [visualized by, for example, clear white rays of light] is envisioned as traveling between the Higher Self, the conscious self, and the inner self. [It is helpful to create a mental picture of the initiating region for each of these selves: an area two-inches below the navel and an area just beneath the solar plexus have both been used successfully in the representation of the home of the inner self; the area of the brain in totality and the area of the crown chakra have both been used successfully in the representation of the conscious self; the area approximately eight-inches above the top of ones head has been used successfully in the representation of the Higher Self.]

The passage can be easily activated via the application of a breathing technique where one visualizes inhaling the life energy of the perfect universe and exhaling the flowing channel connecting the three selves. When the current is flowing freely, one will become aware, usually via an emotional or physical stimulus [e.g., a feeling of clear fresh freedom, a tingling sensation, an invigoration, a impression of warmth, a perception of peace, etc.].

- ♥ After each repetition of this exercise, send love and thankfulness to the inner self, the conscious self, and the Higher Self.

It is recommended that this exercise be repeated for several days prior to initiation of the second exercise. The second exercise involves the recognition and inculcation of ones abiding faith in ones ability to attain the selected desire[s]. Faith and the power of faith is discussed at length in the ancient religious and philosophical doctrines. The amount of faith which one possesses with respect to ones abilities, the more efficient will be the outcome. The degree of strength, conviction, determination, resolution, persistence, and continuity in pursuit determines the success in accomplishment and/or attainment. "Belief" in oneself both mobilizes the conscious self and the inner self to initiate the beginning of those events and conditions which will stimulate the continuance toward manifestation of that which is desired; it further predisposes others to be receptive to, and supportive in, the realization of the desire. The primary objective with the following exercise is to inspire an intuitive perception that ones essential attributes, capabilities, efficiency, and energies are more than sufficient to produce the pre-visioned results. Succinctly, confident anticipation will become a part of ones character, and the laws of attraction and successful achievement will be activated. Faith in the self, with respect to each individual conceived strategy, may be established in the following manner:

♥ One prepares a written message indicating the "belief" in the capabilities of the self to initiate the "plan" and in the subsequent manifestation of same. This missive is placed beneath a smaller version of the "Confidence" array [see page 107, Figure 35].

♥ One then enters the normal array, after centering the self, and initiates deep and circular breathing for several minutes. At this time, a clear mental picture is created which represents faith in oneself; the vision can be the written word which has been placed beneath the small version of "Confidence", a display of the self imparting, to another, information of faith in the self, the repetition of the words similar to those in the children's book "The Little Engine That Could" [i.e., *I know I can ...., I know I can ....]*, etc. The inclusion of that which one "knows one can" do/be [in relation to the conceived strategy] is essential. This activity is continued for at least 30 minutes per day for at least three days, or until verification of faith is received from the inner self.

♥ During the [minimum] three day period, "harmonious time" is initiated and the same process is repeated. This is an excellent time to verbalize ones faith in the self and in the realization of ones desires [e.g., via "mirror talk"]. At the conclusion of this exercise, confidence and faith in the actualization of the "plan" will be assured and fear and worry will have been consumed by trust and surety of purpose.

Verbalization of this faith in the self during lucid communication with another is also recommended in order to speed the process. Recognition that any obstacles which seem to impede progress will diminish with your approach and the pathway to your goal will be unobstructed. After the completion of the exercise, send love and thankfulness to the inner self, the conscious self, and the Higher Self.

The elimination of impoverished thoughts is completed and the birth of confident thoughts has been initiated. After each "plan" is assured confidence in actualization and faith and confidence are deeply implanted with the self, one can explore the avenues of expression through which the Higher Self can expedite the unveiling of the manifestation of ones desires. Remember the aphorism that "belief in the self" is the white magic of ones self-actualization, actualizing that which one desires.

FAR REACH

The "Far Reach" configuration is established by placing the crystals in the pattern shown in Figure 82. This array was adopted from the ancient culture of the Mound Builders of North America; it represents the sum of all of the Higher Selves, the universal benevolent intelligence which will assist one in endeavors. The channels have now been open between the Higher Self and the conscious self and inner self, and faith has been affirmed; now, "Far Reach" will serve to expedite the attainment of ones desires via the utilization of the law of attraction.

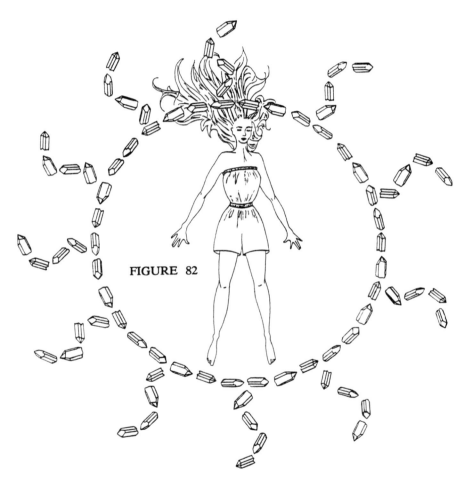

FIGURE 82

The first objective is to define the avenues of expression through which the Higher Self can expedite the unveiling of the manifestation of ones desires. This exercise assists one in yielding to the guidance of the *Infinite Wisdom* during ones travel on the pathway toward the acquisition of that which is chosen.

♥   Two small versions of "Far Reach" are utilized during this exercise: one is placed around a photograph of the self and one is placed upon a written description of the "plan". These two configurations are regarded daily and are permitted to remain in their special location until the desire has been realized.

It should be noted that if the "plan" is consciously modified in any way [e.g., see "The Gate"], one should modify the description of the "plan", remove the outdated "plan" from the array, and place the revised "plan" within the array.

♥   Next, one enters the array after centering the self; deep circular breathing is initiated until one is relaxed and receptive. At this time the intuitive information from the inner self, the illuminating date from the Higher Self, and the intellectual reasoning power of the conscious self are all available and in a state of cohesive cooperation. The law of attraction is now within your direct control and direction.

♥   Envision the "plan" and the results of same, sending the thought currents from the conscious self to the inner self and the Higher Self. This process usually requires approximately thirty-minutes. The concepts and images are transmitted, by a process similar to osmosis, to the *Infinite Wisdom*, through which actualization of ones ambitions can be facilitated; the Faden crystal has enhanced this transmittal.

A vortex has now been established - it surrounds the physical self - and will stimulate ones personal magnetism to attract the "things", persons, circumstances, and conditions which are relative to, and in correlation with, the subject of ones desires. The powerful forces of nature, operating within the consciousness of the *Infinite Wisdom*, are initiated and one is guided and directed toward innovative thoughts, ideas, and strategies, which will lead one in the direction of additional support which will assist in the realization of those insistent desires.

Be attentive to the messages which are given at this time; they are often the initiation of ideas which will further ones "crusade". After the completion of the exercise, send love and thankfulness to the inner self, the conscious self, and the Higher Self. Daily return to "Far Reach" is recommended until the requested result is obtained. "Harmonious time" may also be utilized to further ones venture.

One may progress to "The Gate" at any time after the completion of several experiences of "Far Reach".

THE GATE

"The Gate" configuration is established by placing the crystals in the pattern of four lines, two pillars placed on each side of the subject [See Figure 83].

FIGURE 83

A sphere is placed at the top of each pillar; sugilite, charoite, red hematite, and red jasper spheres have been utilized to enhance the creative actualizations and to bring additional energy to the array; sheen obsidian spheres have provided additional insight to ones desires and to the methods for actualization; rutilated and tourmalinated spheres have promoted depth of perception. The practitioner is encouraged to experiment with a variety of mineralogical spheres. The number of crystals used is left to the intuition of the practitioner.

"The Gate" can be employed after the previous four arrays to impress upon the conscious and inner selves that one does control ones personal reality, and to assist in the maintenance of perseverance and persistence in ones "cause"; it is quite useful for assisting one in recognizing more efficient sub-plans to enhance the attainment of the "true" desire. It can also be utilized, without completing the previous five arrays, to instill tenacity and determination in ones endeavors. It assists one in establishing and exhibiting strength in action and courage and effectiveness in ones life.

The following three applications for "The Gate" have proved to be exceptionally useful to those on the path to the realization of dreams.

Application #1:

Occasionally, the *Infinite Wisdom* may provide for conditions which appear to be strangely indirect with respect to the accomplishment of the goal. In these cases, one may be discouraged and/or it may appear that ones conscious strategies are being overturned and that one is being forced from ones present [and comparatively acceptable] environment; these are the times when "The Gate" can be used to provide impetus to the completion of the cycle:

- ♥ Two small versions of "The Gate" are utilized during this exercise: one is placed around a photograph of the self and one is placed upon a written description of the final desire [including only the preferred end result]. These configurations are regarded daily and are permitted to remain in their special location until the completion of the receipt of insights with respect to the alterations of the sub-plans.

- ♥ One then enters the normal array after centering the self; deep circular breathing is initiated until one is relaxed. Next, one consciously focuses ones thoughts on the end result of that which is desired, believing in the receipt of same, and visualizing the open gate to successful accomplishment. White light is visualized, initiating at the area representing the home of the inner self, and progressing toward the image of the desired end-result. The Faden crystal and the fulgurite have been used during this period to enhance the effects.

- ♥ At this time, insight is presented with respect to modifications of the sub-plans which are a part of the overall "plan", enhancing ones understanding of the "now available" most efficient method for completing that which is necessary for attainment of the desire. The insight also assists one in releasing the disappointments of yesterday, and in inspiring optimistic anticipation for each "tomorrow". The number of days and/or frequency of utilizing "The Gate" for this application is left to the intuition of the user; the employment of "harmonious time" is also recommended.

The array has also been placed to surround the sleeping area, stimulating explicit dreaming and providing insight to the actions which will further ones desires.

After any message has been received, send love and thankfulness to the *Infinite Wisdom* and, when applicable, review and modify the contents of the missive which is placed within the "Far Reach" array. It is recommended that one recognizes that those events and conditions which one may fear, or about which one may worry, will not occur if one places trust in the *Infinite Wisdom* and passes through "The Gate".

Application #2:

This exercise can be used to assist in the transmittal of consciously reinforcement of the desire to the inner self, the Higher Self, and the *Infinite Wisdom*.

- ♥ Two small versions of "The Gate" are utilized during this exercise: one is placed around a photograph of the self and one is placed upon a written description of the "plan", including all of the sub-plans. These configurations are regarded daily and are permitted to remain in their special location until the desire has been realized.

- ♥ Next, one enters the array after centering the self; deep circular breathing is initiated until one is relaxed. Next, one visualizes each of the sub-plans, in succession, envisioning the transfer of each sub-plan to the Higher Self via the channels which were previously opened by the "Higher Self Affinity" array. The image of each sub-plan is intuitively perceived as traveling, from the conscious and inner selves, through the white light of a tributary channel until it reaches the Higher Self.

- ♥ After each sub-plan has been transmitted, the "grand finale" is dispatched through the main channel to the Higher Self. Having relayed all portions of the "plan" to the Higher Self, one shifts from the "personal" view to an "impersonal" view and utilizes the imagination to observe the effects the "plan" will have upon others, the responses which will be issued by others. This visualization assists one in testing the hypothesis that the desire is, in fact, desirable.

♥ Any modifications or additions which are necessary to the plans will be obvious during the "impersonal" viewing of same.

After the information has been received, send love and thankfulness to the inner self, the conscious self, the Higher Self, and *Infinite Wisdom* and, when applicable, review and modify the contents of the missive which is placed within the "Far Reach" array.

Application #3:

This exercise can be used to further the actualization of ones desires.

♥ One enters the array after centering the self and initiates deep circular breathing until one is relaxed. Next, focusing on the third eye, allow the self to become the witness of the thoughts which flow through the mind. One will become no longer ones thoughts [e.g., pain, anger, etc.], but will the witness to the condition which is in the thoughts and will encounter the condition philosophically and impartially. Allow those thoughts which are self-limiting to float out of the mind; instill the concept of peace.

♥ Continue deep circular breathing, visualizing the intake of the vitality of the universe. Allow the essence of this vitality to completely fill the body and mind; it is usually perceived as a continuing flow of pulsing golden light, filling ones totality with purity and freshness. Envision the flow of energy coursing through the body, activating and passing through the crown chakra to operate as a fountain of perfection, showering its energy over body, mind, and spirit, and refreshing the self with inner re-birth.

♥ Focus at the third-eye and imagine that which is your desire. Focused at the third-eye, with the golden vitality surging through ones body, the imagination becomes dynamic and influential.

It is interesting to "watch" the results of this exercise. Testing has shown that when one is visualizing with the attention at the area of the third-eye, the results are actualized in an expedient manner. When one is not focused on the third-eye, that which is imagined is, occasionally, actualized; when this occurs, it is interesting to note that ones attention was, in fact, near the area of the third-eye.

Application #4:

The following exercise has been utilized to facilitate the meeting of, and/or to further communication with, ones spiritual guide[s]:

- A photograph of the self is placed within a smaller version of the array. This acts to initiate further protection in the light and love of the universe.

- After centering the self, one enters "The Gate". Deep circular breathing is initiated.

- One now visualizes a grand version of ones "favorite" crystal [an extremely powerful protective mechanism] located on the spiritual plane. One progresses to the interior of the crystal, envisioning comfortable conditions [e.g., a beautiful lush garden, the top of a mountain, the serenity of the autumn, the vitality of the ocean], and establishes a comfortable location in which to await the arrival of ones guide.

- When the guide materializes, an effusion of energy usually fills the subject. At this time, introduction of the self is recommended [this assists in the relaxation of "formality programming"]. Communication will ensue and one will emotionally understand that the guide is a "best friend". The sojourn may continue indefinitely; one usually terminates the visitation with a verbalized intention to meet again at a future time [either specified or unspecified].

- After the meeting is concluded, one returns to "The Gate".

One may return to within the array whenever, and as frequently, as is desired. Visualization of a different "favorite" crystal located at the end of the center ray of energy has facilitated the encounter of other guides. It is recommended that one visualizes the same "favorite" crystal each time contact with the same guide is desired.

May you proceed through the "Gateless-Gate, achieving control of your reality and actualizing your desires in the light of love and brotherhood with self-fulfillment ♥

APPENDIX A

MINERALOGICAL UPDATE

AN IMPORTANT NUTRITIONAL ELEMENT
WHICH IS CONSUMED
FOR ONES HEALTH
IS COMPRISED OF
NEW IMPRESSIONS TO STIMULATE
AND NOURISH THE SPIRIT

MINERALOGICAL UPDATE

The following information is provided in supplement to this book in order to furnish the reader with additional details relevant to the practice of crystallography.

"NEW" MINERALS

Quartz Faden Crystal   [Astrological Sign of Scorpio]

The Quartz Faden [pronounced as "Fah-den"] crystal is one in which the inclusion of one or more white thread-like fibrous formations of quartz occurs. The name "Faden" is derived from the German translation of "thread". If more than one fiber is encompassed, the fibers are separate from each other. The Faden is visible [as a white thread or fiber] within the quartz structure because it is surrounded by either a fluid-filled or gaseous-filled chamber. The fiber is located [usually] at, or in proximity to, the center of the crystal; the geometrical location is perpendicular to the termination of the crystal and may be linear and undeviating or curved/bent. Faden crystals have been found only in the fissures of metamorphic formations; unlike other quartz crystals, they do not form in pegmatite or in cavities of sedimentary rocks.

Since several of the arrays within this guidebook have recommended the utilization of the Faden crystal, a brief description of the attributes [which are in addition to those given for Quartz in **Love Is In The Earth - A Kaleidoscope Of Crystals**] are given below.

The Faden crystal is one of *connection*, stimulating and furthering connective forces between the self and that which is chosen as the recipient. Delineation of many methods of unification are given within the description of the preceding arrays.

This crystal facilitates the attunement between the self and another, similar to the action produced by the Herkimer diamond. It assists in producing and maintaining the ethereal connection which one has with another [on any planes, in all dimensions].

It is also a stone for astral travel and for the exploration of the parallel dimensions of ones reality. It strengthens the "silver cord" and produces an energy which both promotes and protects one during flight. [It is also currently being used as a protective crystal for those engaged in air travel.]

In the exploration of parallel dimensions and other planes of existence, it stimulates the opening of the pathway and assists one in remembering the activities which one experiences and/or views as a non-participant. It has been used for past-life ascension, allowing one to maintain a strong-hold on the present reality while observing, without participating in, the events which one accesses; it further provides an understanding of the lessons which were [or could have been] learned, such that one may continue progression beyond the limitations of the lesson.

It is a stone for finding ones complement on the physical plane, serving as a magnetic field to attract ones counterpart and to facilitate an unfathomable energy transfer between the self and the other. The Faden crystal may be programmed to assist in bringing to one that which is desired.

It can be used to promote physical, mental, and emotional stability. It is an excellent stone for centering the self and for gridding disturbed areas of the Earth. It has been used in classrooms [similarly to the utilization of Lepidolite] in order to facilitate a stability within the environment. It has also been used to grid [via photograph and through actual physical placement] areas of the Earth which are prone to unsteadiness.

It provides for a continuous [when in ones energy field] alignment of the physical meridians and the nervous system, and for the alignment of the physical, emotional, mental, etheric, astral, etc., bodies, singularly and with one another.

It can be used to cleanse the aura and to stimulate the opening of the chakras.

The structure which exhibits a curved or bent thread-like fiber emanates a gentle, yet powerful, energy and can be used to promote flexibility in ones attitudes, and to provide strength to ones decisions. It allows one to see the inner workings of any situation and to understand the superficial and the deeper meanings inherent in same. It also allows one to access the interior of the physical body in order to understand existing disorders, providing information with respect to the "fix".

It is a stone of "seeking", assisting one in "ferreting-out" information which is either hidden or unknown. It is an excellent stone for future-telling and telepathic activities. It is also quite conducive to the furtherance of ones meditative state, serving to diminish attentiveness to distractions, and to foster the maintenance of same.

The energy of the Faden crystal serves to stimulate molecular bonding and is, hence, applicable to both superficial and internal healing of cellular loss of integrity and cellular abrasion. It is a stone which facilitates "mending" on all levels, assisting one to trace ones actions/belief systems back to the original cause of a disorder, and subsequently, promoting the restoration of same.

The crystals which exhibit the bent or curved faden can also be used in the treatment of disorders relating to inflexibility; they serve to stimulate ones adroitness and dexterity. The crystals containing the linear faden can also act to strengthen, and to ameliorate dysfunctional conditions of, the spine.

An elixir constituting the application of the energies of the Faden crystal can be used to further all of the actions listed above.

Vibrates to the number 2 and the master number 88.

Chevron Amethyst   [Astrological Sign of All]

Amethyst is a variety of quartz which occurs [throughout the world] either in crystalline or massive form. It was discussed in length in **Love Is In The Earth - A Kaleidoscope Of Crystals**. The Chevron Amethyst is of the variety exhibiting one of the deepest colours of the purple hue. There are two primary structures of the chevron - one structure exhibits a chevron of two or more colours [purple and rusty/rose-red/orange/yellow], with additional hues; and, one structure features a chevron containing several hues of purple. It is found in Siberia and in India. Since several of the arrays within this guidebook have recommended the utilization of the Chevron Amethyst, a brief description of the attributes are given below.

In addition to the properties of amethyst which have been previously discussed, this mineralogical formation possesses the energies which allow it to be represented as one of the finest third-eye stones, stimulating vision into unknown realms both within the self and into the exterior worlds.

It can also be used to facilitate both the perception and the interpretation of the aura, assisting in diagnostic techniques and in the furtherance of auric cleansing. It emanates a concentrated energy, allowing for direction such that a larger area than is usual [with terminated crystals] is impacted. The forceful, yet subtle, rays provide for clearing of the aura and for the release and dissipation of negativity. The enhancement of the aura has been shown by Kirlian photography. After the utilization of this stone to cleanse ones aura, one can, literally, become absorbed in the light of its radiance. It further stimulates the "brighter" aspect of the individual, as well as encouraging the emanating warmth and the purity of love within ones being.

Placement of the Chevron Amethyst on a chakra serves to release the tensions of that chakra and to further energize the areas which have heretofore been static.

It is an excellent stone for journeying and for inner-self evaluation and evolution. It brings one the strength and the loving essence to continue in any and all pursuits. It is an energy for psychic research, assisting one to transport and to retrieve [on both the tangible and intangible levels] patterns of force, movement, and space-time relationships. It also allows one to re-trace any negative energies which attempt to penetrate ones protective shield, providing information with respect to the reasons for, and the origin of, the negativity.

It stimulates the understanding of a positive answer to any imaginable problem, assisting one in the selection of the resolution, which would best be suited to ones purpose, and to the doctrine of universal love. It also assists in the implementation of same, bringing forth a perceptible manifestation. It has been called the "breath of life", assisting one to actualize that which is required for personal and universal development.

The Chevron Amethyst allows one to gain knowledge in the arts of spiritual healing; it furthers ones acceptance of the unseen forces which are available to complete the actions to facilitate the perfect state. Carried upon ones person, it can act to repel negativity.

It assists one in the application of the central unity of all religions, all men/women - all of existence. It helps one to understand the abstract forms of ones being and to develop the "resistance to resistance" via the total release of resistance.

With this larger forcefield, the Chevron Amethyst can affect a greater area and can stimulate the emergence of a synthesis between the various organs in the body. It assists the members of the body to act in a cooperative manner, bringing balance to the structure and autonomic and sympathetic nervous systems and the generative systems. It has been used successfully to eliminate headaches, pain, symptoms of viral and infectious dis-ease. It can be used in the treatment of disorders of the lungs, the intestines, the pancreas, and the liver. It further acts to stimulate the thymus and the immune system. It has also been used [via placement upon the closed eyes] to increase the proper functioning of the eyes.

Vibrates to the number 7.

Electric-Blue Sheen Obsidian [Astrological Sign of Sagittarius]

The following properties are in addition to those listed for obsidian in **Love Is In The Earth - A Kaleidoscope Of Crystals.**

Electric-blue sheen obsidian a black obsidian which contains a radiance of electric-blue, ranging from a powder blue [sometimes with a powder pink] to a deep indigo blue. It is an excellent stone for "gazing" and for "journeying". It has also been applied extensively in many of the lay-outs which have been reported within the text of this guidebook.

Used alone, it further assists one in accessing the bases of any difficulties which one is experiencing. It emits an energy conducive to balance the energy fields [personal and those with which one experiences contact] and to assist in the suspension of actions which are ineffectual and/or unavailing.

In "gazing" activities it has been applied to the shamanic and the healing arts, providing for the recognition of the areas within the emotional, physical, and/or intellectual bodies which are creating dysfunctional events/conditions. It further acts to cleanse the mind of contrary and dissenting thoughts of the self and of others, assisting in the promotion of patience and tolerance.

"Electric-blue", configured into spherical formations has served to enhance the activities of "gazing" and "journeying"; the energy transfer, being simultaneously in all directions, has easily facilitated the trance state, and has enhanced all activities associated with psychic communication, astral travel, future-telling, and past-life ascension. It has also promoted a direct access to communication with those of other planetary realms, providing for a direct link to those which whom one *needs* contact.

It is an excellent third-eye stone, stimulating visionary experiences and providing for the activation and energizing of the third-eye chakra. It assists one in traveling deeply within the inner being and in maintaining the depth while integrating the myriad of visual images which are made available. It assists the energy from the third-eye to be transported throughout the body, producing an intuitive understanding of the complete cellular structure.

"Electric-blue" stimulates intuition and enhances awareness. It provides for freedom in accessing pre-determined sites during astral travel and assists one in both lucid dreaming and dream recall. It is an excellent grounding stone [when consciously applied to that purpose]. It has also been applied to the amplification of the auric field, and, via testing with Kirlian photography, has been shown to increase the range and to both intensify and brighten the energies.

It can be used in the application of radionic techniques, enhancing the attunement of the radionics operator and the subject, and enabling the user to more easily recognize the response.

Used as a pendulum, during diagnostic research, the energy of the mineral acts to interfere with the energy of the user and indicates the areas which are involved, as well as, the problems which are implicated [the recognition of the problems is usually expedient].

At this time, spherical configurations have been used primarily in all applications; the smaller pieces of the mineral, when fashioned for the third-eye and additional chakra locations, also work quite well. Jewelry has also been created which includes the "Electric Blue" - wearing the mineral assists one in maintaining a protective field which not only shields one from negativity, but also transforms any negativity to either a positive "thing" or to that which is both meaningless and harmless.

The mineral is of immense benefit in furthering the receptivity of the subject during healing exercises.

It has been used in the treatment of disorders of spinal alignment and to ameliorate the arrangement of impaired vertebrae. It has been used in the treatment of circulatory disorders, to disseminate and disperse growths, to ameliorate toxicity, to enhance and strengthen the structure of the veins, and to allay spasmatic conditions. It can also be used to improve the eyesight; an elixir, taken internally, is recommended for this application. "Electric-blue" is currently being applied to deficient immune systems and dysfunctional cellular structures. Additional applications are currently in the experimental stages.

Vibrates to the number 7.

Nephrite-Quartz   [Astrological Sign of All]

This mineralogical combination was previously reported in **Love Is In The Earth - A Kaleidoscope of Crystals** in the section designated as "Nephrite", subsection designation "Quartz Crystals/Structures within Nephrite". Nephrite-Quartz combines the qualities of quartz and nephrite, and, in addition to the utilization of this mineral in the arrays listed within this book, the further research which has been accomplished is reported below.

Nephrite, a form of jade, is comprised of jade and actinolite. The occurrence of the quartz crystals and quartz crystal structures within the green nephrite is uncommon; the quartz crystal structures have been seen to occur in a state where nephrite replaces the quartz crystal, leaving the outline of the quartz crystal [or a portion of the crystal] as a pattern within the mass.

This combined configuration is one of the "GRAND FORMATIONS", combining the properties, of both the quartz crystal and the structure, totally within the nephrite. The crystals within the nephrite were used in both Lemurian and Atlantian healing ceremonies and retain the records of both the knowledge of use and the methods of facilitation leading to results. This unification of nephrite and quartz will be made available to those who are to work with these advanced energies.

This combination is a catalyst to the acceleration of growth and to the re-awakening and remembering of those with whom one has been closely connected in "previous" lives. It helps one to transcend the third dimension, and to resonate in harmony with the self and with others. It assists one in uniting with the brothers and sisters of this dimension, with those from the realms of the spiritual and astral spaces, and with those from the stars; during these activities, the supreme energies are synthesized to produce the dazzling golden/white radiance of the enlightened state and the shared essence of the heart of the life force.

It further assists one in acknowledging the self as an integral part of the perfection of "All That Is", providing for the empowerment to foster progress toward fulfillment, in love and clarity, of ones final destinies. It has also been called a "stone of luck", assisting one in gaining that which is necessary for ones progression.

The quartz crystals within the nephrite can be likened to arrows of light, assisting one to progress on the path toward the enlightenment of the entire planetary body. The energy of the structure acts as a well-traveled guide, providing mythical arms to encompass all knowledge leading to wisdom. It is an excellent stone for meditation, assisting in ease of entry to, and maintenance of, the meditative state. It has consistently been used, during the planetary convergences toward love and brotherhood, to promote connected-ness between the self and others; it enhances the transmission of loving energy and healing to the world. It further marks the end of separation and denial.

It has been used to remove unwanted implants, concurrently healing breaches within the chakra system and filling the voids which remain after the removal of the implant, with the healing light of love.

The Nephrite-Quartz structure is considered a "stone of the seventh mansion", expediting meditative travel to the realm of "all knowing". It shows one the pathway to higher bliss, providing access to heightened energies which can be used to propel the self into the higher dimensional awareness; this plane of awareness yielding a limitless zone of silence containing greater peace and unity than one has ever known. It is a stone of love and blessings, bringing the positive attributes of the universe to ones life and assisting one in both self-love and other-love. It promotes self-esteem and the culmination of cooperation between the self and others.

The ancient cultures of Indians and tribal natives are said to have used the energies of this structure in shamanic ceremonies to remove the cause of dis-ease. In addition, this mineral has been used in entity detachment and in shamanic ceremonies to heal the inner being. It is an excellent stone for the third-eye, initiating intuitive communication and promoting the sending and the receipt of telepathic messages. The medicine wheel concept, combined with Nephrite-Quartz, has acted as protection, has introduced desired "contact renewal", and has delivered an energy of healing which is both smooth and gradual [i.e., no trauma associated].

Nephrite-Quartz has been used in diagnostic activities and is an excellent stone for facilitation of regeneration and recovery. It can be used to stimulate the thymus and in the treatment of trauma and in the alleviation of disorders of the heart, lungs, arteries, the cerebrum and cerebellum, the eyes, and the emotions. It has provided a beneficial energy in the treatment of disorders of the kidneys and the pancreas, and in the amelioration of water retention.

The Nephrite-Quartz structure vibrates to the number 9.

BEAUTIFY THOUGHT
BEAUTIFY LANGUAGE
BEAUTIFY HEART
BEAUTIFY ENVIRONMENT

APPENDIX B

MASTER NUMBERS

Each time I give something,
I do it freely and willingly.
There are no expectations
of something in return,
for it is in the giving
that I receive my fulfillment.
The INTENT of the give-away
is the GIFT.
The gift that I have given
cannot be returned to me
in any way at all.
If I receive a gift
from the one to whom I gave
it is their gift that they give
and it is given in their way,
whatever that may be.
They alone place the limit
on the fulfillment they receive
in their give-away.
I am thankful and blessed
for the many opportunities
given to me to grow fully
in a free and willing way.

Leroy Anderson
Arizona, USA
1990

MASTER NUMBERS

Supplementary to the doubling of the effects of the qualities attributable to the numbers from one to nine, the "Master Numbers" also possess distinct properties. The following information is given to provide the user with additional details relevant to "Master Numbers".

Master Number 11: The connection between "brotherhood" and "sisterhood" is combined to reflect the androgynous and spiritual connection between all which exists, which has ever existed, and which will ever exist. The concept that "*I am also a you*" is reflected in the "eleven" vibration.

Master Number 22: Actualization of the God within the self, recognition that God is in the totality of existence, and understanding of the God outside of the self, produce a combined vibration in "realization" of the self, of others, and of the whole. The concept of the parallel dimensions with respect to the four cardinal directions is reflected in the "twenty-two" vibration.

Master Number 33: Power over the total physical realm is revealed and the application of same is facilitated. Understanding of the "right time" is expedited and the act of non-action is furthered; patience is a keyword. The concept of ease in actualization and the understanding of the abstraction of manifestation is reflected in the "thirty-three" vibration.

Master Number 44: Metamorphosis and continued change throughout all times is concentrated with determination of both the acceleration and the ease of reformation of the self. The concepts of impetus and catalytic motion are reflected in the "forty-four" vibration.

Master Number 55: The extension of occurrences to facilitate knowledge with ease is advanced such that approach to each event/condition/experience is with absolute precision and beneficial construction. The concept of approach via strategic techniques is reflected in the "fifty-five" vibration.

Master Number 66: Arrangement of the divine order of personal life, the sacred order upon, and within, the Earth, and the celestial order of the universe, is facilitated. The concepts of organization and systematic resolutions, and the implementation of same, are reflected in the "sixty-six" vibration.

Master Number 77: Transcendence of the creation of advancement combines the energies of non-restriction with the application of a devoted stamina. The synthesis of the vibratory messages of "twenty-two" and our Mother Earth and Father Sky brings the correspondence to consummation of all within each dimension. The concept of wholeness in entirety is reflected in the "seventy-seven" vibration.

Master Number 88: The elevation of the personal and the infinite consciousness is facilitated to encompass the actuality of "knowing" <u>and</u> the receipt of meaningful, revealing, and significant revelations [and implementation of same] with respect to ones unlimited and unrestricted capabilities. The concepts of sensitivity and compassion, with the experiencing of each moment, is reflected in the "eighty-eight" vibration.

Master Number 99: Revolution and evolution on all levels are expedited and a comprehension of the appropriate paths to completion is imparted. Flexibility in consciousness and in the unification of past, present, and future actions gains appreciation. The concept of supple adaption to facilitate the integration of all which has transpired, is transpiring, and will transpire, is reflected in the ninety-nine" vibration.

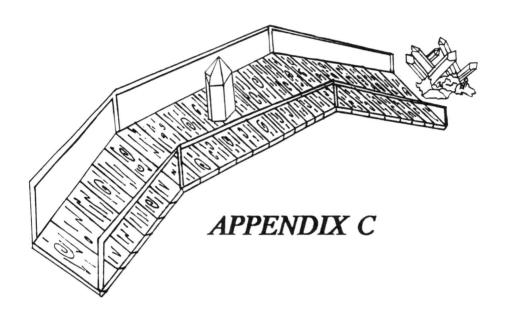

APPENDIX C

CROSS-REFERENCE INDEX

THE UNIVERSE IS PERFECT -
*EVERYTHING HAPPENS AT THE **RIGHT** TIME ♥!♥*
TODAY, AND EVERY DAY, EVERYTHING
*IS POSSIBLE FOR **YOU**!*

CROSS-REFERENCE INDEX
ZODIACAL DESIGNATIONS - MINERALOGICAL ASSOCIATION

This cross-reference index has been developed from the astrological sign designations which were described for each mineral in **Love Is In The Earth - A Kaleidoscope Of Crystals.** Please note that some minerals are related to more than one astrological sign.

ARIES [CONT.]

PITCH
PYROMORPHITE
QUARTZ
RAMSDELLITE
SARCOLITE
SARDONYX
SILLIMANITE
SPINEL - ELEMENTAL
SPINEL - ORANGE
STILBITE
TEKTITE
TEPHROITE
THENARDITE
TOURMALINE - BROWN
  [DRAVIDE]
WILKEITE
ZARATITE
  [EMERALD NICKEL]

CANCER

ADAMITE
ADULARIA
AGATE - TURRITELLA
ANALCIME
ANHYDRITE
AUGELITE
BASALT
BLOEDITE
BORNITE
  [PEACOCK ROCK]
BROOKITE
CALCITE
CAPPELENITE
CARNELIAN
  [SARD]
CHALCEDONY -
  ELEMENTAL
CORAL - PINK
CHEVRON AMETHYST
CUSPIDINE
ENHYDRO
ERIONITE
FERSMANNITE
GOYAZITE
GROSSULAR GARNET
HALITE
ILVAITE
IRIDOSMINE
KATOPHORITE
LEAD
LEAVERITE
LEIFITE

CANCER [CONT.]

LINARITE
MARBLE
METEORITE
MOLDAVITE
MOONSTONE
MORDENITE
MULLITE
NADORITE
NATROLITE
NEPHRITE-QUARTZ
NISSONITE
OPAL - ELEMENTAL
OPAL - FIRE
OPAL - WATER
ORTHOCLASE -
  ELEMENTAL
PEARL
PHILLIPSITE
PYROPE
QUARTZ
RALSTONITE
RASPITE
ROSELITE
RUBY
SILVER
SPINEL - BROWN
SVABITE
TARBUTTITE
TEKTITE
VALENTINITE
XANTHOCONITE

CAPRICORN

AGATE - DRY-HEAD
AMETHYST
ANTHROPHYLLITE
ARAGONITE
AUGITE
AZURITE-MALACHITE
BRAZILIANITE
CAT'S EYE
CORAL - BLACK
CHEVRON AMETHYST
CRISTOBALITE
CUPRITE
CYLINDRITE
ERYTHRITE
FLUORITE
FOURMARIERITE
GALENA
GARNET - ELEMENTAL
HARMOTOME

CAPRICORN [CONT.]

IDOCRASE
  [VESUVIANITE]
JASPER - ORBICULAR
JET
LEAD
LEAVERITE
LEIFITE
MAGNETITE
MALACHITE
MATLOCKITE
METEORITE
MIMETITE
MOLDAVITE
NEPHRITE-QUARTZ
NORTHUPITE
PARACELSIAN
PUMICE
QUARTZ
QUARTZITE
ROSCHERITE
SAPPHIRE - STAR
SMOKEY QUARTZ
  [CARNIGORM]
STIBIOTANTALITE
STIBNITE
TELLURIUM
TIGER EYE
TOURMALINE - GREEN
TOURMALINE - BLACK
  [SCHORL]
  [APHRIZITE]
TRILOBITE
VESZELYITE
WOODWARDITE

GEMINI

AGATE - ELEMENTAL
AGATE - DENDRITIC
ANTLERITE
APATITE
APOPHYLLITE
AQUAMARINE
BABINGTONITE
BERZELIITE
BUTLERITE
CAFARSITE
CAPPELENITE
CELESTITE
CHEVRON AMETHYST
CHROMITE
CHRYSOCOLLA
CITRINE

GEMINI [CONT.]
CRYOLITE
CYMOPHANE
EMERALD
EPIDOTE
ERYTHROSIDERITE
ETTRINGITE
FAUJASITE
FRANKLINITE
LECHATELIERITE
  [NATURAL GLASS]
HARMOTOME
HORNEBLENDE
HOWLITE
HYDROZINCITE
JADE
JASPER - BRUNO
JEREMEJEVITE
KOLBECKITE
LAZULITE
LEAVERITE
LEGRANDITE
LODESTONE
MELIPHANE
METEORITE
MOLDAVITE
NEPHRITE-QUARTZ
NORDENSKIOLDINE
OBSIDIAN - GREEN
OLIGOCLASE -
  ELEMENTAL
OPAL - DENDRITIC
PACHNOLITE
PEARL
PETZITE
PHENACITE
QUARTZ
RUTILE
SALESITE
SANDSTONE
SAPPHIRE - BLUE
SAPPHIRE - GREEN
SERPENTINE
SPHALERITE
  [BLENDE]
SPINEL - BLUE
STILLWELLITE
TANZANITE
THOMSONITE
THULITE
TOPAZ - "RUTILATED"
TOURMALINE -
  WATERMELON
TREMOLITE

GEMINI [CONT.]
TSUMEBITE
ULEXITE
  [T-V ROCK]
VALENTINITE
VARISCITE
WAKEFIELDITE
WILLEMITE
WOLFRAMITE
ZOISITE

LEO
AGATE - ELLENSBURG
  BLUE
AGATE - LAKE
  SUPERIOR
AMBER
ARTHURITE
ASH - VOLCANIC
AZULICITE
BERYL - GOLDEN
BOJI STONE
BOLIVARITE
BRAUNITE
BRAVOITE
CALAVERITE
CARNELIAN
  [SARD]
CHERT
  [HORNSTONE]
CHEVRON AMETHYST
CHILDRENITE
CHRYSOBERYL
CINNABAR
CITRINE
COBALTITE
DANBURITE
DIAMOND
DOUGLASITE
DUMORTIERITE
EOSPHORITE
FILLOWITE
FORSTERITE
GARNET - ELEMENTAL
GOLD
GRANDIDIERITE
GREENOCKITE
HELIODOR
HOMILITE
HUMMERITE
IRIDOSMINE
IRON
JASPER - ELEMENTAL

LEO [CONT.]
JASPER - PICTURE
JASPER - ROYAL
  PLUME
KUNZITE
LABRADORITE
  [SPECTROLITE]
LANTHANITE
LAUBMANNITE
LEAVERITE
LIMB CAST
LINNAEITE
MARCASITE
MESOLITE
METEORITE
MOLDAVITE
MOSANDRITE
NEPHRITE-QUARTZ
OBSIDIAN - RED &
  BLACK
OBSIDIAN - RED
ONYX
OPAL - ELEMENTAL
OPAL - FIRE
OPAL - GOLDEN
OPALIZED NATURE
PECTOLITE
  [LARIMAR STONE]
PERIDOT
  [CHRYSOLITE]
  [OLIVINE]
PETRIFIED WOOD
PIETERSITE
PLANCHEITE
PLATINUM
PROUSTITE
  [RUBY SILVER]
PYRITE
PYROMORPHITE
PYROPE
QUARTZ
RHODOCHROSITE
RHODOLITE
RICKARDITE
RUBY
SAPPHIRE - YELLOW
SAPPHIRE - GREEN
SPINEL - YELLOW
SULPHUR
SUNSTONE
TIGER IRON
TOPAZ - GOLDEN
TOURMALINE -
  YELLOW

LEO [CONT.]
TOURMALINE -
   YELLOW
   [PERIDOT OF
   CEYLON]
   [TSILASITE]
TOURMALINE -
   ORANGE
TUGTUPITE
TUNGSTENITE
WADEITE
WHITLOCKITE
WITHERITE
XONOTLITE
ZIRCON

LIBRA
AGATE - ORBICULAR
AMETRINE
APOPHYLLITE
ARTINITE
BAVENITE
BEAVERITE
BITYITE
BLOODSTONE
   [HELIOTROPE]
BUSTAMITE
CHEVRON AMETHYST
CHIASTOLITE
   [CROSS STONE]
CHRYSOPRASE
CITRINE
CORAL - RED
DAMSONITE
DAPHNITE
DUMONTITE
ERYTHROSIDERITE
EUCHROITE
GOSHENITE
GRANITE
HEINRICHITE
HEMIMORPHITE
HOPEITE
HORNEBLENDE
HYPERSTHENE
   [EULITE]
IOLITE
   [CORDIERITE]
JADE
JOAQUINITE
KATOPHORITE
KOLBECKITE
KYANITE

LIBRA [CONT.]
LEAVERITE
LEPIDOLITE
LEUCOPHOENICITE
MESOLITE
METEORITE
MIXITE
MOLDAVITE
MOONSTONE
MORDENITE
MORGANITE
NEPHRITE
NEPHRITE-QUARTZ
NORDENSKIOLDINE
OBSIDIAN -
   MAHOGANY
OBSIDIAN - RAINBOW
OPAL - GOLDEN
OPAL - WHITE
OPAL - PINK
OPAL - COMMON
   [POTCH]
PECOS DIAMOND
PENNINITE
PREHNITE
QUARTZ
RIEBECKITE
ROSE QUARTZ
SAPPHIRE -
   ELEMENTAL
SAPPHIRE - WHITE
SCHEELITE
SERENDIBITE
SIMPSONITE
SPHAEROCOBALTITE
SPINEL - GREEN
SUNSTONE
TAAFFEITE
TANZANITE
TIN
TOUCHSTONE
TOURMALINE -
   ELEMENTAL
TOURMALINE - LIGHT
   PINK
   [ELBAITE]
TOURMALINE - BLUE
   [INDICOLITE]
RUBELLITE &
   LEPIDOLITE
TREMOLITE
TRIPHYLIT
TRIPLIODITE
WAGNERITE

LIBRA [CONT.]
WOHLERITE
WOLFRAMITE
ZINCITE

PISCES
AGATE - BLUE-LACE
ANGLESITE
ANHYDRITE
AQUAMARINE
BIEBERITE
BIXBYITE
BLOODSTONE
   [HELIOTROPE]
CALEDONITE
CARROLLITE
CHEVRON AMETHYST
CHINESE WRITING
   ROCK
CONICHALCITE
CORAL - ELEMENTAL
CORAL - WHITE
COWRIE
DAVYNE
DIABANTITE
ENARGITE
ENHYDRO
ERIONITE
FLUORITE
GISMONDINE
GMELINITE
HALITE
JOAQUINITE
KAMMERERITE
KAOLINITE
LAMPROPHYLLITE
LAZURITE
LEAVERITE
LINARITE
MESSELITE
MITRIDATITE
MOLDAVITE
NADORITE
NATROLITE
NATROPHYLLITE
NEPHRITE-QUARTZ
NEPTUNITE
NORDENSKIOLDINE
NORTHUPITE
OPAL - ELEMENTAL
OPAL - FIRE
QUARTZ
SENARMONITE

PISCES [CONT.]
SHELL
SMITHSONITE
STAUROLITE
TAVORITE
TOPAZ - GOLDEN
TREMOLITE
TREVORITE
TURQUOISE
VAUXITE
VERDITE
WITHERITE
WOODWARDITE

SAGITTARIUS
AGATE - BOTRYOIDAL
  BLACK
AGATE - FLAME
AGATE - IRIS
AGATE - WOODWARD
  RANCH PLUME
ALABASTER
AVOGADRITE
AZULICITE
AZURITE
AZURITE-MALACHITE
BRANDTITE
BUNSENITE
CASSITERITE
  [TINSTONE]
CATLINITE
CHALCEDONY -
  ELEMENTAL
CHAROITE
CHEVRON AMETHYST
CHLORITE -
  ELEMENTAL
COOKEITE
COPPER
CORAL - BLUE
CORUNDUM -
  ELEMENTAL
COVELLITE
DANALITE
DIOPTASE
DUNDASITE
ELIAT STONE
EPISTILBITE
EUCLASE
GANOPHYLLITE
GAUDEFROYITE
GEHLENITE
GENTHELVITE

SAGITTARIUS [CONT.]
HERKIMER DIAMOND
HEULANDITE
HOLDENITE
HYPERSTHENE
  [EULITE]
IDOCRASE
  [VESUVIANITE]
ILMENITE
IOLITE
  [CORDIERITE]
IVORY
JASPER - BAT CAVE
LABRADORITE
  [SPECTROLITE]
LAPIS LAZULI
LAZULITE
LAZURITE
LEAVERITE
MANGANOSITE
METEORITE
MOHAWKITE
MOLDAVITE
NEPHRITE-QUARTZ
NUUMMIT
OBSIDIAN -
  ELEMENTAL
OBSIDIAN - BLACK
OBSIDIAN - RED &
  BLACK
OBSIDIAN - GREY
OBSIDIAN - BROWN
OBSIDIAN - ELECTRIC-
  BLUE SHEEN
OBSIDIAN - SILVER
  SHEEN
OBSIDIAN - GOLD
  SHEEN
OKENITE
OPAL - FIRE
OPAL - PINK
OPAL - BLACK
OPAL - HONDURAN
OWYHEEITE
PALLADIUM
PAPAGOITE
PERIDOT
  [CHRYSOLITE]
  [OLIVINE]
PETOSKEY STONE
POWELLITE
PSILOMELANE
PYROMORPHITE
QUARTZ

SAGITTARIUS [CONT.]
RICHTERITE
RUBY
RHYOLITE
SAINFELDITE
SAPPHIRE -
  ELEMENTAL
SAPPHIRE - BLACK
SAPPHIRE - STAR
SAPPHIRE - INDIGO
SENARMONITE
SHATTUCKITE
SMOKEY QUARTZ
  [CARNIGORM]
SODALITE
SONOLITE
SPHENE
SPINEL - ELEMENTAL
SPINEL - DARK BLUE
SPINEL -
  "COLOURLESS"
STEATITE
  [SOAPSTONE]
STRENGITE
TANZANITE
THAUMASITE
THOREAULITE
TIN
TOPAZ - ELEMENTAL
TOPAZ - BLUE
TOPAZ - GOLDEN
TOPAZ - "RUTILATED"
TOURMALINE -
  RUBELLITE
  [RED-RED/VIOLET]
  [DEEP PINK]
TRIPLIODITE
TSAVORITE
TURQUOISE
WULFENITE
ZIRCON
ZUNYITE

SCORPIO
ACTINOLITE
AGATE - BOTRYOIDAL
  BLACK
AGATE - BOTSWANA
AGATE - LAKE
  SUPERIOR
AGATE - MONTANA
AGATE - PRIDAY
  PLUME

INDEX

immune system 91
immune system 20, 91, 121, 244, 246
implants 7, 17, 18, 24, 247
impotency 90, 121, 189
incarnate 214
incense 72, 135
incontinence 148
India 94, 103, 124, 243
Indian Ocean 93
indigestion 85, 118
infections 88, 103, 244
infertility 48, 115, 126
infinite wisdom 232, 233, 235-237
infinity 186, 187, 189
inflammation 78, 88, 91, 94, 103, 113, 124,
    132
inflexibility 82, 135, 242
influenza 132
inner self 100, 134, 178, 217, 218, 220-228,
    230-233, 235-237
insomnia 78, 115, 124
inspiration 26, 32, 70, 77, 82, 98, 105, 129,
    137, 191, 204, 230
insulin 126
intestines 83, 91, 97, 103, 108, 115, 118, 121,
    129, 244
intuition 2, 3, 7, 14, 16, 18, 19, 23-25, 27, 28,
    31, 33, 35, 37-45, 47, 48, 52, 53,
    67, 69-71, 77, 79, 81, 84-86, 89,
    92, 95, 98, 101, 107, 111, 114, 116,
    119, 122, 123, 125-127, 130, 133,
    134, 136, 139, 141, 143, 145-149,
    151, 153, 155, 157-159, 182, 185,
    187, 198, 200-202, 207, 217, 229,
    230, 233, 235, 236, 245
investigation 28, 90, 108
investments 126, 150
iodine 80, 135
iris 78, 80
iron 71, 85, 108, 124
Italy 78
jade 121, 135, 138, 202
jasper 234
jaundice 124, 126, 129
jaw 16, 80
jet 129
joints 40, 46, 103, 129
journeying 71, 72, 243-245
journeys 1, 72-74, 208, 228
juniper 72
kahunas 52
karma 6, 8, 128, 158, 160, 204
kidney stones 94, 97, 124
kidneys 13, 83, 94, 97, 106, 118, 121, 124,

kidneys [continued] 126, 129, 132, 247
Kirlian 243, 245
Kundalini 13, 17, 78, 87, 99, 128, 138, 149,
    150, 183-185
lapis lazuli 71, 121
larynx 80
laser wand 138
law of attraction 232, 233
laying-on-of-hands 6, 7, 9, 18, 185
left brain 38
legs 36, 83, 106, 126, 158
Lemuria 61, 93, 134, 246
lesions 132
lethargy 135
leucorrhea 121
leukemia 129
life after work 79
liver 14, 34, 85, 91, 100, 126, 129, 244
lodestone 132
logic 28
loins 94
love 1, 7, 10, 13, 14, 16, 24, 28, 32, 34, 47,
    54, 60, 67, 82, 87, 106, 119, 120,
    132, 137, 142, 144-146, 150, 152,
    154, 177-180, 187, 189, 199, 200,
    210, 211, 220, 221, 225, 227, 228,
    230, 231, 233, 236-238, 241, 243,
    244, 247
lower back 94, 121
luck 34, 99, 113, 154, 247
lumbago 100, 118
lungs 16, 34, 83, 85, 94, 106, 108, 118, 126,
    135, 150, 244, 247
lupus 129
lymphatic system 34, 97, 106, 108, 115, 121
Madagascar 88, 100
magic 54, 96, 126, 132, 134, 137, 231
magnetic forces 16
magnetism 132, 233
malachite 124
malaria 129, 138
malnutrition 91, 126, 129, 132
manifestation crystal 140, 146
manual dexterity 118
marcasite 115
marriage 145, 151
masculine 112, 126, 193, 194
masculine/feminine 193
massage 17, 80
Master numbers 97, 132, 242, 249
mathematics 40, 129
Mayans 71, 134
measles 78, 115
meditation 4, 5, 10, 17, 20, 37, 38, 73, 108,

THE BEGINNING